D0807784

INTERNATIONAL BUSINESS TRANSACTIONS

IN A NUTSHELL®

TENTH EDITION

RALPH H. FOLSOM
Professor of Law
University of San Diego School of Law

MICHAEL WALLACE GORDON
John H. and Mary Lou Dasburg
Professor of Law Emeritus
University of Florida Levin School of Law

MICHAEL P. VAN ALSTINE
Professor of Law
University of Maryland
Francis King Carey School of Law

MICHAEL D. RAMSEY
Professor of Law and Director of International and
Comparative Law Programs
University of San Diego School of Law

WEST
ACADEMIC
PUBLISHING

PREFACE

International Business Transactions in a Nutshell introduces the basic legal aspects of private transactions for international sale of goods and international investment. It commences with a general introduction to international business, followed by a chapter on international business negotiations, and thereafter focuses on documentary international sales and letters of credit, transfers of technology, foreign investment, expropriations, extraterritorial regulation and anti-corruption law. Its concluding chapter provides a brief overview of private transnational dispute resolution, principally through litigation and arbitration.

This Tenth Edition of the Nutshell has been updated to include new cases, legislation, and developments relating to international business through early 2016. It has also been expanded to include an overview of important extraterritorial regulations by the United States and the European Union (Chapter 8) plus a new chapter on the U.S. Foreign Corrupt Practices Act (FCPA) and the OECD Anti-Bribery Convention (Chapter 9).

A closely related resource is *International Trade and Economic Relations in a Nutshell* (6th ed. 2016) by three of the same authors. It focuses principally on government controls on imports and exports, customs unions and free trade agreements, trade remedies, and the law and economic relations of the World Trade Organization, the European Union, and the North American Free Trade Agreement (NAFTA). The two Nutshells together provide a broad introduction to the people and institutions who practice international business law, and the government and multilateral organizations that both encourage and restrict international trade and economic relations.

For those who wish to explore these topics in greater depth, our *International Business Transactions: A Problem-Oriented Coursebook* (12th ed. 2015) provides problems, excerpts from cases and other legal materials, questions and further discussion. An additional resource is our *Principles of International Business Transactions* (West's Concise Hornbook Series, 3d ed. 2013) (the fourth edition is forthcoming in 2016).

In preparing these volumes, we are grateful for the advice and assistance we have received from colleagues at our own law schools and others both in this country and abroad, from student research assistants, and from persons in practice. We welcome continued suggestions for the next edition.

RALPH. H. FOLSOM
rfolsom@sandiego.edu

MICHAEL WALLACE GORDON
Gordon@law.ufl.edu

MICHAEL P. VAN ALSTINE
MVanAlst@law.umaryland.edu

MICHAEL D. RAMSEY
mramsey@sandiego.edu

April 2016

OUTLINE

TABLE OF CASES

XI

INTERNATIONAL BUSINESS TRANSACTIONS

IN A NUTSHELL®

TENTH EDITION

INTRODUCTION

FROM BROCKTON AND BURBANK TO BANGKOK AND BEIJING

Representing a Boston client who sells goods to a buyer in Burbank, California, creates relatively few issues that are not similarly present if the buyer is in the same state as the seller, for example Brockton, Massachusetts. Both sales are likely to constitute a standard, domestic sales transaction. Unlike a face-to-face transaction, the seller will not meet the buyer and hand over the goods at the same time that the buyer pays the agreed purchase price. Instead, the parties' agreement likely will require that the buyer pay when the seller presents *documents* confirming shipment of the goods—not when the *goods* have arrived and the buyer has had an opportunity to inspect them. Occasionally, a seller unfamiliar with the financial situation of the buyer may demand payment by a letter of credit. With this payment arrangement a bank agrees to pay on behalf of the buyer once the seller presents documents proving that it has shipped the contract goods to the buyer. In rare cases, the seller even may demand that a bank in its area confirm the letter of credit and thus also agree to pay on behalf of the buyer. The sale to Brockton will be in dollars, just as will be the sale to Burbank. And the parties will correspond in English.

Perhaps the most significant features unique to the Burbank purchase involve which state's law will apply and which state's courts will be the appropriate forum if a conflict later arises. But the rules of commercial law of Massachusetts and California are nearly identical, because both states have adopted the Uniform Commercial Code. The California lawyer representing the Burbank buyer passed a different bar exam than the Massachusetts lawyer. But nearly all of the substantive law on each exam was the same, rooted in the common law tradition and expressed in state legal systems containing many common features. The two lawyers studied the common law in their respective law schools, and they may even have gone to the same law school, located in a third state such as Maryland. Although a continent apart, the Massachusetts and California lawyers for the buyer and seller could exchange practices, and quickly function with little loss of efficiency and skill on a common subject such as a sale of goods.

The situation changes in significant ways, however, if the sale from Boston is not to Brockton or Burbank, but instead to a buyer in Bangkok. Among myriad other things, this *international* transaction will involve two different business and social cultures, and two different legal systems. The economy of Thailand is less developed than the economy of the United States, and may present some problems unique to developing nations, such as a less efficient infrastructure at the port of entry for unloading the goods. Risk of damage thus is greater, and insurance rates will be higher. Customs rules and procedures may be strikingly different, and officials might demand "unofficial" payments to admit the goods. As in the sale to Brockton or Burbank, the parties may agree that the buyer must pay upon presentation of documents confirming shipment, but much more commonly they agree on payment by an international letter of credit. The challenge in such a case is that the local law and practices on documentary sales and letters of credit may differ, perhaps greatly. Commonly used commercial terms (such as FOB and CIF) may have different meanings and may allocate the risks between the buyer and the seller in different ways. For its part, the Bangkok buyer may worry that the goods shipped in fact will not conform to the requirements of the sales contract. It thus may demand that a third party inspect the goods before shipment and issue a certification of conformity. Such certification would be required before the buyer would be obligated to pay the seller.

The letter of credit in an international transaction also is more complex. If the Bangkok buyer arranges for its local Bangkok bank to issue the letter of credit, the Boston seller is almost certain to require that a U.S. bank, very likely with an office in Boston, confirm the credit. The Boston seller does not wish to have to go to Bangkok to challenge the Bangkok bank if a conflict over the letter of credit arises. The Boston seller will prefer to go to a Boston bank to present the documents for payment, thus avoiding having to send the documents to an agent in Bangkok for presentation to a Bangkok bank. Additionally, letters of credit may be irrevocable or revocable. The Boston seller almost certainly will insist that the credit be irrevocable, but practice in Bangkok might be to issue revocable letters.

Numerous challenges also arise from the simple facts that the buyer in Bangkok is both geographically more distant and in a different country (with a different legal system). The greater distance almost always requires the involvement of a third-party carrier. To be sure, the sale to Burbank also likely will involve a carrier. But the law and practice on the obligations of the carrier may differ substantially as between Burbank and Bangkok. Thus, the Boston seller in the sale to Burbank can avoid any international issues simply by shipping the goods with a domestic carrier across the continental United States to California. Selling to Bangkok does not offer that option. The shipment to Bangkok might be on a vessel with stops in several foreign nations before reaching Bangkok, creating additional and different risks. Furthermore, the laws and rules applicable to the shipment may differ.

A major difference in many international transactions involves the choice of *currency*. This issue of course does not arise in a sale from a Boston seller to a Burbank buyer. For the Bangkok sale, the Boston seller probably also will insist on payment in U.S. dollars, not Thai bahts. But even if the Bangkok buyer agrees, the Thai government later may impose exchange restrictions limiting (or even prohibiting) the removal of hard currency from Thailand. If the Boston seller instead agrees to accept Thai bahts, it of course cannot pay suppliers with them, nor give them to workers as salary. Even if the Thai currency is freely exchangeable, the rates of conversion from bahts to dollars might change between the time of the conclusion of the sales contract and the time of the exchange, causing either an unexpected gain or an unwelcome loss. Moreover, the seller's bank may offer a very unfavorable exchange rate for Thai bahts and also impose substantial exchange fees.

Not only the currency but the *language* of the contract will have to be decided. Even if the contract terms are expressed in English, as preferred by the Boston seller, the Bangkok buyer may believe the contract terms say something quite different than does the Boston seller. While differences in the meaning of terms also may occur in purely domestic transactions, the likelihood and magnitude of differences in the international transaction are likely to be more extensive.

If the sale from Boston is to Beijing rather than to Bangkok, the Boston seller will address most of the same issues as noted above with the sale to Bangkok, plus issues of dealing with an economy that possesses some *nonmarket* economy characteristics. There are fewer nonmarket economies today than a decade ago, and many nonmarket economies are in a stage of transition to various forms of a market economy, including China. Thus, there may be a question regarding the character or nature of the buyer's economy. It may be a nonmarket economy and also a developing nation, such as Cuba. It may be an advanced developing country (ADC) or newly industrializing country (NIC), but still be a nonmarket economy, such as China (if it is fair to currently characterize the PRC as beyond a mere developing nation). It may be a nonmarket economy trying to become a market economy, but having difficulty overcoming decades of central planning and government involvement in the production and distribution of goods. Or it may be a nonmarket economy which prefers to remain a nonmarket economy, but which finds it necessary to do business with market economies and opens the door to market economy characteristics only enough to achieve specific goals. Such remains the policy of Cuba (although much may change in coming years due to the recent warming of relations with the United States).

Where the buyer is located in a nonmarket economy, a major difference is that the purchaser may be the government rather than a private entity. Furthermore, the purchaser may not be the end user of the goods, but a centralized government agency, frequently called a foreign or state trading organization (FTO or STO). Most nonmarket economies have very strictly controlled currencies. The currencies tend to be nonexchangeable in international currency markets, and are usually artificial in value. They are sometimes so strictly controlled that they may not be removed from the country.

We have noted only a few differences in a commercial sale of goods where the seller and buyer are in different countries. There are many other new issues to confront. The differences noted above tend to be attributable to different legal and economic systems in the two nations. There also may be differences in the cultures of the two nations which affect the transaction. Misunderstandings of cultural norms may create minor embarrassments, or constitute serious improprieties that terminate negotiations. The result is lost business. If the Boston seller or its counsel has gone to Bangkok or to Beijing to negotiate or sign the contract, what conduct is expected? Do people greet each other by shaking hands, or is touching inappropriate? Is it proper to discuss business over breakfast? Should spouses be invited to a business dinner? Should one sit with legs crossed? Are nominal gifts appropriate or distasteful? How does the calculus change in this regard when one country's laws prohibit payments intended to influence government officials (such as the Foreign Corrupt Practices Act in the United States)?

Our Boston seller may begin to sell sufficient products to Bangkok or Beijing that it decides to establish some form of agency or distributorship abroad. It may have experience with the use of agents or distributors in its sales to Brockton or Burbank. The buyer might have used an *agent* to represent it. The agent would not possess title to the goods; title would pass directly from the Boston seller to the buyer. The agent would be said to have had the goods "on consignment." Or the Boston seller might have used a *distributor*. The distributor takes title to the goods, and passes that title upon the sale to the buyer. The Boston seller will have to make the same choice between an agent and a distributor when selling abroad, but it may learn that quite different laws may apply. The foreign state may have a special distributorship law, which reduces some of the seller's choices available in U.S. law. The foreign law is likely to favor the local distributor, especially regarding matters of the right to, and rights upon, termination. Even where there is no special distributorship law, the applicable laws may be different. Those laws may be included among the many provisions of the local civil or commercial code, if the foreign state has a civil law legal system. Establishing a foreign distributorship also may raise issues of questionable trade restraints under the foreign law, when the distributor becomes the exclusive agent, or is limited to certain territory, or must sell at seller established prices.

Depending upon the form chosen for the sale of goods abroad, the Boston seller may become enough of an employer in the foreign country to be subject to the foreign state's labor law. Labor law in many foreign states differs dramatically from labor law in the United States. Foreign states often are particularly protective of their workforce, and the Boston seller may encounter far stricter rules regulating the employment relationship, especially termination. A "once hired, can't be fired" rule is perhaps the most troublesome for employers. In addition to foreign labor laws, the Boston seller will have to deal with the movement of business persons across borders. Even a brief *business* visit to Bangkok or Beijing may require entry papers far more complex than a *tourist* visa. Much business is undertaken using tourist visas, but such use may create a risk if a contract is breached. As business persons cross borders for longer stays, visa requirements are likely to increase. Beyond the immigration rules of Bangkok or Beijing, our Boston seller looking to develop international business relations also may face obstacles in the U.S. immigration rules. The Boston seller may wish to bring Bangkok or Beijing business associates to Boston for training. That may require a business visa, or perhaps an education visa.

As our Boston client's trade evolves and increases, from an isolated sale, to occasional sales, and perhaps to the creation of a distributorship agreement, it may begin to consider manufacturing its products abroad. Manufacture abroad may follow the major step of creating a direct foreign investment, or perhaps by licensing a foreign producer in Bangkok or Beijing to manufacture the goods. Licensing production to a company in Brockton or Burbank would involve only the negotiation of the licensing agreement by the Boston licensor and the Brockton or Burbank licensee. But if the Boston seller licenses the production to a developing or nonmarket economy nation, the transfer of technology agreement may be subject to careful scrutiny by the host government. The Boston licensor will be most concerned with protecting its intellectual property, while the foreign government may be more concerned with regulation of the transfer of technology.

Even if the foreign licensee is a privately owned enterprise, the government may mandate that all technology agreements be registered, and sometimes be reviewed for approval to ensure that they do not include provisions considered detrimental to the economic development of the foreign state. Among other issues, such a governmental review may examine the duration of the agreement, royalty amount, grant-back requirements, territorial restrictions on sales, the availability of comparable technology in the local marker, and choice of law and forum.

The Boston licensor of the technology also will be very concerned about the existence and adequacy of laws protecting intellectual property in the foreign country. The Boston licensor has invested considerable time and money in developing its products, and wants the fullest protection offered by patent, trademark, copyright and trade secret laws. If the products are licensed to be manufactured by a Brockton or Burbank licensee, the Boston licensor is protected by a scheme of U.S. (mostly federal) law protecting intellectual property. But if the license is to Bangkok or Beijing, the licensor may confront very different views about rights to intellectual property. Such rights may not be recognized at all, because they are considered not subject to private ownership, at least to the extent in U.S. law. Even if intellectual property is acknowledged to be private property, practical issues of enforcement arise. If local tradition or economic interests run to the contrary, it may be difficult or impossible to gain the assistance of local authorities and courts to combat counterfeiting or prevent outright theft of intellectual property rights.

The above business transactions illustrate some of the differences in selling to or licensing the production of goods in foreign states. These differences occur every day in international business. The differences may create additional transaction costs. One transaction cost all business persons hope to avoid is the cost of resolving disputes. That is accomplished by avoiding them. But we are yet to find a way to assure that all transactions will occur without conflict, and thus must be prepared to assume some costs of dispute resolution, and to understand the nature of dispute settlement in international transactions.

If a conflict arises between the seller and the buyer, the choice of law and choice of forum issues become extremely important. It should come as no surprise to the Boston lawyer and client that the contract law of Thailand differs from that of Massachusetts much more than does the contract law of California. Furthermore, the legal system of Thailand, including procedural law, may have very different characteristics than the legal system of Massachusetts. Even if both countries have adopted an international treaty on the subject—such as the UN Convention on Contracts for the International Sale of Goods (CISG), *see* Chapter 2—a Bangkok court will use a copy of the law in Thai, while a Boston court will use one in English. Different meanings to terms may result from different translations. Furthermore, the method of judicial interpretation in Bangkok will differ from that in Boston, far more so than that in Brockton or even Burbank. The Bangkok court will interpret the statutory provision, with some assistance from scholarly treatises, but with less attention to Thai cases than the Boston lawyer may expect. The Boston court is likely to focus on past Massachusetts decisions, and, if none are found, decisions of other states which interpret the particular provision. Harmonization of law does not mean harmonization of the legal systems, and therefore of methods of judicial interpretation.

Because of the very different attitudes towards dispute resolution, the parties may choose to include a provision in their contract for mandatory arbitration. Considered essential when dealing with some foreign states because of inefficient or corrupt judicial systems or a failure to enforce foreign judgments, arbitration often is chosen even when judicial systems function efficiently. Court back-logs, litigation costs, and more relaxed rules of evidence are often the reasons parties prefer arbitration even in a domestic setting, for example for disputes arising in the sale from Boston to Burbank. Those same reasons exist in the international setting, plus a sense of fairness provided by third party arbitration.

International litigation and arbitration add many new dimensions to the same issues when part of domestic litigation. Choosing Burbank (meaning California) law rather than Boston (meaning

Massachusetts) law is a much less significant decision than choosing Bangkok (meaning Thailand) law or Beijing (meaning PRC) law. The same is true in choosing a forum. Initiating suit in a foreign country almost certainly will involve different rules of jurisdiction (ones quite different from U.S. notions of subject matter and personal jurisdiction). Service of process in many foreign states is a more formal process than in the United States. The extensive process of discovery in the United States is essentially nonexistent abroad; and a U.S. litigator likely will not find a sympathetic ear in a foreign court when seeking to obtain discovery in aid of a lawsuit in the United States. If the Boston seller is able to obtain jurisdiction over the Bangkok or Beijing buyer in a Boston court, and obtains a judgment, it may have little value unless the foreign courts will recognize and enforce the Boston judgment. Recognition and enforcement rules vary throughout the world. In the United States recognition and enforcement varies state-to-state, often confusing to foreign lawyers. The Full faith and Credit clause of the U.S. Constitution mandates recognition of a judgment rendered in another state of the United States. But Thailand and the PRC of course will have their own domestic law on the subject. Thus, the near certainty of enforcement of a Boston judgment in a Brockton or Burbank court will contrast markedly from the substantial doubt about enforcement in a Bangkok or Beijing court.

Our Boston client has entered the world of international business transactions, and has learned quickly of the complexities of dealing with Bangkok or Beijing rather than Brockton or Burbank. It might decide not to deal with developing nations or nonmarket economies, but only to sell to, or license or establish a direct investment in, only those developed foreign states with more established market economies. For example it may sell to buyers in Brussels. In selling goods to a Brussels buyer it will not confront import licenses; and it will receive a strong, convertible currency. But it may have to deal in another language and, depending on the nature of the product, may confront European Union import rules (*e.g.*, on health, safety, privacy) that differ from those in the United States. If the Boston company licenses a Brussels firm to make its products, it will have its intellectual property protected, but with some variations as compared to the law of the United States. If it creates a subsidiary in Belgium it will not have to adopt a joint venture. But it will face civil law tradition corporate concepts and possibly some workers' rights not present in the United States. The company will have to learn something about dealing in an economically integrated market, in this case the European Union. The similarities with dealing in Brockton or Burbank are as prevalent as the disparities in dealing with Bangkok or Beijing. That is partly why a very large part of U.S. trade and investment abroad is with developed, market economy nations.

What follows in the chapters ahead is an introduction to some of the laws and policies, the organizations and entities, and the people involved in what we believe are the principal forms of international business transactions. (A companion book, International Trade and Economic Relations in a Nutshell, covers the government-imposed restrictions on imports and exports, the GATT/WTO, free trade agreements and customs unions, and economic integration with an emphasis on the European Union and the North American Free Trade Agreement.)

We begin in Chapter 1 with an examination of the special issues—cultural, linguistic, and otherwise—that arise in negotiating international business transactions. Chapter 2 then reviews in detail the UN Convention on Contracts for the International Sale of Goods, which by far is the most important law for international sale of goods transactions. Next, Chapter 3 addresses how parties typically structure international sale transactions, with a special focus on commercial terms, the traditional "payment against documents" transaction, and the important role of international bills of lading. Chapter 4 turns to the financing of international sales transactions through letters of credit (both in the form of standard, commercial credits and standby credits). Chapter 5 takes up the subject of the international law governing transfers of technology (especially intellectual property rights).

Chapters 6 through 9 next examine how things change when a party decides to move assets or business operations to a foreign country. Chapter 6 addresses the basic laws and practices relevant to the decision to undertake a foreign investment. Chapter 7 then reviews the difficult subject of defining—both in legal and practical terms—a "taking" of property by a foreign state and the possible remedies for an investor when this occurs. Chapter 8 reviews the extraterritorial regulation of international business (*e.g.*, the application of U.S. antitrust law to foreign activities). Chapter 9 (new to this 10th edition of the IBT Nutshell) explores the law prohibiting corrupt payments to foreign public officials, especially the U.S. Foreign Corrupt Practices Act (FCPA) and the OECD Anti-Bribery Convention.

Finally, Chapter 10 addresses the resolution of international business disputes. Of special relevance here will be issues of jurisdiction, choice of law and forum, international arbitration, and the enforcement of foreign judgments and arbitral awards.

CHAPTER 1

NEGOTIATING INTERNATIONAL BUSINESS TRANSACTIONS

Nearly all business transactions, domestic and international, begin with a negotiation in some form. But significant, and often subtle, differences exist in the international context. A sensitivity to these differences—in style, timing, procedure, language, and above all culture—is a valuable, indeed indispensable, skill for an international business lawyer.

Negotiating styles differ—often substantially—from culture to culture, enterprise to enterprise, person to person, and even context to context. A substantial body of research and literature has examined the principles of successful negotiation. But at least two general styles may be observed in international settings: the competitive (or adversarial-standoff) style and the consensus-building style. Each can be effective in its own context.

NEGOTIATING STYLES: COMPETITIVE OR CONSENSUS-BUILDING

The Competitive Style. The adversarial-standoff approach to negotiation may be illustrated by reverting to medieval Europe and imagining two opposing armies drawn up in battle array. Although their common purpose is to secure a resolution about who is to have what, they will bludgeon each other to achieve that resolution while parrying, shouting provocations, and carrying out diverting sorties along the way. The common elements of such a style are viewing the other side as an adversary; seeking concessions as a condition of any relationship; beginning with a healthy level of distrust of the intentions of the other side; limiting disclosure of goals and interests; seeing all issues as subject to negotiation, including ones previously settled; applying pressure to secure tactical advantage; demanding one-sided gains as a price of agreement; regarding the process as a "zero-sum" game; and ultimately setting a goal of "victory."

This style may be counterproductive when negotiating an international business transaction. Its emphasis upon pressing maximum advantage to the point of conquest is frequently inappropriate when measured against other, more important factors. These factors include the efficient use of time, political and cultural differences, the volatility of international markets, currency exchange fluctuations, and expenses that must be paid by a client along the way to shaping a satisfactory agreement. Moreover, the ill will engendered by this style may prejudicially color the opponent's judgment, in some cases killing the deal. In short, the adversarial-standoff style can have too high a cost for the "winner."

The Consensus-Building Style. A second broad negotiating approach seeks to build a rolling consensus toward an agreement. An experienced,

U.S. negotiator from the past, W. Averell Harriman, once suggested in this vein that "You have to put yourself in the other fellow's shoes . . . You also have to consider how to make it possible for him to make a concession . . . But the idea that you can whip your negotiating opposite into agreeing with you is nonsense . . . If you call a hand, you must recognize that you may lose it."

The consensus-building style places an emphasis upon negotiators finding kernels of agreement and expanding upon those areas with a view to building a momentum toward complete agreement. This momentum may overcome differences about how to resolve difficult issues. This approach is marked by viewing a negotiation not as a battle of adversaries, but rather as an effort to solve a shared problem; insisting on arguments based on objective criteria; engaging in "active listening" for the principled arguments of the other side; searching for common ground founded on mutual interests; beginning with a basic level of trust in the good faith of the other side; considering available options when confronted with apparent impasses; avoiding fictional "bottom lines"; and ultimately seeing the goal as a mutually acceptable outcome achieved in an efficient way.

Preparation is particularly important to the success of this approach. That is, the key to the consensus-building style is an advance determination of: (a) what your negotiating opposites really want; (b) what they really must have; (c) what they may offer in return; and (d) what they really cannot offer either because they lack authority to do so or because it would be unacceptable for enterprise, national, or international reasons.

Ultimately, however, the two styles—competitive and consensus-based—are not mutually exclusive, at least not in all respects or in all circumstances. Rather, aspects (or degrees) of each may be appropriate in a given negotiation. In cultures in which a cooperative style predominates, combative tactics may derail a deal even before substantive talks begin. Other cultures expect a more candid, no-nonsense approach. The key for skillful negotiators is careful preparation founded on a detailed understanding of the cultural, political, financial, and historical background of the opposite side in a potential business deal. So armed, they tailor their techniques, tactics, methods, and manners to the particulars of each negotiation—with the ultimate goal of securing an agreement (or not) in a way that best advances the client's goals and interests.

THE IMPORTANCE OF CULTURE

Cultural Competence. Perhaps—and maybe even certainly—the most important requirement for success in international negotiations is a deep and refined awareness of cultural differences. This basic point may seem obvious, but certain fundamental aspects of culture are worthy of special emphasis here. And in a broader sense, the significance of this issue is worthy of a lawyer's career-long commitment to learning, understanding, and appreciating culture as a necessary foundation for negotiating international business transactions.

Broadly captured by the modern notion of "cultural competence," the essential point here is that a negotiator must appreciate that the expectations, requirements, limitations, and even form (etiquette, tone, manner, level of formality, etc.) for international business negotiations may vary considerably depending on the cultural context. Indeed, significant differences exist even over the expected or allowed participants. In some cultures, for example, lawyers are directly involved in negotiations; in others, the practice is frowned upon or even seen as an insult. Duties or expectations of disclosure likewise vary across cultures and even enterprises. In some countries, such as Japan, it is considered courteous to tell people what they want to hear (irrespective of actual reactions, positions, or interests). In others, excessively indirect communication of information or interests may be seen as devious or even deceptive.

At a more personal level, expectations of courtesy, manners, and comportment may influence negotiations before they begin. Self-praise is deprecated in virtually all cultures, but what qualifies in this regard can vary significantly. The act of presenting and accepting business cards in many Asian countries (especially China and Japan) reflects a ritual that has been finely tuned over many decades. A failure to follow that ritual risks leaving an impression of a lack of sophistication, or even boorishness. Another commonly told story is of a multinational investor in Africa who inserted certain "whereas" clauses into a negotiated agreement to the effect that the local government was unable to perform a task and that the investor possessed worldwide management and technical success at the same task. An African newspaper published those "whereas" clauses as evidence of "imperialist attitudes."

In a similar vein, gift-giving reflects an essential, deeply ingrained component in the development of business relations in some countries (*ttokkap* in South Korea, *guanxi* in China, *baksheesh* in India and the Middle East, to pick just a few). Certain gifts, such as books depicting the natural beauty of the investor's home area, are generally appreciated, while more specialized gifts may be preferred in a particular country. In other cultures (and legal systems), however, "gift-giving" quickly transforms into a "bribe" that may be punishable as a crime.

There also is an almost universal cultural importance attached to sharing a meal with a negotiating opposite. Mealtime affords a good opportunity for a foreign business partner to show an interest in and sensitivity about the host's culture. But here again, substantial differences exist about the significance of dinners in "negotiating" business deals. In the United States, it is common to conduct business over lunch or dinner. In many cultures, however, talking about business matters during a meal is considered at least inappropriate, if not impolite or offensive. In still others, in contrast, *most* important decisions are made over the "informality" of a business dinner.

Considerable cultural diversity also exists about the meaning of silence and delay in international negotiations. In some countries silence may mean "no," while in others, periods of silence are a sign of respectful consideration of a proposal. For example, one familiar tale is of an investor in Indonesia who brought the final draft of a completely negotiated agreement to a counterpart for signature and, following some pleasant conversation, placed the agreement on the desk. In complete silence, the counterpart simply returned the document, unsigned, to the investor. The investor later learned that the specific day was not considered propitious in Indonesia for signing one's name. The agreement was signed the next day. Delays of days or even of months may not be signs that a negotiation is in difficulty, nor an indication of efforts to secure a tactical advantage. Such delays simply may be the minimum time period for bringing about a necessary consensus within a foreign negotiating team. Thus, the common law notion that, in some circumstances, silence may amount to acceptance may have little or no relevance when negotiating with someone from another culture.

Timing. This last point highlights the importance of the substantial differences across cultures with respect to time and timing. Understanding the overall timing framework for a successful negotiation may be particularly difficult for U.S. attorneys and business executives. People from some cultures—especially in Asia—negotiate with a recognition that what cannot be settled today perhaps can be settled tomorrow or next week. In some cultures, a substantial amount of time, discussion, and interaction, both formal and informal, is required before business relationships can develop. It may take weeks spent together on a golf course, in dinners, and in a variety of other forms of personal contact before such trust is engendered. People in other countries prefer not to negotiate during certain times of the year, *e.g.*, Ramadan in Islamic nations, or the period between Christmas and New Year's Day in some European countries. In some countries the "weekend" is on days other than Saturday and Sunday. Standard "business hours" in the United States (9:00 a.m. to 5:00 p.m.) are not considered appropriate for doing business in other countries. In parts of Africa "noon" may be any time between 10:00 a.m. and 2:00 p.m. The hours between 2:00 p.m. and 5:00 p.m. are inappropriate for doing business in Saudi Arabia. (Even the reference system may be different, with many countries preferring a 24-hour clock— "military time" in the United States—instead of "a.m." and "p.m.")

In short, cultural differences may play a substantial, even decisive, role in the success or failure of an international business negotiation. But a variety of valuable resources are available for lawyers and businesspeople to develop a deeper understanding of this important subject. One valuable tool for educating yourself about the field is a commonly used assessment (originally developed

by David A. Victor) known as "LESCANT." The
LESCANT analysis identifies the following
significant cultural variables in international
negotiations: language; environment and
technology; social organization; contexting (a
measurement of explicit and implicit
communications); authority conception; non-verbal
behavior; and temporal conception (the subject of
timing discussed above). Another valuable resource
is the AMERICAN BAR ASSOCIATION GUIDE TO
INTERNATIONAL BUSINESS NEGOTIATIONS: A
COMPARISON OF CROSS-CULTURAL ISSUES AND
SUCCESSFUL APPROACHES (3rd ed., 2009).

THE IMPORTANCE OF LANGUAGE

The Language of Negotiations. Differences in
language skills between negotiating opposites
likewise may be a source for tension in international
business transactions. Each negotiating party quite
naturally prefers to use the language whose
nuances are best known. Words that have a clear
and culturally acceptable meaning in one language
may be unclear or culturally offensive in another.
The converse may be true as well. Many foreign
words do not have simple or clear counterparts in
English. Likewise, linguistic *faux amis* ("false
friends") abound. And even subtle mistranslations
may undermine trust or even scuttle an entire deal.
Body language may be equally important. Some
hand gestures and body movements are acceptable
in one culture yet deeply offensive in another; as a
result, they are rarely an appropriate
communication aid in international negotiations.

For example, raising an open hand in the direction of another party in North Africa can mean that you hope that the person will lose all five senses. Touching of heads is offensive in many Asian cultures.

The use of interpreters substantially slows the pace of negotiations and may spawn further difficulties. The simple reason is that, however talented, the interpreter is one more fallible person involved in the negotiations. Interpreting is exhausting work and rarely exact, with the result that inaccuracies creep in and disputes crop up. During an international commercial arbitration in Los Angeles, for example, a witness testified in German with the help of a skilled interpreter. Inevitably, however, disputes arose over the accuracy of the oral translation. This forced the arbitrators to wait while the interpreter, a U.S. lawyer fluent in German, and a German lawyer fluent in English were able to agree on a sufficiently accurate translation.

The peril of language difficulty can be equally acute in negotiations between a lawyer from the United States and a negotiating opposite who speaks English well. Each party may be embarrassed to raise a language question. Certain foreign enterprises require their negotiators to speak English when negotiating with Americans. The problem is that their English seldom tracks American English, and embarrassing moments occur when U.S. negotiators must delicately seek clarification of the opposite's words. Such clarifications must be undertaken with the utmost politeness and goodwill in order not to insult or intimidate the foreign party.

Even exceptionally able interpreters may have difficulty if a U.S. lawyer or executive uses American slang in communicating during an international negotiation. The American penchant for using "ball park" figures may not be shared or understood in countries where baseball is not a popular sport. Slow and distinct patterns of speech combined with simple declarative sentences will always facilitate international business negotiations.

The Language of the Agreement. Similar challenges arise over the language in which the parties will express their final agreement. The person who controls the drafting of an international business agreement often drives the negotiations. U.S. lawyers almost always will seek to perform this leading role. But the careful language normally used by American lawyers in commercial contracts may prove controversial. While legally trained persons in some countries share an affinity for written contracts that set out the full extent of every right and duty of each party, the practice in many other countries tends toward more generally worded agreements that leave it to the parties (*e.g.*, in Japan) or to the courts (*e.g.*, in Germany) to supply any necessary details. A detailed, exhaustively worded, draft contract proposed in negotiations with Japanese or German persons thus may arouse distrust. To them, a contract relationship is perceived as something that is shaped mutually as an understanding develops over time. Shorter contracts are the norm in Germany, with the premise that the parties' agreement is founded on good faith (*Treu und Glauben*) and that any gaps in the express deal are to be filled based on notions of reasonableness and mutual interests. With this foundation, German lawyers are much more willing to have a court resolve disputes as they arise.

This attitude may trap unwary parties. Chinese negotiators, for example, may resist bargaining on the details of a contract or joint venture, saying "All that is of course understood" or "a part of our law." They may even show resentment at attempts to detail business agreements. However, during performance at a later date, other representatives of a Chinese entity may not hesitate to say: "That is not written expressly in the contract and is not our duty." Many attorneys involved with Chinese business transactions have learned the hard way. This is not to say that such an approach is wrong— it is simply different and a skilled lawyer must take such differences into account in international business transactions.

Similarly, permissible contract clauses in one country may be impermissible in another. For example, penalty clauses, which are not legally enforceable in the United States, are enforced routinely by French, German, and, to a lesser extent, Italian courts. One-sided (adhesion) contracts may be fun for lawyers to draft, but they may serve only to raise suspicion by identifying the drafter as an adversary or to generate hostility and ill will. Draft adhesion contracts do not promote the consensus-building style of international business negotiations. German courts will eviscerate an unfair adhesion contract without mercy.

One of the most frustrating features of international business agreements is the presence of texts in different languages, each of which is considered authoritative. Counsel to a U.S. enterprise will always seek to make English the sole language of the agreement, and may sometimes succeed, since English has become a predominant language of international business. Especially when negotiations have been conducted exclusively in English, time, expense, clarity, and mutual understanding favor such a result. Even parties who are not native English speakers may use it as the language of agreement for these reasons. Agreements between Japanese and Indonesian businesses, for example, are often in English. But cultural pride (especially with French speaking negotiators) or fear of unfair dealing (especially with Chinese negotiators) may leave multiple texts in different languages the only acceptable solution once "agreement" is reached.

Another important linguistic feature of international transactions of particular concern to lawyers is the existence of different language texts of relevant laws. In the European Union, for example, there are fully 24 official, authoritative texts for every treaty, regulation, directive, parliamentary report, etc. The North American Free

Trade Agreement (NAFTA) exists in three authoritative versions: English, French, and Spanish. Treaties concluded under the auspices of the United Nations Commission on International Trade Law (UNCITRAL)—such as the hugely successful UN Convention on Contracts for the International Sale of Goods covered in Chapter 2— have six official language versions. The nuances of languages can significantly affect the legality of any business transaction. Those same nuances can undermine any carefully constructed consensus international negotiators have worked hard to create.

THE IMPORTANCE OF PROCEDURE

It may be, and often is, that the procedure employed in international business negotiations is the single most important reason for their success or failure. The careful lawyer or executive will make advance inquiry about whether contacts preliminary to the negotiation are advisable and about which locations may be preferable for conducting negotiations. Procedures calculated to facilitate the building of personal relationships increase prospects for a successful negotiation, especially in Asia. In tough moments during a negotiation, courtesy alone may preserve the momentum. Enduring courtesy is the essential lubricant of international negotiations.

A negotiating opposite may not want to admit that an apparent unwillingness to agree to a suggested point is caused by bureaucratic foot dragging, lack of coordination, lack of technical understanding, or simple confusion. Procedures that are flexible enough to allow time to work out such problems may cultivate respect, avoid a loss of "face," and ensure continued participation in the negotiations. For example, negotiating opposites may be unwilling to disclose that a failure to reach quick agreement flows from the fact that— notwithstanding a lofty title—they do not have authority to make a final agreement or will not assume personal responsibility for the consequences of an agreement. The latter case is not uncommon in Japan.

Procedures that cause surprise can engender hostility and distrust. Obvious examples include emotional displays used as smoke screens, changing the agreed agenda for negotiation, unannounced or late arrivals or departures of negotiating personnel, and retreating from agreements already made. The surprise introduction of a written document (such as an investor's initial proposal) together with an insistence of prompt action often causes similar reactions. A mutual decision to prepare a written summary of points of agreement in a negotiation may support the consensus-building process; but the surprise presentation of such a document to a negotiating partner can have the opposite effect. Of course, the latter tactic may be useful if one is negotiating by contest rather than by consensus. But even then, because the intimidating nature of a written document increases with its thickness (especially if in a foreign language), a one page summary of the contents stands a better chance of being read, and thus of contributing to a successful negotiation.

PLANNING FOR RENEGOTIATION

An international business agreement, once achieved, must be monitored and maintained in good order. An agreement, particularly one spanning a substantial period of time, should be negotiated and written with a recognition that it may be renegotiated and rewritten repeatedly. Business persons (like other people) live with unbalanced agreements only until they can change or terminate them. A multinational enterprise may perform a contract with a foreign government carefully and faithfully in accordance with a negotiated agreement, but unexpected events may work to change a host country's attitude. For example, OPEC's rapid revision of the price of oil affected economic parameters of contract arrangements worldwide. The People's Republic of China has been known to cancel or slow payment under contracts with foreign investors when currency exchanges or market prices fluctuate.

Broader geopolitical events also may intervene. For example, marked shifts in the political climate of a host country may change its government's attitude toward foreign investment in general, or certain types of international business transactions, or even specific multinational enterprises. Media discovery of contract terms unfavorable to a host country may focus local attention on a foreign investor. Thus, an enterprise that is highly visible in a host country may become an easy vehicle for venting local resentment against foreign investors.

Where plant, machinery and other assets are already in place, renegotiation is one of several, relatively unattractive alternatives. Political developments in a number of countries, especially in South America, over the last decade have left a much less favorable environment for foreign investors. The pressure of possible expropriation or other unilateral adjustments to the investment may prompt renegotiation as an alternative to even less attractive solutions.

In short, much more than in purely domestic deals, international business transactions operate in a fluid legal and factual environment. The prepared, informed, and prudent lawyer or executive will accept this important context as a fact of international business life, and tailor both the form of negotiations and the substance of the final contractual deal accordingly.

CHAPTER 2
INTERNATIONAL SALES OF GOODS

BACKGROUND: DOMESTIC CHOICE
OF LAW RULES

By far the most common form of international business transactions is the sale of movable things (everything from pencils to copper to automobiles). In the United States, the relevant law for sale of goods transactions is found in Article 2 of the Uniform Commercial Code (UCC), which the legislatures of all states (except Louisiana) have adopted as statutory law to ensure uniformity throughout the country. *See* §§ 2–102 (providing that Article 2 applies to "transactions in goods"), 2–105 (defining "goods" as things that are "movable"). Students who have taken a first-year Contracts course thus often come away with the belief that UCC Article 2 governs all contracts for the sale of goods, both domestic and international.

This assumption about the scope of the UCC provides an opportunity to explore what is perhaps the most fundamental issue in international business (and other) transactions: Of its very nature, a transaction that touches the interests of two or more countries requires a choice of which country's laws will govern if any disputes arise— and for this choice, of course, we need a set of legal rules. In the United States, we refer to these as "choice of law" (or "conflict of laws") rules. The parallel term in civil law countries is the "rules of private international law."

The challenge is that each legal system has its own choice of law rules, and often they are quite different. This raises a kind of pre-question: Which jurisdiction's choice of law rules will govern the question of which jurisdiction's substantive laws will apply? Thankfully, broad agreement exists on the answer to this question: A court will apply its home choice of law rules (which also will cover whether the parties may agree to displace the otherwise-applicable law, see below). Thus, where a lawsuit is filed determines which jurisdiction's choice of law rules will apply.

If a lawsuit on a subject within the scope of the UCC—such as a sale of goods—is filed in a U.S. court (whether state or federal), the UCC has a simple choice of law rule: The UCC of the state where the court is located will govern if the transaction in dispute bears an "appropriate relation" to that state. *See* UCC § 1–301(b)(former § 1–105). Of course, other countries have their own choice of law rules to determine which body of domestic law applies to a particular transaction. One prominent example is the European Union's Regulation on the Law Applicable to Contractual Obligations (2009), which applies in all twenty-eight EU member states. For sale of goods transactions, this so-called "Rome I" Regulation chooses "the law of the country where the seller has his habitual residence." Article 4(1).

The choice of law rules of most countries nonetheless generally permit private parties to agree on the law that will govern their transaction (so-called "party autonomy"). The EU's Rome I Regulation places no limitation on such a choice (*see* Article 3), except with regard to mandatory rules such as on the protection of consumers. The UCC in contrast permits such a party agreement on the application of a foreign country's laws only if the transaction "bears a reasonable relation" to that country. *See* § 1–301(a). Other countries may apply more or less stringent rules.

This legal situation leaves substantial uncertainty for parties engaged in international sale of goods transactions. Because they cannot know in advance where a lawsuit will be filed, they cannot know which country's choice of law rules will apply if any dispute arises. And because of this, they cannot know in advance what substantive legal rules apply to their transaction. And without knowing the answer to this question, they cannot know whether they even have formed a contract, and if so, whether any attempt to choose the governing law by one or both of them will have any legal effect.

The solution to such legal uncertainty is an international treaty that creates uniform legal rules across as many countries in the world as possible. For international sale of goods transactions, such a treaty (thankfully) in fact exists: The UN Convention on Contracts for the International Sale of Goods (1980). As explored below, the United

States and over eighty other countries have ratified or otherwise accepted this treaty. The parties to a contract may "opt out" of the treaty, but it must be the starting point for any analysis of international sales transactions.

THE BACKGROUND OF THE UN SALES CONVENTION (CISG)

The UN Convention on Contracts for the International Sale of Goods (which is commonly known, even internationally, by the acronym CISG) governs the sale of goods between parties in the United States and those in over eighty other countries. The CISG entered into force on January 1, 1988, thirteen months after the ratifications of the United States, China, and Italy exceeded the Convention's prescribed threshold of ten member states.

Under U.S. law, the CISG operates as a so-called "self-executing treaty." This means that it functions as directly applicable federal law without implementing legislation by Congress. And because ratified international treaties function as supreme federal law under Article VI of the Constitution, the CISG preempts all state law within its scope, including Article 2 of the UCC. The CISG also creates a federal cause of action in favor of aggrieved buyers and sellers in ordinary commercial litigation before federal courts in the United States. Thus, a sale of goods transaction between a private party in the United States and one, for example, in Canada would be governed by the CISG, and not by the UCC or otherwise-applicable Canadian sale of goods law.

As of March 1, 2016, eighty-four countries are "Contracting States" to the CISG (the term the treaty uses for countries that have ratified or otherwise accepted it). These states account for over ninety percent of the world's trade in goods. The list includes countries from all parts of the world and from all legal traditions, as well as nearly every major trading partner of the United States, from Canada and Mexico, to Japan and China, to Germany and France, and to South Korea and Singapore. (The few notable exceptions are the United Kingdom, India, Ireland, and South Africa.) The list of countries that have ratified or otherwise accepted the CISG continues to grow at noteworthy pace. This will increase the impact and effectiveness of the CISG in unifying international sales law. A current and complete list of Contracting States to the Convention is available at www.uncitral.org.

The CISG was adopted and opened for signature and ratification by a U.N.-sponsored diplomatic conference held at Vienna in 1980. It resulted from the work of a specialized body of the UN, the United Nations Commission on International Trade Law (UNCITRAL), whose mandate is to advance the unification and harmonization of international trade law. The purpose of such unification is to reduce legal obstacles to international trade, decrease transaction costs, enhance predictability and certainty, and promote the orderly development of new legal concepts as international commerce evolves in the future.

OTHER EFFORTS TO UNIFY INTERNATIONAL COMMERCIAL LAW

In addition to the CISG, UNCITRAL is responsible for a series of further treaties in the field of international commercial law. The most significant of these for present purposes is the 1974 Convention on the Limitation Period in the International Sale of Goods (as amended by Protocol in 1980). This Convention, which the United States and over two dozen other countries have ratified as of 2016, provides special rules for what American lawyers would call the statute of limitations for international sale of goods transactions. (For more detail on this treaty, *see* below.) Other such UNCITRAL treaties—which thus far have had substantially less success in attracting ratifications—include the Convention on Transparency in Treaty-based Investor–State Arbitration (2014); the Convention on the Use of Electronic Communications in International Contracts (2005); the Convention on the Assignment of Receivables in International Trade (2001); the Convention on Independent Guarantees and Stand-by Letters of Credit (1995); and the Convention on International Bills of Exchange and International Promissory Notes (1988). In addition, a Convention on the Recognition and Enforcement of Foreign Arbitral Awards (1958) (the "New York Convention"), which preceded UNCITRAL's formal creation, plays a significant role in international dispute resolution (*see* Chapter 10).

Separately, UNCITRAL has prepared "model laws" for consideration by individual countries as domestic legislation. Prominent among these are a Model Law on Public Procurement (2011); a Model Law on International Commercial Arbitration (1985, as amended in 2006), which has inspired legislation in nearly seventy countries, eight states of the United States, and every province of Canada; a Model Law on International Commercial Conciliation (2002); a Model Law on Cross-Border Insolvency (1997), which the United States implemented through Chapter 15 of the Bankruptcy Code; a Model Law on Electronic Commerce (1996), which has influenced more than forty national laws, uniform acts in nearly every state of the U.S. and every province of Canada, and various European Union directives; and a Legal Guide on Drawing Up International Contracts for Construction of Industrial Works (1987). UNCITRAL is continuing its work on promoting international uniformity in other areas of commercial law, with present projects on the enforcement of international settlement agreements, on secured transactions, and on the recognition of cross-border insolvency judgments.

UNCITRAL is not the only international organization involved in proposing legal instruments for the unification and harmonization of commercial law. Another prominent body, the International Institute for the Unification of Private Law (UNIDROIT), has prepared a variety of formal treaties in the field, including a Convention on International Factoring (1988), a Convention on International Financial Leasing (1988), and a promising (and as of 2016 already quite successful) framework Convention on International Interests in Mobile Equipment (2001). The Organization of American States (OAS) also has been active in this field on a hemisphere-wide basis.

In addition, UNIDROIT has prepared and issued the Principles of International Commercial Contracts. The Principles provide rules for all types of international commercial contracts, not just sales of goods, and their provisions are set forth in more general terms. If the CISG is the international analog to UCC Article 2 in U.S. law, then the Principles are the international analog to the Restatement of Contracts in U.S. law. They are not intended to be adopted as a convention or enacted as formal domestic law. Instead, they are designed for use principally by international commercial arbitrators, and even by judges where local law is ambiguous (and so permits). A separate section below reviews the structure and role of the Principles as well as some of their more significant concepts.

THE CISG's SPHERE OF APPLICATION

The goal of the UN Sales Convention is to create a uniform set of legal rules to operate in the place of the diverse domestic legal systems of its Contracting States. The Convention does not even permit Contracting States to declare reservations to limit the effect of any of its substantive provisions (but for a short list of expressly stated exceptions). In addition to rules governing its scope, the CISG contains provisions on contract formation; the respective rights and performance obligations of sellers and buyers; the rights and remedies upon breach; the passing of the risk of loss from the seller to the buyer; as well as most other significant subjects in international sales transactions. The CISG is structured in four principal parts:

Part I on scope and general principles (Articles 1–13);

Part II on contract formation (Articles 14–24);

Part III on the substantive rights and obligations of the buyer and the seller (Articles 25–88); and

Part IV on the non-substantive "diplomatic" provisions relating to ratification, permitted reservations, withdrawal, etc. (Articles 89–101).

The first six articles of the CISG define its sphere of application, but the principal rules are found in Article 1. That Article provides that the CISG will apply if a transaction (1) involves a sale of goods; (2) is international (as defined there); and (3) bears a stated relation to at least one Contracting State.

(1) On the first requirement, the CISG unfortunately does not define "sale" or "goods." Nonetheless, it is generally understood that the subject matter of the transaction must involve an

actual "sale"—that is, the passing of title for a price (and thus not a bailment, gift, or lease). The term "goods" means things that are both tangible (*i.e.*, have a physical existence) and moveable at the time of delivery.

(2) In contrast, the CISG clearly defines the requirement of an "international" sale of goods. This is determined not by whether the goods cross a national border, but rather by the "places of business" of the parties involved in the transaction. Specifically, under Article 1(1) the transaction must be "between parties whose places of business are in different states" (with "states" being sovereign countries, not the states of the United States). The fact that the parties are from different states will be disregarded, however, if this does not appear from information available to them upon the conclusion of the contract. Article 1(2).

Although the Convention does not define "place of business," its drafting history suggests that the term means a location with at least (a) some permanence and (b) the authority to make independent business decisions. Thus, neither a simple warehouse nor the office of a seller's agent qualifies as a "place of business." Interpretive case law has established, on the other hand, that a branch office may suffice as long as it has some level of independent decision-making authority. If a party does not have a formal place of business, then the relevant location for purposes of CISG Article 1 is his "habitual residence." Article 10(b).

For emphasis, Article 1(3) also declares that neither the nationality of the parties (*e.g.*, where a business is incorporated) nor their "civil or commercial character" (*e.g.*, whether or not domestic law would consider a party a "merchant") is relevant in determining whether the CISG applies.

The "place of business" criterion may cause difficulty where a party has more than one relevant business location. In such a case, CISG Article 10 provides that the relevant place of business is the one with the "closest relationship to the contract and its performance." The reference to these two different factors, however, may leave some ambiguity. Thus, where one office is more closely associated with the formation of the contract and a second more closely associated with a party's performance of its contractual obligations, courts will need to weigh the relative significance of both considerations to determine which office is the relevant "place of business." Nonetheless, Article 10(a) limits the usable facts in such cases to those circumstances "known to or contemplated by the parties" at or before the conclusion of the contract. The use of the plural here is important, for in choosing the relevant place of business a court may consider only those facts that were known to *both* parties at the time of contract formation. As a more general matter, Article 10(a) should permit well-advised parties to resolve possible ambiguities by stating in the contract which office of each party they believe to have the "closest relationship" to their transaction.

(3) Finally, the CISG governs only those contracts for the international sale of goods that have a substantial relation to one or more Contracting States—that is, the countries that have ratified, accepted, or otherwise acceded to the Convention before the relevant transaction (or, if contract formation is at issue, the making of the offer, *see* Article 100). The CISG defines two different ways to satisfy this requirement. First, under Article 1(1)(a) the Convention will apply if the parties have their places of business in different states and *both* of these states are CISG Contracting States. Under this option, therefore, the CISG will govern a contract of sale if one party has its place of business in the United States and the other has its place of business in France, China, Mexico, or any of the other eighty-plus CISG Contracting States.

Second, under Article 1(1)(b), the CISG also applies if the applicable domestic conflict of law rules (again, known by the civil law term "the rules of private international law") lead to the application of the law of a Contracting State. As an illustration of this option, assume that a seller based in France (which has ratified the CISG) contracts to sell batteries to a buyer based in the U.K. (which has not). If one party files a lawsuit in France, the Rome I Regulation would require application of French law as it is the home state of the seller (see above). But because France is a CISG Contracting State, under Article 1(1)(b) the French court should apply the CISG (again, even though the U.K. has not accepted the CISG).

The Article 1(1)(b) option does not apply, however, for lawsuits filed in the United States. When it ratified the CISG, the United States declared an allowed reservation under Article 95 that it would not be bound by Article 1(1)(b). The effect of this reservation is that courts in the United States will apply the CISG *only* when the parties' respective places of business are in different states and *both* of those states are CISG Contracting States (*i.e.*, only when Article 1(1)(a) is satisfied). Thus, for example, the CISG will not apply to a sale transaction between a seller located in the United States and a buyer located in the United Kingdom (a non-Contracting State to the CISG), even if under appropriate choice of law rules a U.S. court would apply U.S. law. What law should the court then apply? Instead of the CISG, the court would apply the otherwise-applicable choice of law rule for sales transactions (UCC § 1–301) in order to determine which domestic law will govern the transaction. The Article 95 reservation was included at the insistence of the U.S. delegation, because it was believed that the UCC is a superior approach to sales law as compared to the CISG. At the time, the CISG was considered helpful to U.S. interests only where it provided uniform law as between two countries that had adopted the CISG.

The U.S. reservation under Article 95 also has some unexpected consequences. The drafting history of the reservation indicates that even a foreign court should not consider the United States as a CISG "Contracting State" for purposes of Article 1(1)(b). Thus, in our U.S.–U.K. example above, even if the litigation somehow were brought in France (which has not declared an Article 95 reservation), such that the Rome I Regulation would point to the application of U.S. law (the home of the seller), the French court should apply the UCC (not the CISG)—because, again, the U.S.'s Article 95 reservation would mean that it would not be considered a CISG Contracting State *for purposes of Article 1(1)(b)*. Nonetheless, with the growing world-wide acceptance of the Convention (and thus the increasing application of Article 1(1)(a)), the Article 95 reservation of the United States is rapidly decreasing in significance.

PARTY AUTONOMY AND CHOICE OF LAW CLAUSES

One of the most important provisions for understanding the basic philosophy and scope of the CISG is Article 6. That provision states the core principle of "party autonomy," that is, the power of the parties to "exclude application of th[e] Convention" and to "derogate from or vary the effect of any of its provisions." The agreement of the parties, in other words, takes precedence over the provisions of the CISG. In its most fundamental sense, this includes the power of the parties to declare that the CISG will not govern their transaction (the power to "opt out" of the Convention).

Special care is required, however, in the exercise of this power. First, and most important, CISG Article 6 grants the opt out power to the parties (in the plural). As a result, an international trader cannot be assured that a unilateral choice of law clause in its standard business terms will be effective. The recent case of *Hanwha Corp. v. Cedar Petrochemicals, Inc.*, 760 F. Supp. 2d 426 (S.D.N.Y. 2011), illustrates this point. There, a South Korea-based buyer and a New York-based seller exchanged standard business forms that had conflicting choice of law clauses. Even though both parties tried to choose domestic law (and not the CISG), the absence of an agreement between them on one choice meant that the court applied the CISG, and especially its contract formation rules.

Moreover, even an express choice of a specific domestic law will not suffice. Thus, for example, a simple statement that a contract "shall be governed by New York law" will not effectively exclude the CISG. Indeed, courts addressing such clauses now commonly hold that a choice of the domestic law of a CISG Contracting State merely means a choice of the CISG. As a federal Court of Appeals declared in a case where the parties had agreed on the application of Ecuadorian law, "[g]iven that the CISG *is* Ecuadorian law, a choice of law provision designating Ecuadorian law merely confirms that the treaty governs the transaction." *BP Oil Int'l, Ltd. v. Empresa Estatal Petroleos de Ecuador*, 332 F.3d 333 (5th Cir. 2003)(emphasis in original). The same rule applies, under preemption doctrines, if a party attempts to choose the law of a state of the United States.

As a result, if the parties wish to exercise their Article 6 "opt out" power, they must do so through express language that excludes the Convention by name. To avoid difficult choice of law issues they also should agree on the applicable domestic law. (*E.g.*: "The parties hereby exclude application of the UN Convention on Contracts for the International Sale of Goods (CISG). The law of the State of New York, including as applicable the New York Uniform Commercial Code, shall govern all disputes relating to this transaction."). Note also that, even if the parties do not wish to exclude the CISG, they are well advised to designate a default domestic law, because the CISG, like any other single legal instrument, does not represent a complete legal regime for all issues that may arise between the parties.

Many attorneys seek to opt out of the CISG for all contracts under all conditions, simply because they do not understand it as well the UCC. Such an action may work a disservice to their client's interests. If an attorney represents the seller in an international transaction, for example, the UCC and its "perfect tender" and "implied warranty" rules may be less favorable than the corresponding rules under the CISG (*see* below). In such cases, automatic rejection of the CISG may prejudice the client's interests, unless the attorney can be assured that comparable seller-friendly rules will make it into the express terms of the contract. One prominent author has observed in this vein that routinely opting out of the CISG, or even simply negotiating an international sales contract without understanding how the treaty affects the client's interests, may constitute malpractice.

OTHER SCOPE ISSUES

Hybrid Transactions. A variety of other issues may arise concerning the CISG's sphere of application. A prominent example is so-called "hybrid" (or "mixed") transactions, under which the seller both sells goods and provides services to the buyer as part of the same contract. CISG Article 3(2) addresses such situations based on which aspect of the deal—sale of goods or services—predominates. It states that the Convention does not apply to such transactions if "the preponderant part" of the seller's obligations concerns "labour or other services." For goods not yet produced, the Convention also does not apply if the buyer undertakes to supply a "substantial part" of the materials necessary for the seller's subsequent manufacture or production of the goods. Article 3(1).

The CISG's Express Exclusions. In addition, CISG Article 2 expressly excludes a variety of transactions that otherwise might fall within the definition of a "sale of goods." The most important exclusion is a sale of goods to consumers. *See* Article 2(a)(excluding sales of goods "bought for personal, family, or household use"). The same Article also declares, however, that this exclusion does not apply—and thus the CISG does—if at the time of contract formation the seller "neither knew nor should have known that the goods were bought for any such [consumer] use." This limitation aside, the goal of the Article 2(a) exclusion is to avoid conflict with domestic consumer protection laws, which are often mandatory law. CISG Article 5 provides in the same vein that the Convention does not govern causes of action against the seller "for death or personal injury," even if they arise out of a sales transaction, because of concerns over conflicting with core public policy values of domestic law. Articles 2(b) and 2(c) also exclude auctions and goods sold on execution "or otherwise by authority of law."

The remaining subparts of Article 2 provide that the Convention does not apply to contracts for the sale of investment securities or negotiable instruments; of ships, vessels, hovercraft, or aircraft; or of electricity. Unfortunately, these express exclusions unintentionally may create ambiguity about the proper understanding of the term "goods" for the rest of the Convention. As noted above, a broad consensus holds that "goods" are things that are both tangible and moveable. But few if any legal systems would consider negotiable instruments to be "goods" in any event. By expressly referring to negotiable instruments, Article 2(d) may leave ambiguity over the CISG's application to other documents or intangibles not expressly excluded. In addition, the exclusion of ships, etc., arose because such vessels are usually subject to registration and regulatory legislation. But timber to be cut, growing crops, and railroad rolling stock may be subject to the same conceptual and regulatory difficulties, and CISG Article 2 does not expressly exclude these forms of potential goods.

Software Transactions. Transactions involving computer software are especially challenging. Certainly, the CISG may apply to the sale of computer hardware. Likewise, software sold in physical discs, including off the shelf at a store, may be "goods" within the contemplation of CISG Article 1. But courts and commentators seem to disagree over whether a contract to develop software, if ultimately delivered in physical form, is a contract for the sale of goods or not. It nonetheless would seem clear—although some commentators argue otherwise—that the CISG should not apply to a sale of pure software, especially if downloaded directly over the internet (although, again, Article 2(a) excludes sales to consumers in any event).

Other Transactions. As noted, the Convention does not define "contract of sale," so its application to some types of transactions is unclear. Nonetheless, a general consensus now exists on a variety of once-uncertain issues: Thus, the CISG does not apply (a) to franchise agreements (the essence of which is the temporary transfer of intellectual property rights); (b) to "turn-key" contracts (the essence of which is that a contractor must complete a work, typically a building, for immediate operation); (c) to financial leasing arrangements (which involve a transfer of only temporary rights); (d) to pure "consignments" (in which the "buyer" does not assume legal ownership of the goods and may freely return them to the owner); or (e) to barter ("countertrade") transactions (in which goods are exchanged for other goods and not for money). With respect to conditional sales (in which the seller seeks to retain title to the goods to secure payment of the purchase price), the authorities seem clear that the CISG may govern the sale of goods, but not the security aspects of the transaction. Finally, most courts have concluded that the CISG does not apply to framework distribution contracts (which merely define the parties' basic relationship, but do not (yet) involve a sale of goods).

Express Gaps in the CISG. One further limitation on the application of the CISG is that it expressly does not address all issues that may arise even under a contract otherwise within its scope. Under CISG Article 4, the Convention governs "only the formation of the contract" and the "rights and obligations" of the parties to the contract. Thus, the CISG should preempt state law claims based on the contract law notion of promissory estoppel (although some U.S. courts wrongly have held otherwise); but it should not preempt any related business tort claims.

Under the same provision, the CISG does not govern the "validity" of the contract, or its effect on title to ("property in") the goods. This exclusion presumably includes most rights and obligations of third parties to the contract. The restriction concerning "validity" arose because the CISG was not designed to police sales contracts for fairness or otherwise address core defenses to contract enforcement. Originally created to avoid conflicts with regulatory law, the case law indicates that Article 4 also excludes at least issues arising out of fraud, negligent misrepresentations and omissions, duress, illegality, incapacity, mistake, and similar basic contract defenses.

THE GENERAL PROVISIONS OF THE CISG

CISG Articles 7 through 13 contain the Convention's "general provisions." These articles deal with interpretation of the Convention and filling gaps in its provisions (Article 7); interpretation of party expressions and conduct as well as usages of trade (Articles 8 and 9); a few definitions (Articles 10 and 13); and a general removal of form requirements (Articles 11 and 12). Article 7 is designed to assist in interpretation of the Convention itself, while Articles 8 and 9 provide rules on interpretation of party intent, both pre-formation and as reflected in their contract. In turn, Article 8 concentrates on the parties' own statements and conduct, while Article 9 concentrates on customs and usages external to the parties.

Interpretation of the Convention. Beyond the "party autonomy" principle of Article 6 (see above), the most important provision for understanding the legal nature of the CISG is Article 7. At first glance, this Article seems merely to state standard rules of interpretation. But a more careful examination reveals that it declares the fundamental principles that define the Convention's relationship with domestic law.

At its most basic, Article 7(1) is designed to inhibit local courts from applying local norms and rules, rather than the Convention, to international sales disputes governed by the CISG. It first directs that interpretation of the Convention must heed its "international character." The purpose of this provision is to ensure that local courts respect the fact that the Convention reflects a broad international compromise among domestic legal systems. Courts thus must interpret the CISG on its own ("autonomously"), without resort to domestic interpretive norms or substantive rules. Unfortunately, some courts in the United States have missed this essential message when they have turned to the domestic UCC to assist in interpreting the CISG.

The requirement of an international perspective is stressed further by a second directive in Article 7(1)—that interpretation of the CISG must "promote uniformity of its application." This principle serves both to highlight the persuasive authority of foreign decisions interpreting the CISG and to emphasize (again) that local precedent on domestic sales law should not be relevant. Even the doctrine of "good faith" under the CISG is muted. Although UCC § 1–304 (former § 1–203) imposes an obligation of good faith on the parties to sales (and other) transactions, CISG Article 7(1) only refers to good faith in the interpretation of the Convention, not of the parties' contract. (Some courts nonetheless have shown recent flexibility on this score via Article 7(2), *see* immediately below.)

Article 7(2) continues the internationalist approach with respect to apparent gaps in the express provisions of the Convention. Reflective of a civil code interpretive approach, this provision states as a primary rule that gaps in the CISG "are to be settled in conformity with the general principles on which it is based." This approach (unlike that of the domestic UCC) thus again mandates that courts first attempt to fill regulatory gaps on an "autonomous" basis—that is, with reference to the broader principles reflected in the *Convention itself* (such as notions of reasonableness and timeliness). Based on this approach many courts have found a "general principle" that the CISG includes an obligation of "good faith" *by the parties* in the formation and performance of international sales contracts.

It is only if the required search for internal general principles fails that Article 7(2) permits resort to domestic law determined under applicable choice of law rules. The danger to uniform application is that local courts will discover many "gaps" in the CISG and no usable internal "general principles," and then readily fall back on their own familiar domestic rules. The fundamental philosophy of the CISG is that local courts must assiduously resist this impulse.

Interpretation of Party Intent. Article 8 establishes rules for interpreting party expressions and conduct as well as any final contract between them. The Convention's approach to this issue reflects significant differences with prevailing norms under domestic U.S. law—a fact recent U.S. courts fortunately have recognized and applied in the CISG disputes before them. Article 8 establishes a three-tier hierarchy: (1) Although not expressly stated there, basic principles of party autonomy mean that if the parties in fact have a common understanding concerning their intent or the meaning of a provision, that common understanding will prevail. The difficulty with this obvious point, however, is that a supposed shared intent is very difficult to prove once a dispute arises between the parties. (2) The essence of the CISG's interpretive scheme instead is found in Article 8(1). That provision mandates as a primary principle that a party's actual (*i.e.*, subjective) intent governs where the other party "knew or could not have been unaware" of that intent. The idea here is that a party's *actual* intent should prevail where the other party knows—actually or constructively—of that *actual* intent. This is a blunt rejection of the strict objective standard of interpretation applied by many U.S. courts. (3) Finally, if this search for actual intent fails Article 8(2) applies the traditional objective approach. Under that provision a party's manifestations (both statements and conduct) are to be interpreted "according to the understanding that a reasonable person of the same kind as the other party would have had in the same circumstances."

Article 8(3) then further highlights the contrast of the CISG's interpretive rules with those of many U.S. courts. That provision declares that in interpreting party intent—including disputed provisions in written contracts—a court must consider "all relevant circumstances of the case." And this includes—in a clear rejection of the American "parol evidence rule"—"the negotiations" of the parties as well as their prior practices, usages, and subsequent conduct.

As noted, U.S, courts fortunately seem to have taken this hierarchy to heart. In an early significant case, *MCC-Marble Ceramic Center, Inc. v. Ceramica Nuova d'Agostino, S.p.A.*, 144 F.3d 1384 (11th Cir. 1998), for example, a federal Court of Appeals interpreted Article 8(1) to require consideration of a party's subjective intent in interpreting its statements and conduct in the formation of a contract.

Article 8(3) also can direct a court to a very different approach to contract interpretation than is usual in domestic U.S. contract cases. Its requirement that a court give consideration to all relevant circumstances is a clear direction to consider parol evidence, even in interpreting a subsequent and final written agreement (as *MCC-Marble* and a number of more recent courts also have held). Some courts and scholars likewise have relied on the interpretive rules in Article 8 to promote the actual intent of the parties in "battle of the forms" situations and thus to avoid mechanical application of the traditional "last shot" doctrine (*see* "Contract Formation" below).

Trade Usages. CISG Article 9 addresses express and implied acceptance of usages of trade. Article 9(1) first gives effect to "any usage" on which the parties have agreed. The drafting history indicates that the focus of this language was on express agreements by the parties to include a trade usage (although the express agreement need not be written). Article 9(1) also binds the parties to "any practices which they have established between themselves." Where the parties have established such practices, they prevail over common industry usages. Further, "any" such usage or practice may be so incorporated, including local ones that may differ from international standards. If so incorporated, the usage is considered to be part of the express contract items. This is significant, for under Article 6 the actual agreement of the parties will prevail even over the provisions of the Convention. (The one exception to the last statement—as with Article 6 as a whole—is Article 12, which limits the power of party autonomy where a Contracting State has declared a reservation relating to writing requirements under domestic law, see below).

Article 9(2) concerns the incorporation of usages by implication. In the drafting of the CISG, both less developed countries and nonmarket economies expressed strenuous concerns about the application of unfamiliar trade usages on this basis, and the careful language of Article 9(2) reflects those concerns. It states that "unless otherwise agreed," the parties are considered "impliedly" to have accepted a usage for their contract only if (a) they "knew or ought to have known" of it; (b) it is international (not merely local) in nature; and (c) it is both "widely known to" and "regularly observed by" other parties to "contracts of the type involved" in the "particular trade concerned." This seems to set a very high standard for a party seeking to rely on an implied trade usage, and in particular with regard to the identification of the specific *international* trade involved.

Rejection of Writing Requirements. CISG Article 11 rejects any writing or other form requirements for contract formation. It broadly states that a contract for the international sale of goods "need not be concluded in or evidenced by writing and is not subject to any requirement as to form." For emphasis—and fully consistent with the flexible interpretive rules of Article 8 discussed above—a second sentence of Article 11 declares that a contract "may be proved by any means, including witnesses." Thus, there is no equivalent in the Convention of the Anglo-American Statute of Frauds.

Nonetheless, Articles 12 and 96 allow a Contracting State to declare a reservation that the local law of that Contracting State will govern the form requirements for a sale contract "where any party has his place of business in that State." Such a reservation, however, is applicable only to the extent that the domestic law of the declaring State "requires contracts of sale to be concluded in or evidence by writing." Article 96. Nonetheless, an Article 96 reservation may extend not only to the contract of sale itself, but also to "its modification or termination by agreement" as well as to "any offer, acceptance or other indication of intention." Article 12.

The United States has not declared an Article 96 reservation, and thus the Statute of Frauds provisions in UCC § 2–201 do not apply for contracts under the Convention. In fact, only eight Contracting States have declared an Article 96 reservation; but prominently included among these are Russia, Chile, and Argentina, with the result that their domestic law on writing requirements would continue to apply for CISG contracts. (China and three other states initially declared, but then withdrew, Article 96 reservations.)

Some dispute nonetheless exists on when such an Article 96 reservation actually applies. Courts have adopted different approaches where one party is located in a reservation state and one is not. The majority view requires application of the forum state's conflict of law rules. A reserving state's law then will apply only if those rules lead to the application of its law. Under what appears to be the minority view, in contrast, if one party has its relevant place of business in a reservation state, that state's writing requirements always apply.

If a Contracting State's Article 96 reservation applies, any party agreement under Article 6 to the contrary is not effective. Indeed, Article 12 expressly states that the parties "may not derogate from or vary the effect of" any such reservation. This gives the local law the effect of mandatory law under the Convention. (Article 13 states that a telex or telegram may satisfy a writing requirement, but such methods of course long ago yielded to electronic communication, so the effect of Article 13 is quite limited.)

CONTRACT FORMATION

Part II of the CISG sets forth its contract formation provisions. *See* Articles 14–24. Under Article 92, a Contracting State may declare a reservation at the time of ratification that it will not be bound by Part II, even though it is bound by the rest of the CISG. Only the Scandinavian countries initially did so, but even these—other than Iceland—have since withdrawn their reservations.

Every first-year American law student studies about offer, acceptance, and consideration, but these three elements of contract formation are not present in other legal systems. Civil law emphasizes the agreement process, and does not include a consideration requirement. Nonetheless, an examination of the consideration cases will show that few such disputes arise in true commercial transactions. Rather, they tend to involve family members arguing over failed promises (uncles attempting to induce nephews not to smoke and the like). Thus, it should not be surprising that the CISG has no requirement of consideration in its contract formation provisions.

As the previous section noted, writing requirements such as in the Statute of Frauds also do not apply for CISG contracts, unless one of the parties has a place of business in a Contracting State that has declared an Article 96 reservation. Further, Articles 8(1) and 8(3) clearly reject the principles of the U.S. parol evidence rule (and especially the notion of agreement being integrated into a final writing).

Part II of the CISG focuses on "offer" (Articles 14–17) and "acceptance" (Articles 18–22). In Convention terminology, a contract "is concluded at the moment when an acceptance of an offer becomes effective." Article 23.

Offer. Article 14 defines three requirements for an effective "offer." First, it must be "a proposal for concluding a contract," which is a standard notion. Second, it must indicate "an intention to be bound in case of acceptance," which will distinguish an offer from a general sales catalogue, an advertisement, or a purchase inquiry. Article 14(2) elaborates on this concept by making proposals addressed to the general public presumptively not offers "unless the contrary is clearly indicated." Third, an offer must be "sufficiently definite." A proposal satisfies this definiteness requirement if it "indicates the goods" and "expressly or impliedly fixes or makes provision for determining the quantity and the price." By implication, other terms can be left open, but not those three.

The requirement that an offer at least "make[ ] provision for determining" the price seems more restrictive than the comparable UCC provision on open, or flexible, price contracts (§ 2–305). This was intended, because many civil law states do not recognize such contracts. Nonetheless, it seems clear that a contract sufficiently "makes provision for determining the price" where it identifies a specified index, or is subject to an escalator clause, or is to be set by an independent third party. Arguably, the latter also would include "lowest price to others" clauses.

CISG Article 55 also may provide a foundation for flexible pricing arrangements. If a contract does not expressly or impliedly set the price, that provision permits reference to the price "generally charged at the time of the conclusion of the contract . . . under comparable circumstances in the trade concerned." But Article 55 only applies where a contract already "has been validly concluded," which assumes a valid offer. The Convention's language is flexible enough, however, to authorize most forms of flexible pricing, and some courts have expressly so held. That is, these courts have utilized Article 55 as a "subsidiary method" for determining the price, especially where the parties have begun performance of the contemplated transaction. One court similarly enforced an apparently price-less contract because the parties had established a payment practice under prior contracts. Other courts, however, give precedence to the express requirements of Article 14, and thus do not permit Article 55 to "save" a deal where the parties have not expressly or impliedly agreed on the price.

Open quantity contracts, such as those for requirements, output, or exclusive dealings, should cause less difficulty. In each such contract, a "provision for determining the quantity" likely will arise through party performance, even if the precise number cannot be fixed in advance. However, in view of the requirements of CISG Article 14, parties are well advised to include either estimated or minimum quantity amounts, in order to set a reference point for a "fixed or determinable" quantity.

Assortment deals, under which one party has discretion over the choice of goods from among an assortment, is a final problem concerning "definiteness." (The UCC covers this subject in § 2–311.) The challenge for such arrangements is Article 14(1)'s requirement that the offer "indicate[ ] the goods." That article does not require, however, that the offer "specify" the goods; thus, a clause that permits either the buyer or the seller to select the goods from an assortment presumably should satisfy Article 14, provided that the contract in fact identifies the assortment—*i.e.*, the type or range of goods—from which the designated party must choose. In a case involving the sale of an airplane, for example, a Hungarian court held that a seller's proposal was an offer under CISG Article 14, even though it gave a choice to the buyer as between two types of engines and two types of airplanes. The court reasoned that the offer sufficiently indicated the goods and fixed the quantity under Article 14(1) because it gave the buyer a choice between only two specific engines for each of only two specific airplanes. Thus, the parties concluded a contract when the buyer indicated its acceptance.

The three articles following Article 14 address the withdrawal, revocation, and termination of an offer. Under Article 15, an offer is effective when it reaches the offeree, but may be "withdrawn" by a corresponding declaration that reaches the offeree first. After the offer becomes effective, however, the only recourse for a regretful offeror is to attempt to "revoke" the offer. Under Article 16(1), it may do so effectively if a corresponding declaration *reaches* the offeree before the offeree has *dispatched* an acceptance. The offeror does not have such a power, however, in all circumstances (see below). Finally, even it is irrevocable, an offer "terminates" under Article 17 when a rejection by the offeree reaches the offeror.

Revocation of an Offer. One of the consequences of the CISG's rejection of the "consideration" requirement is that there is no foundation for the strict common law approach to the revocability of an unaccepted offer. Traditional common law doctrine makes an offer freely revocable until accepted, unless the parties conclude a contract supported by consideration to keep it open (a so-called "option contract"). In many civil law systems, in contrast, an offer is binding and irrevocable unless the offeror states that it is revocable. These two approaches are in conflict, and the compromise adopted by the CISG uses neither.

Under CISG Article 16(2), the offeror in principle may revoke the offer, but this power is subject to two important exceptions. First, Article 16(2)(a) states that an offer is not revocable if it "indicates" that it is irrevocable "by stating a fixed time for acceptance or otherwise." The first reference seems relatively clear, and would include a statement that an offer will be held open for a specified period. The words "or otherwise," in contrast, leave substantial room for interpretation. They may well include a general statement that an offer will lapse after a specified period. In any event, the "or otherwise" language should require (under the interpretive rules of Article 8) consideration of the other terms of the offer as well as the surrounding circumstances and the prior dealings between the parties.

Second, the offeror loses the power of revocation in the case of reasonable and actual reliance by the offeree. Article 16(2)(b). This possibility for limiting the offeror's power of revocation is similar in concept to (but should not be influenced by) the notion of an "option contract" through offeree reliance under Section 87(2) of the Restatement (Second) of Contracts. For emphasis, however, the requirements of § 87(2) are idiosyncratic to U.S. domestic law and courts should not consult them for guidance in developing the autonomous law required by the CISG (for no gap exists as contemplated by CISG Article 7(2)). Thus, what is "reasonable" reliance for purposes of CISG Article 16(2)(b) must be determined on an international level and not based on domestic law practices or precedents.

In any event, in either of the two categories of irrevocability under Article 16, the offer also must meet the Article 14 requirements, including an indication of the goods and a fixed or determinable price and quantity. The simple reason is that an offeree cannot accept a proposal that is not an offer in the first place.

Acceptance. CISG Articles 18 through 23 provide the rules for an "acceptance" of an offer. Article 18(1) first defines "acceptance" as a statement or "other conduct" by an offeree "indicating assent to an offer." Silence or inactivity alone does not suffice, but the negotiations and other prior conduct of the parties may establish an implicit understanding that lengthy silence followed by an absence of an affirmative objection indicates an acceptance. *See also* CISG Article 8(3).

Under Article 23, a contract is "concluded" when an acceptance of the offer "becomes effective." Thus, as in most legal systems the timing question for an acceptance can be quite important. As a basic rule, Article 18(2) declares that an acceptance becomes effective when it "reaches" the offeror. This is yet another situation in which the CISG differs from the traditional rules in the United States. At U.S. common law, "the mailbox rule" passed the risk of loss or delay in transmission of an acceptance to the offeror once the offeree has dispatched the acceptance. It also chose that point in time to define the moment of contract formation, and thus to terminate the offeror's power to revoke the offer and to terminate the offeree's power to withdraw the acceptance.

The CISG's approach to this issue is more nuanced. As noted, under CISG Article 18(2) an acceptance is not effective until it "reaches" (*i.e.*, is delivered to) the offeror. The same article also provides, however, that an acceptance is not effective if it does not reach the offeror "within the time he has fixed or, if no time is fixed, within a reasonable time" under the circumstances. (A late acceptance nonetheless may be effective if the offeror so informs the offeree without delay, *see* Article 21.) Thus, risk of loss or delay in transmission generally is on the offeree, which must now take care to inquire with the offeror about the actual receipt of the acceptance.

Nonetheless, this rule is balanced by CISG Article 16(1), which—as briefly noted above—provides that the offeror's power to revoke the offer ends upon dispatch of the acceptance. However, the offeree's power to withdraw the acceptance terminates only when the acceptance reaches the offeror. Article 22. Thus, an acceptance sent by a slow transmission method allows the offeree to speculate for a day or two while the offeror may not revoke the offer. An email message will release the offeree from the not-yet-received acceptance.

A different timing rule may apply for an acceptance by conduct alone. Article 18(1) states that such an acceptance is possible. Under the Article 18(2) rule, such an acceptance would become effective only when it "reaches" the offeror, although this may occur indirectly through third parties such as banks or carriers. Article 18(3) states, however, that acceptance by conduct is effective "at the moment the act is performed" (such as dispatch of the goods or payment of the purchase price). Nonetheless, such an acceptance without notice to the offeror is possible only if it is allowed by the offer, by usage, or by the parties' prior course of dealing. Thus, a careful offeree—at least one worried about a revocation of the offer after, for example, the goods have been dispatched but have not yet arrived—will notify the offeror that acceptance by conduct is forthcoming.

Finally, CISG Article 29(1) provides that a contract may be modified by the parties through a "mere agreement." If a contract in writing permits modification only in writing, however, Article 29(2) declares that the contract cannot be otherwise modified, unless a party by its conduct induces the other party to act in reliance on an unwritten modification.

Battle of the Forms. One of the most vexing of modern contract formation issues is the "battle of the forms." This "battle" arises when the respective lawyers of the buyer and the seller prepare carefully crafted forms, but the parties themselves pay little attention to the forms when they actually negotiate their contract. The parties focus on the business terms (price, specification and quantity of goods, performance time); it is only if and when a dispute arises that the parties pull out the forms and review them carefully (most often, for the first time). The CISG's approach to the "battle of the forms" differs markedly from that of the UCC (the infamous § 2–207).

To begin the battle, the CISG, although in a circular fashion, generally follows the traditional "mirror image" analysis. Under Article 19(1), if the buyer's purchase order form and the seller's reply order acknowledgment form—the typical arrangement—differ in any respect, the reply functions not as an acceptance, but instead as a rejection and counteroffer. Article 19(2) seems to inject some flexibility, for it states that a reply may operate as an acceptance—and thus form a contract—even with additional or different terms as long as they do not "materially alter" the terms of the offer (and the offeror does not timely object to them). What Article 19(2) gives, however, Article 19(3) takes away almost entirely. The latter defines as "material" nearly every term of interest to the parties, including "among other things," those relating to "price, payment, quality and quantity of the goods, place and time of delivery, extent of one party's liability to the other or the settlement of disputes."

In the great run of battle of the forms cases under the CISG, therefore, the reply document (again, usually the seller's order acknowledgement form) does not function as a legal acceptance of the buyer's offer. Instead, it operates as a rejection of the offer and a counteroffer. The rejection also terminates the original offer under CISG Article 17. Thus, the parties do not "conclude" a contract by exchanging forms, and if one party reneges on its promises, before performance, it likely will not be liable for breach.

Nonetheless, in the vast majority of transactions involving exchanges of such forms, the parties fail to notice, or intentionally disregard, the technical conflicts in their respective standard business terms and perform the contemplated transaction. Once the seller ships the goods and the buyer accepts and pays for them, there is little doubt—on the basis of the party autonomy principle of CISG Article 6— that the parties have formed a contract governing their transaction. But what are its terms?

The common law analysis would give effect to the terms of the last form sent by either party, since that last form (usually the seller's) would be a rejection and counteroffer, and thereby terminate all prior unaccepted offers. The only offer left to accept through conduct, therefore, is this last counteroffer. This is the "last shot" principle, and, on the surface, CISG Article 19(1) & (3), together with Articles 17 and 18(1) & (3), seem to follow it. The reflexive initial response of some scholars thus supported the traditional "last shot" approach for the CISG as well. The drafting history of the CISG, however, is at best ambiguous. It instead shows that the drafters simply were unable to come to an agreement on this difficult issue, and thus consciously left the matter unresolved. By near universal consensus of courts and scholars, this does not, however, represent a gap in the CISG that would permit resort to domestic law. Thus, the answer must be found within the structure and principles of the Convention itself.

A recent and growing trend of opinion among courts and scholars has rejected a strict application of the last shot rule. Instead, they have relied on the flexible interpretive rules of the Convention (*see* Article 8 and the discussion above) and the core principle of party autonomy (*see* Article 6) to assess more carefully the actual intent of the parties.

This is particularly true regarding the standard business terms the parties routinely exchange but rarely discuss. A growing chorus of federal courts now holds that a party must have actual knowledge, or at least reasonable notice, of the attempted inclusion of standard business terms by the other party. Even an express reference will not suffice if the party has not actually received the terms. In absence of this, the other party's standard business terms will not become part of the contract. This approach is fully consistent with CISG Article 8's primary reliance on the actual intent over inflexible notions of objective intent.

The approach of foreign courts tends to be in accord. Some French and several German court decisions—including one from the Federal Court of Justice of Germany (*Bundesgerichtshof*)—have held that standard business terms become part of a contract only if the other party had notice of them and "easily" could have taken notice of their contents. Where both parties send standard business terms without a formal agreement on either, these recent courts have applied an "overlap" rule, under which the boilerplate provisions in the parties' respective forms become part of the contract only to the extent the provisions agree in substance. The CISG's provisions fill the resulting gaps in the contract. The courts have reached this result based on the principle in CISG Article 6 that the parties' actual agreement prevails over the terms of the

Convention and on the flexible interpretive rules for determining that agreement in CISG Article 8. Indeed, the German Federal Court of Justice has described this approach as "probably" the prevailing view. A few courts, however, have hewn closely to the limited language of Articles 17, 18, and 19, and applied the mirror image and last shot doctrines. These courts have thus ignored the more sophisticated analytical tools available for resolving the battle of forms under the CISG.

In summary, the CISG generally follows the traditional offer–acceptance scheme. But, at least as compared to U.S. domestic law, it reduces the flexibility of the parties by prohibiting some open price terms, and it imposes more restrictions on the ability of the offeror to revoke the offer. On the battle of the forms, the CISG also may delay the formation of a contract through the "mirror image" rule, and may use the "last shot" principle to make the offeree's (usually the seller's) terms control the transaction. However, on the last point, both the courts and the authors who have analyzed the subject have suggested ways of avoiding this traditional analysis in a manner consistent with deeper principles in the Convention.

SELLER'S PERFORMANCE OBLIGATIONS

Part III of the CISG sets forth the basic performance obligations of the seller and the buyer. After some initial general provisions (such as on the core notion of "fundamental breach" in Article 25), Part III contains separate chapters for the obligations of the seller (Articles 30–52) and of the buyer (Articles 53–65).

CISG Article 30 defines the fundamental obligations of the seller. Under that provision, the seller is obligated to deliver the goods and any related documents as provided in the parties' contract and to transfer to the buyer "the property in the goods" (*i.e.*, title). In addition, the seller is obligated to deliver goods that conform to the contract as to quantity, quality, description, and freedom from third-party claims.

Domestic law may influence the content of some of these obligations, because under Article 4(b) the Convention "is not concerned with" the effect of the contract on "the property in the goods sold." Domestic law, therefore, determines whether "the property" passes from the seller to the buyer at the conclusion (formation) of the contract, upon delivery, or at some other time; whether a certificate of title is required; and whether the seller may retain title as security for the purchase price or other debts.

Place of Delivery. "Delivery" under the CISG is a limited concept, and relates only to transfer of possession of or control over the goods. The CISG's drafters did not attempt to consolidate all incidents of sale—physical delivery, passing of risk of loss, passing of title, liability for the price, and ability to obtain specific performance, etc.—into a single concept or make them turn on a single event, as some domestic law does. Instead, they generally followed the approach of the UCC—although not the specific rules—by providing separate rules for each of these incidents.

As to the place of delivery, the CISG recognizes four distinct types of delivery terms: (1) delivery contracts, under which the seller must deliver the goods at a specified distant place; (2) shipment contracts, which "involve carriage of the goods," but do not require delivery at any particular distant place; (3) sales contracts where the goods are at a known location and are not expected to be transported; and (4) sales contracts without a specified place of delivery and where goods are not expected to be transported. CISG Article 31. Each of these options is examined below.

(1) In a delivery contract, the seller may be obligated to deliver the goods at the buyer's place, or at a sub-buyer's place, or at any other specified distant location. However, the CISG has no provisions directly describing the seller's duties in delivery contracts, for Article 31 expressly addresses only those contracts under which the seller "is not bound to deliver the goods at any other particular place." As a result, the identification of the seller's specific delivery obligations is left to interpretation of the contract terms. A common practice in international sales transactions is to define such obligations through commercial terms such as DAP, DAT, or specific forms of FOB. *See* Commercial Terms below.

(2) In a shipment contract, the seller has no obligation to deliver the goods at any particular place, but it is clear that transportation of the goods

by a third party carrier is involved. Subject (as always) to the parties' contractual agreements, a shipment contract may require the seller to take more than one action to accomplish its obligation of "delivery." First, Article 31(a) requires that the seller transfer ("hand over") the goods to a carrier—the first independent carrier. (Because the seller must "hand over" the goods to the carrier and not to the buyer, transactions requiring the buyer to assume responsibility for carriage seem excluded from this provision.) Thus, unlike UCC § 2–504, the CISG does not impose a duty on the seller to arrange for the carriage of the goods. Second, Article 32(1) provides that if the goods are not "clearly identified to the contract" by the shipping documents or by their own markings, the seller must "give notice to the buyer of the consignment specifying the goods." Third, Article 32(2) states that if the seller is bound to arrange for carriage of the goods, it must make such carriage contracts as are "appropriate in the circumstances" and according to the "usual terms" for such transportation. Finally, Article 32(3) requires, depending upon the contract's terms, that the seller either "effect insurance" coverage of the goods during transit or, at the buyer's request, give the buyer the information necessary to effect insurance.

CISG Article 31 then has different rules for transactions where carriage of the goods is not "involved."

(3) First, absent a contrary agreement, if the parties knew at the time of the conclusion of the

contract where the goods were or were to be produced, the buyer is expected to pick them up at that location. The seller's obligation then is merely to put the goods "at the buyer's disposal" at that location. Article 31(a)(b). The Convention is not clear on whether this requires notification to the buyer, but it would require notification to any third party bailees to allow the buyer to take possession.

(4) Second, in all other cases where transportation is not involved, Article 31 provides that delivery is required only at the seller's place of business. Again, the seller then is obligated merely to put the goods at the buyer's disposal at that place.

Where the delivery of the goods is to be accomplished by tender or delivery of documents (typically, a bill of lading), Article 34 requires only that the seller adhere to the terms of the contract. The second and third sentences of Article 34 also establish the principle that a seller that delivers defective documents early may cure the defects until the date due for delivery of the documents under the contract, provided that this does not cause the buyer "unreasonable inconvenience or unreasonable expense." Of course, in such a case the buyer nonetheless will retain a right to any damages caused by the original defective delivery and the cure.

Time of Delivery. CISG Article 33 defines the time requirements for the seller's performance. Not surprisingly, the primary focus is on the contract terms. Thus, the seller must deliver the goods as follows: (a) if a specific date is fixed by or determinable from the contract, on that date; (b) if a period of time is fixed by or determinable from the contract, within that period, unless the circumstances indicate that the buyer has a power to choose a specific date; or (c) in all other cases, within a "reasonable time." "Reasonable time" is not defined, and will depend on the surrounding circumstances and trade usage, but at least it should preclude a demand for immediate delivery.

The Convention has no express provisions on the seller's duties regarding export and import licenses and taxes, and thus leaves the determination of these incidents of delivery to the contract terms, or usage. Where these issues are not covered by the contract terms or usage, the nature of the seller's delivery obligation often will provide the needed guidance. Thus, if the seller is not obligated to arrange transportation, these responsibilities should fall to the buyer; if, in contrast, the seller is obligated to deliver at a particular destination inside the buyer's country, the seller generally will have the responsibility to obtain export and import licenses. In any event, it is quite common in international transactions for the parties to agree on an international "commercial term" (FOB, CIF, etc.), which expressly address export and import licenses and related issues. *See* Commercial Terms below.

Quality of the Goods. With respect to the goods themselves, CISG Article 35 (not surprisingly) obligates the seller to deliver goods that conform to the parties' contractual agreement. In determining whether the quality of the goods conforms to the contract, the Convention eschews such separate and independent doctrines as "warranty" and "strict product liability" from U.S. law, as well as the doctrines of "fault" or "negligence" from civil law. Instead, the CISG focuses on the simpler concept that the seller is obligated to deliver the goods as "required by" the contract. Article 35(1). It then defines certain default obligations of the seller and creates certain related presumptions. Article 35(2). Thus, notwithstanding certain facial similarities to the UCC, the CISG follows its own distinctive approach, with the result that courts should not apply idiosyncratic UCC notions, precedents, and practices to transactions governed by the CISG.

The basic obligation of the seller under Article 35(1) is that the goods must conform to the contract requirements regarding "quantity, quality and description" as well as in their packaging. To this, the CISG adds certain presumptions that apply unless the seller secures a contractual limitation. First, the goods must be fit for "the purposes for which goods of the same description would ordinarily be used" and be "contained or packaged in a manner usual for such goods." Article 35(2)(a), (d). The CISG imposes no conditions on this obligation of the seller relating to fitness for ordinary use. And because the CISG generally applies only to commercial contracts, there is no need for the UCC limitation to "merchant" sellers.

Nonetheless, this leaves one important unresolved issue—whether the "ordinary use" is defined by the seller's location or the buyer's location, if the "ordinary use" in the two is different. Although some scholars support a contrary position, an early decision of the German Federal Court of Justice declared the now prevailing view that the seller generally is not obligated to deliver goods that conform to public laws and regulations enforced at the buyer's place of business, subject to three important exceptions: (1) if the public regulations of the buyer's state are identical to those enforced in the seller's state; (2) if the buyer informed the seller about those regulations; *or* (3) if, due to "special circumstances," the seller knew or should have known about the regulations in the buyer's state. A U.S. federal court subsequently endorsed this approach in *Medical Marketing Int'l, Inc. v. Internazionale Medico Scientifica, S.R.L.*, 1999 WL 311945 (E.D. La. 1999), as have courts of other jurisdictions. One might also add that the seller likewise should be liable where a use is "ordinary" in the international trade of the goods involved. To secure a broader obligation, the buyer must conclude an express contractual agreement under Article 35(1) or satisfy the criteria for fitness for a "particular purpose" under Article 35(2)(b).

Second, Article 35(2)(b) requires that the goods be fit for any particular use made known to the seller at contract formation. From its structure, this provision prescribes an interesting arrangement for the burden of proof. First, the obligation will arise only if the buyer can prove that its "particular purpose" was "expressly or impliedly" made known to the seller at or before "the time of the conclusion of the contract." If the buyer satisfies these factual predicates, the burden of proof switches to the seller. That is, the seller will not be liable if it can prove either that the buyer in fact did not rely or that it was unreasonable for the buyer to rely on the seller's skill and judgment (which switches the burden of proof on this element as compared to UCC § 2–315). Article 35(2)(b) states no express requirement that the buyer inform the seller of the buyer's reliance; the seller need only know of the buyer's particular purpose. More important, there is no requirement that the buyer inform the seller of any of the difficulties involved in designating or designing goods to accomplish the particular use. Courts may address abuse of this issue through a careful application of the "reasonable reliance" criterion.

Finally, Article 35(2)(c) requires that the goods conform to any goods the seller "has held out to the buyer as a sample or model." This is in addition to any express contractual description of the goods.

Each of these obligations, however, arises out of the contract, with the result that the parties may "agree otherwise" and limit the seller's obligations concerning quality (a more flexible concept than "disclaimer of warranties" under UCC § 2–316(2)). And as a federal Court of Appeals correctly held in *Chicago Prime Packers, Inc. v. Northam Food Trading Co.*, 408 F.3d 894 (7th Cir. 2005), the buyer has the burden to prove any such a nonconformity (although some foreign courts unfortunately have left some ambiguity on the point).

The obligations of the seller under Article 35(2) relating to non-conformities of quality do not apply where the buyer is aware or "could not have been unaware" of a defect at the time the contract was "concluded." *See* Article 35(3). Thus, knowledge gained at the time of delivery or inspection of the goods will not affect the seller's obligation. Courts have held, however, that the seller may not rely on this exemption where, although the buyer has general knowledge of a defect or state of quality in the goods, the seller knows of specific facts not disclosed to the buyer.

CISG Article 36(1) states that the relevant time for assessment of a nonconformity of the goods is "when the risk [of loss] passes to the buyer"—a concept explored in more detail below. Thus, any nonconformity concerning the goods that exists at the time the risk of loss passes is actionable, even if discovered long after delivery. The buyer must prove, however, that the defect actually was present at that point (typically, at delivery) and was not caused by third parties or the buyer's own use or lack of oversight of the goods. The buyer need not prove what caused the goods to be defective, only that they are, in fact, defective.

Buyer's Inspection and Notice of Nonconformities. The CISG also imposes certain conditions on the buyer's right to rely on nonconformities in the goods. First, the buyer must inspect the goods "within as short a period as is practicable" under the circumstances. Article 38(1). Where the contract involves the carriage of goods, the buyer may defer the inspection until the goods have arrived at their destination. Article 38(2). Finally, the buyer loses the right to rely on a nonconformity in the goods if it does not give notice to the seller "specifying the nature of the lack of conformity" within a reasonable time after the buyer discovered or "ought to have discovered it." Article 39(1). The CISG also contains an interesting rule that requires such a notice by the buyer "at the latest within a period of two years from the date on which the goods were actually handed over to the buyer." Article 39(2). As a special protection for remote or unsophisticated parties, however, the buyer retains a right to reduce the contract price or to claim damages (but not lost profits), if it has "a reasonable excuse" for the failure to give the required notice. Article 44.

There has been more litigation over the effectiveness of notices of nonconformity than over almost any other single issue. The results, however, usually are not surprising. Several courts have attempted to set "presumptive periods" for notices of nonconformity, but the measuring points have differed: Some have set a presumptive period—from as short as eight days to as long as six weeks—measured as of the time of delivery (thus encompassing both the inspection period and the notice period). Others have set a presumptive period—from as little as a few days to as much as a month—measured only with reference to the duty of timely notice. On the latter, some courts have indicated that one month should be a presumptive period of adequate notice under normal circumstances. The German Federal Court of

Justice (*Bundesgerichtshof*) also held in one case that the seller waived a right of notice when it agreed to take back the goods after the buyer raised potential concerns.

CISG Article 40, however, mitigates the effects of the notice obligations in Articles 38 and 39 with respect to facts of which the seller knew or "could not have been unaware" and did not disclose to the buyer. In such a case, Article 40 precludes the seller from relying on a failure of the buyer to give a notice of any related nonconformity in the goods. Thus, even if the buyer would lose its right to rely on a nonconformity due its own failure to inspect or notify, the right remains if the seller knew of facts underlying the nonconformity and did not give notice of them to the buyer.

The Seller's Right to Cure. If the buyer discovers a nonconformity in the goods, the seller often will wish to effect a cure, even after delivery. It is for this reason that the Convention requires early notice by the buyer to the seller of any defects in the goods. The Convention has different rules for cure which depend upon whether the defects were discovered before or after the contract date for delivery.

Where a non-conforming tender is made *before* the contract date for delivery, Article 37 gives the seller an option to remedy any lack of conformity, "provided that the exercise of this right does not cause the buyer unreasonable inconvenience or unreasonable expense." But even if the seller does so, it is still liable to the buyer for any damages caused by the defects.

After the date for delivery has passed, the seller may remedy "any failure to perform his obligations," but its right to do so is subject to more exacting conditions. *See* Article 48. Again, the seller may cure only if it is able to do so "without unreasonable delay and without causing the buyer unreasonable inconvenience or uncertainty of reimbursement of expenses." But under Article 48(1), the seller has a right to cure after the delivery date only if it can do so "without unreasonable delay." Finally, a cross-reference to Article 49 makes clear that such a post-delivery-date cure is subject to the buyer's right to declare an "avoidance" of the contract, especially for a "fundamental" breach (on both notions, see below).

Provided these conditions are satisfied, Article 48(2) also permits the seller to state a reasonable time within which it will effect the cure and then request that the buyer "make known" whether it will accept that performance. If the buyer agrees or does not respond at all, the seller has a right to cure within the stated period. And in the interim the buyer may not resort to any inconsistent remedy (including avoidance of the contract). In any event, even if the seller cures the non-conformity, it again will be liable to the buyer for any damages caused by the delay in providing conforming goods. Article 48(1).

Exclusion of Quality Obligations. May the seller exclude the Article 35 obligations concerning the quality of the goods by terms in the contract—and, if so, how? As a basic rule, CISG Article 6 states that the parties may, by agreement, derogate from *any* provision of the Convention. Article 35(2) expressly affirms this point with specific reference to limitations on the seller's obligations concerning the quality of the goods with the statement that such obligations apply "except where the parties have agreed otherwise." Nonetheless, it is also clear that the standard formulation under the UCC— "disclaimer of implied warranties"—will be inapposite, because the CISG describes the seller's obligations neither as "warranties" nor as "implied." Careful international sellers will need to employ different verbal formulations, ones that deal directly with the description of the goods and their expected use as defined in the CISG (not the UCC).

One continuing issue of controversy in this regard is the extent to which local law regulating disclaimers might apply for international contracts governed by the CISG. Such local law covers a spectrum, from prohibitions on "unconscionable" disclaimers (especially in printed standard terms) to the special linguistic and similar requirements set out in UCC § 2–316. Today, however, there seems to be agreement that the former raises a question of "validity" (*see* CISG Article 4), and thus that relevant domestic law applies even for contracts governed by the CISG. The latter, in contrast, do not raise questions of "validity" as contemplated by CISG Article 4(a). As a result, the UCC's statutory requirements for an exclusion of warranties do not apply for CISG contracts. The distinction depends upon whether the local public policy prohibits conduct completely, as opposed to allowing the parties to limit the seller's obligations within certain specified conditions. Accordingly, the courts should draw a distinction between general contract defenses (such as unconscionability and fraud) and the specific UCC provisions that set requirements for exclusion of the express or implied warranties created by the UCC itself (*e.g.*, that the disclaimer be "conspicuous" or use particular words such "merchantability").

Obligations Concerning Title to the Goods. The seller's obligation under CISG Article 41 concerning title is to deliver goods not only free from any encumbrances on their title, but also free from any claim of a third party. Thus, the prevailing view holds that the seller is obligated to protect the buyer even from spurious claims and, if such arise, the seller must indemnify the buyer for the costs of defense. The parties may derogate from the terms of these provisions of the CISG by agreement, but the buyer's knowledge that the goods are subject to a bailee's lien does not necessarily imply such an agreement. Instead, the buyer may expect the seller to discharge the lien before tender of delivery. This rule does not apply, however, if the buyer agreed to take the goods subject to the right or claim.

In addition to good title, the seller is obligated to deliver the goods free from patent, trademark and copyright claims founded on the law of the "buyer's place of business" or the place where both parties expect the goods to be used or resold. Article 42. This obligation is subject, however, to a number of qualifications. First, the seller's obligations arise only with respect to claims of which "the seller knew or could not have been unaware." Article 42(1). Second, the seller has no obligation with respect to intellectual property rights of which the buyer "knew or could not have been unaware" when the contract was formed. Article 42(2)(a). Third, the seller is not liable for claims that arise out of its use of technical drawings, designs, or other specifications furnished by the buyer, if the seller's action is in "compliance with" the buyer's specifications. Article 42(2)(b). It is clear that this provision applies when the seller is following specifications required by the contract; but its application is not clear when the seller is merely following "suggestions" of the buyer as to how best to meet more general contract requirements. Fourth, the seller is excused from these obligations if the buyer does not give timely notice of a related breach (Article 43(1)), unless the seller actually "knew" of the claim and "the nature of it" in the first place (Article 43(2)).

A seller also might argue that mistake of law will provide an excuse, or at least that it has performed its obligations concerning intellectual property rights, if it has relied on trustworthy information from a lawyer. If it entered the transaction on the basis of such trustworthy information that the use or resale of the goods would not infringe on third-party intellectual property rights, the seller may be able to argue that it could not have "known" of the possible infringement claims.

The UCC approach to these problems (*see* § 2–607(5)) is to allow the buyer, when sued by a third party claimant, to "vouch in" the seller, so as to allow the seller to defend itself directly. Given the differences in local procedural rules, the CISG understandably contains no such "vouching in" provision. Thus, buyers that are confronted with third party claims are left to local procedural devices for protection.

BUYER'S PERFORMANCE OBLIGATIONS

CISG Article 53 defines two primary obligations of the buyer in a contract governed by the Convention: (a) to pay the price and (b) to take delivery of the goods. The former duty is the more important of the two. In addition, there are several derivative preliminary duties which might be referred to as "enabling steps." These include taking such actions as are required to enable payment or enable delivery (Article 54), and providing specifications on "the form, measurement or other features of the goods" (Article 60).

Time of Payment. Unless the parties have agreed on payment at some other time, Article 58(1) assumes a cash sale, and the seller may make payment a condition for handing over the goods or the related documents. Thus, payment is due when the seller places the goods, or documents of title controlling them, "at buyer's disposal" in accordance with the contract and the Convention. If the sales contract involves carriage of the goods, Article 58(2) gives the seller the right to ship on terms under which the goods, or (more commonly) negotiable documents of title controlling them, are not released to the buyer except against payment of the purchase price—even if the parties agreed on no particular method of payment. Article 58(3) generally grants the buyer an opportunity to inspect the good before payment, but not if "the procedures for delivery or payment agreed upon by the parties are inconsistent with such an opportunity." The principal example of this latter clause is a "payment against documents" transaction as discussed in Chapter 3.

Place of Payment. If the buyer is to pay against "handing over" of the goods or of documents controlling them (see immediately above), then under Article 57 the place of payment is where that event occurs (unless, as always, the parties' contract provides otherwise); in all other cases, the buyer must pay the price to the seller at the seller's place of business. In effect, this approach requires the buyer to export the funds to the seller, which is a critical issue when the buyer is from a country with a soft currency, or with other restrictions on the transfer of funds. In addition, the buyer has an obligation under Article 54 to cooperate and take all necessary steps to enable payment to be made, including the satisfaction of whatever formalities may be imposed by the buyer's country to obtain administrative authorization to make a payment abroad. Failure to take such steps may reflect a breach by the buyer even before payment is due.

The Buyer's Inspection Rights. Nonetheless, in general the buyer has a right to withhold payment until it has had an "opportunity to examine the goods." Article 58(3). If, however, the parties have agreed on a "payment against documents" transaction (such as through the use of the commercial terms CFR or CIF, see Commercial Terms below), the buyer thereby has agreed to pay upon tender of the documents (regardless of whether the goods have yet arrived) and without an advance right to inspect the goods. On the other hand, as noted above the buyer *must* inspect the goods "within as short a period as is practicable" under the circumstances (Article 38(1)), and loses the right to rely on any nonconformities if it does not timely notify the seller of them (Article 39(1)).

Acceptance of Delivery. The buyer's second obligation is to take delivery, that is, to take physical possession of the goods from the seller at the time and place of delivery (*see* Seller's Performance Obligations, *Place of Delivery*, above). Article 60 refers to this as the obligation to "tak[e] over the goods" (or, as applicable, the documents controlling the goods). This obligation also carries duties of cooperation. These include a duty to make the expected preparations to permit the seller to make delivery and may include such acts as providing for containers, transportation, unloading, and import licenses. The obligation also may have significance for the passing of the risk of loss when the contract contemplates shipment of the goods. In such a case, Article 69(1) provides that the risk of loss of or damage to the goods passes to the buyer when it fails to "take over" the goods in due time and thereby commits a breach by failing to take delivery.

RISK OF LOSS

The identification of the moment at which the risk of loss of or damage to the goods passes from the seller to the buyer is especially important for transactions governed by the CISG. This is because significant geographical distances often separate the parties, and as a result most contracts governed by the CISG will involve a transportation of the goods.

The basic rule under the CISG is that the buyer bears the risk of loss to the goods during their transportation by a carrier, unless (as always) the contract provides otherwise. Such a contractual agreement to allocate the risk of loss typically comes through the inclusion of a "commercial term" (such as FOB or CIF, see Commercial Terms below), and (under the party autonomy principle of Article 6) such agreements supersede the CISG provisions on the subject.

In absence of a contrary contractual agreement, CISG Articles 67 through 70 set forth specific risk of loss rules that depend on the nature of the seller's delivery obligation.

A first set of rules relates to transactions that "involve[ ] carriage of the goods":

(a) If the contract does not *at all* obligate the seller to hand over the goods "at a particular place" (a "shipment contract"), the risk of loss will pass under Article 67(1) when the goods are delivered "to the first carrier" for shipment to the buyer. But if the contract obligates the seller to hand over the goods *to the carrier* "at a particular place," then the risk of loss passes under the same Article when the seller hands over goods to the carrier at that place. Under either, the goods need not be on board the means of transportation—any receipt by a carrier will do. Further, the seller need not "hand over" the goods to an ocean-going or international carrier— possession by the local trucker who will haul them to the port is sufficient. However, if the seller uses its own vehicle to transport the goods, the seller bears the risk until the goods are handed over to an independent carrier, or to the buyer.

(b) If, however, the contract requires the seller to deliver the goods *to the buyer* at the buyer's location or "at" some other distant location (a "destination contract"), the seller bears the risk of loss until it puts the goods at the buyer's disposal at that location at the delivery time and the buyer becomes aware of that fact. Article 69(2).

Thus, in a contract between a Buffalo, N.Y., seller and Beijing, China, buyer: (1) in a shipment contract under the CISG, the risk would pass to the buyer when the goods were delivered to the first carrier in Buffalo; (2) in a destination contract (where the seller is obligated to deliver at Beijing), the seller would bear the risk during transit, and the risk would not pass to the buyer until the goods were put at the buyer's disposal in Beijing. (Again, specific commercial terms—such as FOB, FAS, and

CIF—have more detailed rules on risk of loss and these will have precedence over the CISG rules if incorporated in the parties' contract; see Commercial Terms below.)

A second set of risk of loss rules relates apply to transactions that do not involve carriage of the goods from the seller to the buyer.

(c) If the goods are not to be transported by a carrier (*e.g.*, when the buyer or an agent will pick up the goods), the risk passes to the buyer when it "takes over" the goods or, if it is late in doing so, when the goods are "placed at [its] disposal" and it commits a breach by not taking delivery. Article 69(1). The goods cannot, however, be "at [its] disposal" until they have first been identified to the contract. Article 67(2).

(d) If the goods are already in transit when sold, the risk passes under Article 68 when the contract is "concluded." If, however, "the circumstances so indicate"—especially if the buyer has obtained insurance during transit—the risk of loss will pass when the goods are delivered to the carrier that has issued documents governing the transit. On the other hand, if at the conclusion of the contract the seller knew or ought to have known of a loss or damage in transit and did not disclose this to the buyer, the risk of loss to that extent remains with the seller. Article 68.

The challenge for the buyer under this latter rule is that it may be practically impossible to determine whether damage to goods in a ship's cargo hold occurred before or after the parties concluded the sales contract.

In most situations, title and risk are treated separately. Thus, manipulation of title through the use of documents of title, such as negotiable bills of lading, is irrelevant and has no effect on the point of transfer of risk of loss. *See* Article 67(1). Just as title and risk are treated separately, so also breach and risk generally are treated separately. The one exception to this approach (noted above) is where the buyer is obligated to pick up the goods and commits a breach by failing to do so in a timely manner. *See* Article 69(1). In all other cases, including any breach by the seller, the basic risk of loss rules are not changed by claims of breach (which is contrary to the position of UCC § 2–510). Thus, a breach by the seller, whether a "fundamental beach" under Article 25 or not, is irrelevant to determine risk allocation or the point at which the risk of loss passes to the buyer. In specific, if the seller in fact already has committed a fundamental breach, the risk of loss rules in Articles 67, 68, and 69 will not impair the remedies available to the buyer on account of that breach (and especially the right to avoid the contract). Article 70.

EXCUSE FOR NON-PERFORMANCE

A common issue in the sometimes turbulent world of international trade is that events occur (wars, civil unrest, trade sanctions, etc.) that make one party's performance of a contract more difficult than anticipated, and maybe even impossible. To address such a situation, the CISG has a general provision, Article 79, that recognizes an "exemption" from liability for non-performance. Unlike UCC § 2–615, CISG Article 79 applies to a performance either by the seller or by the buyer, and extends to "any" obligations (not just the seller's delivery obligation).

A party asserting an exemption under CISG Article 79 must prove three elements: (a) First, it must prove that the failure to perform was due to an external impediment beyond the party's control. Although Article 79 refers to an "impediment," the standard for exemption is not strict impossibility. Rather, the prevailing view is that an extreme hardship will suffice, that is, such extreme difficulty in performance as constitutes impossibility as a practical matter under the circumstances. (b) Second, it must prove that it could not reasonably be expected to have taken the impediment into account at the time of the conclusion of the contract. (c) Finally, it must prove that it could not reasonably have avoided or overcome the impediment or its consequences. The non-performing party also must give reasonable notice of the excuse to the other party.

Article 79(2) extends the excuse for a contract party to a failure to perform by "a third party whom [it] has engaged to perform the whole or a part of the contract." This provision is narrower, however, than appears at first glance. According to the consensus view, Article 79(2) extends only to persons employed to perform the specific contractual obligation in dispute and thus does not cover, for example, the failure of an upstream supplier to perform under a separate contract.

In any event, Article 79(5) makes clear that any covered impediment only provides an exemption from liability for *damages* claimed by the other party. It does not deprive the other party of any other rights or remedies, such as avoidance of the contract for fundamental breach.

Reliance on One's Own Acts or Omissions. CISG Article 80 separately declares that a party may not rely on a failure to perform "to the extent that such a failure was caused by" its own acts or omissions. Thus, where a party's own actions are the cause of a breach by the other party, the breach does not provide a ground to assert rights under the Convention. Courts have applied this principle in Article 80 to prevent a party from relying on a variety of remedies otherwise permitted for nonperformance, including a right to damages, to avoid the contract, and to use the non-performance as a contractual defense.

BREACH AND REMEDIES—IN GENERAL

Breach in General. The CISG provides no formal definition for the traditional concept of breach of contract. Rather, it states simply that if the seller fails to perform "any" of its obligations, the buyer has a general right to damages as well as a right to certain more specific remedies. Article 45(1)(a), (b). Likewise, it states that if the buyer fails to perform "any" of its obligations, the seller has a general right to damages as well as a right to certain other more specific remedies. Article 61(1)(a), (b).

The CISG sets forth the rules for the buyer's and the seller's respective remedies upon breach in separate, though parallel, chapters. The buyer's remedies are in Part III, Chapter II (Articles 45 through 52). The seller's remedies are in Part III, Chapter III (Articles 61 through 65). The rules for determining damages for both parties, however, are combined in still another chapter, Part III, Chapter V (Articles 74 through 77).

The following paragraphs will first review the Convention's fundamental principles on breach and remedies that are common to both an aggrieved buyer and an aggrieved seller.

Right to Suspend Performance. Under CISG Article 71(1), a party that has yet to perform may suspend its performance in the case of prospective nonperformance by the other party. This right to suspend performance runs in favor of either the buyer or the seller. It arises if it "becomes apparent" that the other party will not perform a "substantial part" of its obligations because of either (1) a "serious deficiency" in its ability to perform or its "creditworthiness" (Article 71(1)(a)), or (2) its conduct in preparing to perform or in actually performing (Article 71(1)(b)).

The right to suspend performance nonetheless has the greatest significance for sellers. This is so because the sellers often must ship goods before payment, and thus assume the risk of later nonpayment by the buyer. Separately, the CISG permits a seller to suspend performance after shipment but before delivery of the goods—a so-called right of stoppage in transit. Article 71(2). The CISG does not require the carrier to comply with a seller's request; instead, it leaves the carrier's obligations to other law. Thus, it may give the seller the right, but not a practical ability, to prevent delivery by a carrier.

Under CISG Article 71(3), a party that suspends performance must notify the other party of that decision. The same provision declares that the right to suspend performance ceases if the other party "provides adequate assurance" that it will perform. Although not expressly stated, the assurance must come within a reasonable time, as this is a "general principle" of the Convention under Article 7(2).

Avoidance and Fundamental Breach. Either a buyer or a seller may declare a contract "avoided" in the event of certain forms of nonperformance or defective performance by the other party. Articles 49(1), 64(1). The specific situations of buyers and sellers will be analyzed in separate sections below.

Nonetheless, the concept of "avoidance of the contract" is central to the general breach and remedial scheme of the CISG and appears in a variety of provisions applicable to both buyer and seller. In its essence, a justified declaration of avoidance brings a contract to an end and releases both parties from their obligations under it, but preserves the right to damages by the aggrieved party. Article 81(1). To be effective, a declaration of avoidance must be made by notice to the other party. Article 26.

The principal ground for declaring a contract avoided under the CISG is in the event of a "fundamental breach." *See* Articles 49(1)(a) (for the buyer), 64(1)(a) (for the seller). What constitutes a "fundamental breach"? Article 25 defines the term as "such detriment to the other party as to substantially deprive him of what he is entitled to expect under the contract." Thus, a fundamental breach requires more than a failure of a party to perform a contractual obligation (whether from the terms of the contract itself or from the default rules of the CISG). It includes of course a complete failure to perform an essential contract duty (*e.g.*, final nondelivery or final nonpayment). Other possibilities of their nature will depend decisively on the facts of each case, but may include a failure to perform beyond a reasonable time where time is of the essence, defects in the goods such that they are unusable and cannot be resold, and an unjustified denial of contract rights. Accumulation of several violations also may suffice if as a result the aggrieved party loses the principal benefit of, or interest in, the expected contract performance.

Article 25 nonetheless requires consideration of the perspective of the breaching party. In specific, it declares that a breach is not fundamental if "the party in breach did not foresee and a reasonable person of the same kind and in the same circumstances would not have foreseen such a result." The relevant time for assessing this question of foreseeability is the conclusion of the contract.

Anticipatory Breach. Article 72(1) states a general right to declare a contract avoided in the event of an anticipatory breach of contract. The preconditions for such a declaration are few, but stringent. First, the conduct of the other party must make clear that it will commit a "fundamental breach" (as discussed above) when its performance comes due. Second, the mere possibility of a breach in the future does not suffice; it must be "clear" under the circumstances that the other party will commit the required fundamental breach. Third, the declaring party must give reasonable notice to the other party, but only "if time allows." Finally, after receipt of the notice, the other party must fail to give an "adequate assurance" that it in fact will perform. Where the other party actually declares that it will not perform its obligations when due, the requirements for avoidance under Article 72 seemingly are less stringent. In such a case, CISG Article 72(3) provides that a party need not give notice of an intent to declare an avoidance.

Installment Contracts. The CISG has special rules for breach of an "instalment contract"—that is, where the contract involves at least two successive deliveries of the goods. With respect to a breach of such contracts, CISG Article 73 defines different rules for an individual installment as opposed to a breach that affects the whole contract. For an individual installment, if a party fails to perform in such a way as to constitute "a fundamental breach of contract with respect to that instalment," the other party may declare the contract avoided "with respect to that instalment." Article 73(1). If, in addition, such a breach gives the aggrieved party "good grounds to conclude" that a fundamental breach will occur in the future installments, it may declare the contract avoided for the future as well (provided it does so within a reasonable time). Article 73(2).

The CISG then grants a special right to an aggrieved buyer to declare an avoidance of the whole contract (or affected portions) if a breach on one delivery has a broader effect on the contract performances. Under Article 73(3), if the buyer can show that, "by reason of their interdependence," past or future deliveries "could not be used for the purpose contemplated by the parties at the time of the conclusion of the contract," it may declare an avoidance with respect to those past or future deliveries as well.

Damages in General. CISG Articles 74–78 provide an aggrieved buyer or seller an action for damages. There is no requirement that either party prove that the party in breach was at "fault" as a prerequisite to a recovery of damages. Both direct and consequential damages are recoverable; and expectancy, reliance, and restitutionary interests are all protected.

Article 74 defines the basic principle that an aggrieved party is entitled to "a sum equal to the loss, including loss of profit, suffered as a consequence of the breach." But that Article also limits consequential damages in three familiar ways: (a) First, the damages may not exceed the loss that the party in breach "foresaw or ought to have foreseen at the time of the conclusion of the contract . . . as a possible consequence of the breach of contract." This rule has a facial similarity to the traditional common law as famously articulated in *Hadley v. Baxendale*, 156 Eng. Rep. 145 (Ex. Ct. 1854). Careful review reveals, however, that it may be quite different, for recovery is available under the CISG if the loss suffered is foreseeable as a "possible consequence" of the breach, in contrast to the "probable result" test of the common law. *See* Restatement (Second) of Contracts, § 351. (UCC § 2-715 uses neither term.) (b) Second, under Article 77 the aggrieved party must take "reasonable measures" to mitigate its damages. (c) Third, although not expressly stated, the consensus (and perhaps obvious) view is that the aggrieved party must prove its damages to a reasonable degree of certainty. Incidental damages relating to interest are allowed separately in Article 78 (although substantial dispute exists over how to calculate the interest rate).

Articles 75 and 76 then state alternative specific measures of recovery for an aggrieved party. Article 75 first allows the recovery, in addition to the general damages under Article 74, of the difference between the contract price and the "price in [a] substitute transaction." As an alternative, Article 76 permits recovery based on the difference between the contract price and the "current price" (*i.e.*, the market price) for the goods.

In most civil law countries, the litigation loser also pays part of the winner's attorneys' fees, typically according to a statutory formula. This is regarded as part of the damages necessary to make the aggrieved party whole. Courts in the United States generally have rejected such an award on the ground that rules relating to attorneys' fees are procedural, not substantive. The problem with such decisions is that they have engaged carefully neither with the interpretive rules in CISG Article 7 nor with the thoughtful analyses of foreign courts on the subject (which is required by Article 7(1)).

BUYER'S REMEDIES UPON
SELLER'S BREACH

CISG Articles 45 through 52 define the remedies available to the buyer upon a breach by the seller. As described below, if the seller breaches any of its obligations, the buyer has four basic types of remedies: (a) specific performance; (b) "avoidance" of the contract; (c) a special remedy that allows a "self-help" reduction in the price due; and in any event (d) an action for damages. In general, the drafters of the remedy provisions of the CISG faced special challenges because of the divergent approaches of civil and common law legal systems. These challenges are illustrated by two facts: First, specific performance is the preferred remedy at civil law, while an action for damages is preferred at common law. Second, at civil law, a finding of "fault" is usually required for imposition of any recovery of damages, while under the common law an aggrieved party need show only breach of any nature. The CISG drafters attempted to bridge both gaps.

(a) Specific Performance. CISG Article 46 gives a buyer that has not received the agreed performance from the seller a specifically enforceable right to "require performance"—such as delivery of the goods—subject to two important qualifications: First, under Article 28 a court need not grant such a remedy "unless the court would do so under its own law" for comparable contracts. This limitation is quite significant in the United States, where under the traditional approach specific performance is an "extraordinary remedy." Interestingly, the result of the rule in Article 28 is that a U.S. court will grant a remedy of specific performance only as allowed by UCC § 2–716. Second, the buyer must not already have resorted to an "inconsistent" remedy. Thus, a buyer is not entitled to specific performance if it has already declared an avoidance of the contract; effected a reduction in price; or sought damages tied directly to the seller's failure to deliver the goods (as opposed to consequential damages).

In short, the CISG gives the buyer the right to seek specific performance, rather than damages, but does not compel it to do so; and it permits a court to grant such a remedy, but does not compel it to do so. Even in civil law jurisdictions, buyers often will prefer a damages remedy because of the expense and delays inherent in seeking and enforcing formal court orders requiring performance.

If the remedy of specific performance is available, the buyer may require performance by seller of any of its breached obligations. Article 46(1). Where the goods have not been delivered, this would mean a requirement that the seller deliver the goods. If the seller has delivered, but the goods do not conform to the contract, the buyer may require delivery of conforming substitute goods if the nonconformity amounts to a "fundamental breach" (*see* below). Article 46(2). Likewise, the buyer may require the seller to repair nonconforming goods, unless this is "unreasonable having regard to all the circumstances." Article 46(3). In any event, the buyer will lose any right to specific performance if it has declared an "avoidance" of the contract (*see* below), which is an inconsistent remedy.

(b) Avoidance of the Contract. The CISG provides two separate grounds for the buyer to declare an "avoidance of the contract" upon a breach by the seller. First, CISG Article 49(1)(a) permits the buyer to use this remedy in the event of a "fundamental breach," regardless of when the breach occurs. Second, in the specific case of a non-delivery, CISG Article 49(1)(b) allows the buyer to declare an avoidance if the seller does not perform within an additional deadline set by the buyer.

As an essential background for both, recall first that an "avoidance of the contract" by the buyer is a method of refusing to accept or to keep defective goods, with a corresponding right not to pay for the goods. In this respect, "avoidance" under the CISG is comparable to the rights of a buyer under the UCC to "reject" the goods actually delivered before "acceptance," or to "revoke the acceptance" of goods previously accepted. However, the CISG does not adopt the distinctions between "acceptance of the goods," "rejection," and "revocation of acceptance" contained in the UCC, and thus any domestic precedent on those concepts is irrelevant for transactions governed by the CISG. The CISG's concept of "avoidance of the contract" also is quite different from the limited notion of "avoidance" under the UCC. *See* § 2–613. Further, the CISG does not attach special legal significance to the concept of "acceptance" of the goods; as a result, the buyer's taking delivery of the goods is not a crucial factual or legal step in the analysis of the buyer's position under the CISG.

Avoidance for Fundamental Breach. Instead, the core concept under the CISG is to limit use of this remedy to situations that involve "fundamental breach." Thus, Article 49(1)(a) gives the buyer a right to declare an avoidance of the contract, regardless of when the breach occurs, if the seller fails to perform "any" of its obligations and this amounts to a fundamental breach. As noted above, such a breach is one that "substantially deprive[s]" the buyer of what it is "entitled to expect under the contract." Article 25. Such a declaration of avoidance must be made by notice to the seller. Article 26. But the right to declare an avoidance for a fundamental breach is lost if the buyer does not make the declaration (a) in respect of late delivery, within a reasonable time after the buyer has become aware of delivery, or (b) in respect of all other breaches, within a reasonable time after the buyer knew or ought to have known of the breach. Article

49(2)(b)(i). The purpose of this notice is to give the seller an opportunity to cure the defects (as examined in detail above)—although even with a cure, the buyer retains a right to damages caused by the defective goods. Article 48(1).

Even if the buyer seeks to avoid the contract after a "fundamental breach" by the seller, the latter has a right under CISG Article 48(1) to "cure" any defect in its performance. As discussed above, if the seller's nonconforming tender is early, the seller may cure by making a conforming tender up to the delivery date in the contract, whether the nonconformity would create a fundamental breach or not. *See also* Article 37. The seller's right to cure in such a case also survives the buyer's declaration of "avoidance of the contract," because it will be very difficult to sustain a finding of fundamental beach where the seller has made a timely offer of cure. If the seller's tender or offer of cure is made *after* the delivery date in the contract, it still has a right to cure through late performance, but only if it can do so "without unreasonable delay," and without causing the buyer unreasonable inconvenience or uncertainty of reimbursement of expenses. Article 48(1).

Must performance offered as a cure meet a strict "nonconformity" test, or is it still subject to the "fundamental breach" test? The CISG has no provision on this issue. However, it has been held that, if the seller's offer of cure is defective, the buyer may procure cure on its own. In any event, the entire thrust of these CISG provisions on the buyer's remedies is to require cooperation between the parties in resolving disputes over timeliness of delivery and conformity of the goods. Moreover, as noted above and discussed again below, CISG Article 77 imposes an obligation on an aggrieved party to take reasonable steps to mitigate its damages.

The CISG's rules on avoidance and cure may leave the seller of goods in a significantly better position as compared to the UCC, if the buyer claims a relatively minor fault in the goods. First, under the UCC the buyer may reject the goods merely because a tender is not "perfect" (*see* § 2–601); this is definitely not allowed under the CISG. In addition, although the seller has a right to cure defects under both regimes, the right under the UCC has either time limitations or knowledge requirements (*see* § 2–508) that do not exist under the CISG. Finally, although the buyer will have a right to damages under either regime, under the CISG it may return the goods only in the event of a "fundamental breach." Thus, the seller is less likely to find the goods rejected for an asserted minor nonconformity, and stranded an ocean or continent away.

Avoidance and "Nachfrist." Given the inherent uncertainties of the "fundamental breach" test, it often will be very difficult for the buyer, or its attorney, to know how to react to a particular breach—and thus whether "avoidance" of the contract is permissible or not. Incorrect analysis could mean that the buyer has committed a fundamental breach through its response. CISG Articles 47 and 49(1)(b) attempt to address such uncertainties by offering the buyer a power to compel timely and conforming performance by the seller: Based on the German law notion of *Nachfrist* ("additional deadline"), if the seller fails to deliver the goods on the agreed delivery date, the buyer may notify the seller that performance is due by a stated new date. If the seller fails to perform—or declares that it will not perform—by the new deadline, the buyer has a right to declare an avoidance of the contract even if no fundamental breach has yet occurred. Article 49(1)(b). But if the seller has already delivered the goods, the buyer loses the right to declare an avoidance on this basis unless it does so within a reasonable time after the expiration of the *Nachfrist*. Article 49(2)(b)(ii).

However, by its express terms, Article 49(1)(b) allows this *Nachfrist* alternative only for "nondelivery" by the seller, not for delivery of nonconforming goods. Avoidance also is available only if the seller does not deliver during the additional period allowed by the notice. During the additional notice period, the buyer may not resort to any other remedy for breach of contract. Article 47(2).

How long of an additional period must the buyer give the seller? Article 47 requires that it be "of reasonable length," but unless there is a custom on this issue the buyer will have no certainty that the period given in the *Nachfrist* notice is long enough, especially if long distances are involved. In one

German decision, the court found that an additional period of eleven days fixed by an aggrieved buyer under CISG Article 47(1) was "too short to organize carriage by sea." The court nonetheless upheld the buyer's declaration of avoidance seven weeks later because the seller had offered only a partial delivery of conforming goods in the interim.

Conditions and Limitations on the Buyer's Avoidance Rights. The CISG also imposes certain important conditions and obligations on a buyer that wishes to declare a contract avoided. First, the buyer loses the right to make such a declaration—or require delivery of substitute goods—if it cannot return the goods to the seller "substantially in the condition in which he received them." Article 82(1). This rule does not apply, however, if (a) the buyer was not at fault for the inability so to return the goods, (b) the harm to the goods was a result of a proper inspection upon delivery, or (c) the buyer sold or otherwise consumed the goods in the ordinary course of its business. Article 82(2). Even if one of these exceptions does not apply, the buyer retains all of its other remedies for seller's breach. Article 83.

In addition, CISG Articles 85 through 88 impose certain obligations on the buyer to preserve the goods pending their return to the seller. A buyer that declares an avoidance after delivery of the goods must take "reasonable" steps to preserve them (Article 86(1)), which may include depositing the goods in a warehouse at the seller's expense (Article 87). If the seller has no agent in the buyer's location, but the goods have been "placed at [the buyer's] disposal at their destination," the buyer must take possession of them "on behalf of the seller" if this can be done without payment of the price (*i.e.*, without paying for a negotiable bill of lading) and without "unreasonable inconvenience or unreasonable expense." Article 86(2). After such a taking of possession on behalf of the seller, the buyer must again take "reasonable" steps to preserve them. If the goods are perishable or their storage unreasonably expensive, the buyer must take reasonable steps to sell them (and then apply to the proceeds to its expenses and damages, with any surplus presumably for the seller). Article 88(2). The CISG does not, however, contain any provisions that would require an aggrieved buyer in possession to follow the seller's instructions, such as to resell on the seller's behalf, whether seemingly reasonable or not.

Finally, recall that the buyer also must meet the following conditions in order to preserve any remedy for a delivery of nonconforming goods by the seller: it must inspect the goods in "as short a period as is practicable" (Article 38); it must notify the seller of the nonconformity "within a reasonable time" (Articles 39, 49); it must permit the seller to attempt to cure any nonconformity, if the cure does not cause "unreasonable delay" or "inconvenience" (Articles 37, 48); and it must give timely notice of the avoidance to the seller (Article 26).

After it has declared a proper avoidance of the contract, the buyer is entitled to a return of any purchase price paid under the restitutionary provisions of Article 81. In return, however, that Article grants the seller a concurrent right to recover any goods delivered to the buyer.

(c) Reduction in Price. Separate from the power of "avoidance," an aggrieved buyer has an informal remedy that appears to give it a power of "self-help." Under CISG Article 50, a buyer that receives nonconforming goods "may reduce the price" it pays to the seller. There is no requirement of prior notice to the seller. This remedy is available whether the buyer has already paid or not, but if the buyer has paid, the remedy is likely to require an action in court. The buyer may not resort to this remedy, however, if the seller has cured any defects in the goods or the buyer wrongfully refuses to grant the seller an opportunity to make such a cure. Article 50. A buyer that has claimed a price reduction may not, however, *simultaneously* demand that a defect be remedied by repair or delivery of substitute goods, although it may combine a price reduction with a claim for damages to obtain full compensation.

Article 50 also spells out a formula for calculating the permissible amount of the price reduction: The buyer is entitled to reduce the price "in the same proportion as the value that the goods actually delivered bears to the value that conforming goods would have had at that time." Thus, the buyer may reduce the price according to the difference between the actual value of the nonconforming goods and the contractually required value of those goods.

Nonetheless, there is little guidance on how to determine the value of the actual goods delivered at the time of delivery, or as to what evidence of value the buyer must provide to the seller. In any event, the Article 50 remedy seems best suited to deliveries that are defective as to quantity, rather than quality, although it clearly is available for the latter as well. This type of self-help provision is familiar at civil law, and also appears in the UCC (§ 2–717).

(d) Action for Damages. As sketched above, CISG Articles 74–78 grant an aggrieved buyer an action for damages. This is true even when the buyer has avoided the contract and when the seller has successfully cured defects in its performance. Again, there is no requirement that the buyer prove that the seller was at fault as a prerequisite to a recovery of damages. Nor is there a requirement that the buyer prove what caused the defect, only that the goods were nonconforming (as described above).

Under Article 74 an aggrieved buyer is entitled to "a sum equal to the loss, including loss of profit, suffered as a consequence of the breach." But as noted, such damages may not exceed the loss that the seller "foresaw or ought to have foreseen at the time of the conclusion of the contract." The aggrieved buyer also must take "reasonable measures" to mitigate its damages under Article 77. Finally, it must prove its damages to a reasonable degree of certainty.

An aggrieved buyer also has a right to the alternative measures of damages stated in Articles

75 and 76. If the buyer avoids the contract (see above), Article 75 first grants it the right to buy replacement goods if it does so "in a reasonable manner and within a reasonable time after avoidance." The aggrieved buyer then is entitled to damages—in addition to consequential damages under Article 74—corresponding to the difference between the contract price and the price the buyer paid in this "substitute transaction."

As an alternative, Article 76 grants the aggrieved buyer that has declared an avoidance of the contract the difference between the contract price with the seller and the "current price" (*i.e.*, the market price) for the goods. This, again, is in addition to consequential damages under Article 74. Where this current price differential is used, the price in the market is to be measured at the time of "avoidance," unless the buyer had already "taken over" the goods. In the latter case, the market price is measured at the time of "taking over."

Although the Convention provides for recovery under either measure, if the buyer actually makes a replacement purchase, presumably it may use only the first. The general requirement of "reasonable measures" to mitigate damages under Article 77 would seem to require this result. The Convention gives no guidance, however, on how to determine whether any particular purchase by the buyer is a replacement purchase, or is instead an ordinary buildup of inventory.

SELLER'S REMEDIES UPON BUYER'S BREACH

The CISG provisions on the seller's remedies for a breach by the buyer parallel the structure for the buyer's remedies upon breach discussed above. CISG Articles 61 through 65 provide that if the buyer breaches any of its obligations, the seller has three basic types of remedies: (a) an action for the price; (b) "avoidance" of the contract; and in any event (c) an action for damages.

(a) Action for the Price. The preferred remedy for an aggrieved seller upon breach by the buyer is a cause of action for the price. This remedy is the functional equivalent of an action for specific performance. A cause of action for damages, but not the price, is distinctly secondary. In addition, the seller may wish to reclaim the goods if they are delivered or obtain some protection for them if it "avoids" the contract after delivery to the buyer.

As to the seller's recovery of the price, CISG Article 62 gives the seller an unqualified right to require the buyer to pay the price (although no CISG Article expressly states that the seller has a cause of action for payment of the price). Of course, there are implicit conditions on this right: First, the seller must itself have performed as required by the contract (Article 30); second, the payment of the price must actually be due (Article 58); and, third, the seller must not already have resorted to an "inconsistent" remedy (such as reselling the goods with an eye to recovering corresponding damages, see below).

Such an action for the price, however, may constitute a claim "for specific performance." This is significant because, as noted above, Article 28 imposes the important restriction that a court need only grant such a remedy if it would do so under its domestic law. If it is an action for specific performance, therefore, then an aggrieved seller before a U.S. court would have to meet the requirements of UCC § 2–709, as well as of CISG Article 62, before the court could order the buyer to pay the full price rather than damages. If, however, an action for the price does not require the entry of a "judgment for specific performance," then it would seem that CISG Article 28 would not apply, and the seller could seek this remedy directly under CISG Article 62. Today, however, there is near universal agreement that an action for the price reflects a claim to specific performance. As a result, an aggrieved seller seeking the full contract price must meet the requirements of UCC § 2–709, as well as those of CISG Article 62, before a U.S. court could order this remedy as opposed to calculating a general right to damages.

(b) Avoidance: Fundamental Breach and "Nachfrist." In parallel with the rights of an aggrieved buyer, the CISG provides two separate grounds for the seller to declare an "avoidance of the contract" upon a breach by the buyer. First, Article 64(1)(a) permits the seller to make such a declaration in the case of a "fundamental breach" by the buyer—again, as defined in Article 25 (*see* above). Second, if the buyer does not pay the price or accept delivery of the goods, Articles 63 and 64(1)(b)

give the seller a right to set a *Nachfrist* (see the discussion of this notion for an aggrieved buyer above)—that is, to notify the buyer that performance is due by a stated new date after the contract date for performance. If the seller sets such an additional deadline for performance, it may not resort in the interim to any remedy for breach of contract, unless the buyer declares that it will not perform within the deadline. But a failure by the buyer to perform by the new date automatically constitutes a fundamental breach. Like the corresponding limitation on aggrieved buyers, however, after the buyer has paid the price the seller loses the right to declare an avoidance if it does not do so within a reasonable time as defined in Article 64(2).

To assert either option for avoidance, the seller must make a corresponding declaration by notice to the buyer. Article 26. Under either option, the effect of an "avoidance of the contract" by the seller is a right not to perform its contractual obligations, and especially to refuse to deliver the goods to the buyer. In either case, the seller also retains its right to any damages caused by the buyer's breach. Article 61(2).

Avoidance and Seller's Right of Reclamation. If an unpaid seller is unable (for any reason) to obtain the price, may it reclaim the goods from the defaulting buyer, *after* delivery, by "avoiding" the contract? Such a reclamation is difficult under the UCC (*see* UCC §§ 2–507 and 2–702). The Convention, however, seems to allow such reclamation, because Article 64—which again gives the seller the power to declare the contract "avoided"—does not distinguish between pre- and post-delivery situations, and Article 81 requires "restitution . . . of whatever the first party has supplied" after avoidance. This analysis, however, is available only so long as third parties are not involved (*e.g.*, the buyer's creditors and trustees in bankruptcy), for the CISG "is not concerned with" title to the goods or third party rights (Article 4), and again does not require a court to order "specific performance" if it would not do so under its own law. Article 28.

Restitution and Obligation to Preserve Goods. Like the buyer's situation upon breach by the seller, avoidance of the contract releases both parties from their contractual obligations. Article 81(1). If the seller has already delivered the goods, it also has a right of restitution against the buyer. Article 81(2).

If the buyer fails to take delivery of the goods, the CISG also imposes certain obligations on the seller regarding their preservation. In specific, if the seller is in possession of or otherwise controls the goods, it must take reasonable steps to preserve them pending ultimate delivery to the buyer. Article 86(1). It may do so by depositing the goods in a public warehouse at the expense of the buyer (Article 87) and then make reimbursement of the corresponding expenses a condition to delivery of the goods. Article 85. If, however, there is an "unreasonable delay" in the buyer taking delivery or paying the price, the seller may sell the goods to a third party "by any appropriate means" and must do so if the goods are subject to rapid deterioration. Article 88.

(c) Action for Damages. As to damages, CISG Articles 74–78 grant the aggrieved seller an action for damages and the general principles are the same as in the discussion of the buyer's remedies for a breach by the seller. The same two alternatives also exist for the measurement of the seller's specific damages: (a) the difference between the contract price and the price in a "substitute transaction," which in the case of an aggrieved seller is a resale of the goods (Article 75); and (b) the difference between the contract price and the "current price" (*i.e.*, the market price) for the goods at the time of avoidance of the contract (Article 76). The Convention provides for recovery according to either of these measures, but if the seller actually resells the goods, only the first measure should be available in light of the general mitigation requirement of Article 77.

The major practical problem concerning unpaid sellers is that the "lost volume" seller is not adequately protected by the above two measures of damages. The idea here is that if an aggrieved seller resells the goods, the breaching buyer will argue that the seller has mitigated its losses and thus has not suffered any damages. This argument overlooks the possibility that the seller would have concluded *both* sales. Properly understood, CISG Article 74 covers this situation as well. It states as a general principle that an aggrieved party is entitled to all damages "including loss of profit" suffered "as a consequence of the breach." Thus, the courts have granted full protection to the lost volume seller by awarding lost profits damages on the breached first sale contract. Such a recovery requires, however, that the seller actually had the intent and capacity to conclude the second sale in addition to the breached first sale contract.

In parallel with the rules for recovery by the buyer, certain familiar limitations apply to a recovery of contract damages by an aggrieved seller: First, recoverable damages may not exceed the loss that the buyer "foresaw or ought to have foreseen at the time of the conclusion of the contract" (Article 74); second, the seller may not recover damages that it could have avoided through "reasonable measures" (Article 77); and third, the seller must prove its damages to a reasonable degree of certainty.

THE LIMITATIONS CONVENTION

Following its acceptance of the CISG, the United States in 1994 also ratified a parallel treaty that addresses the limitation period for international sales contracts (which U.S. lawyers would know as the "statute of limitations"). As noted above, over two dozen other countries have ratified this Limitations Convention (as amended by a 1980 Protocol).

The provisions on the scope of the Limitation Convention in large measure parallel those of the CISG. Under Article 1(1), the Limitation Convention applies to "claims based on contracts for the international sale of goods." Similar to the

CISG, a contract of sale is "international" under the Limitation Convention if: (a) the parties have their "places of business" in different states (and if a party has more than one, the relevant place of business is the one with the "closest relationship" to the contract and its performance); and (b) either both of those states are Contracting States to the Convention *or* the relevant conflict of law rules lead to the application of the law of a Contracting State. *See* Article 2. Unlike the CISG, the United States has not declared a reservation on the latter option. This means that it is entirely possible for the Limitations Convention to apply even though the CISG does not. In parallel with CISG Article 6, Article 3(2) of the Limitations Convention permits the parties to exclude its application to their transaction.

Under Article 8, the standard period of limitation is four years, and under Article 9 this period begins to run when the claim "accrues." Article 10 then defines when a cause of action accrues: (a) A cause of action for a standard breach of contract accrues at the time of breach; (b) one based on defects or other non-conformities, in contrast, accrues on the date the goods are "actually handed over to, or their tender is refused by," the buyer; and (c) a cause of action for fraud accrues when the fraud "was or reasonably could have been discovered."

Articles 11 and 12 then state special accrual rules for two specific situations. First, Article 11 contains an analog to the UCC's "warranty of future performance" exception (*see* § 2–725(2)). Under that

Article, if the seller has given an "express undertaking" relating to the goods "which is stated to have effect for a certain period of time," a cause of action arising from that undertaking does not accrue on delivery or tender of delivery, but rather on the date the buyer "notifies the seller of the fact on which the claim is based." Recall in this regard that CISG Article 39 requires that the buyer give the seller timely notice of any breach. Putting the two rules together, if the buyer satisfies its notice obligation, a cause of action for breach of an express undertaking that extends to the future will accrue at the latest within a reasonable time after the buyer "discovered or ought to have discovered" the breach.

Article 12 has a special rule for when one party has a right to declare a termination of a contract before the other party's performance is due. *Compare* CISG Article 72. If a party exercises such a right, the limitations period begins on the date on which the declaration is made to the other party. Otherwise, the period begins on the date on which the performance was due.

Articles 13 through 20 also have a number of—in part familiar—provisions on the "cessation and extension" of the defined limitations period. These include rules governing the effect of commencing a lawsuit, acknowledgement of an obligation by the defendant, and impediments to an assertion of a claim by an injured party.

The Limitation Convention nonetheless has certain rules that differ from U.S. concepts in important particulars. First, Article 22 precludes the parties from modifying the Convention's limitation period in advance, even by an express contractual agreement. The party in breach may extend the period, but only after it has begun to run. The Convention also sets an absolute ten year limitation period from when any particular period has "commenced to run." *See* Article 23. Finally, and unusually, the Limitations Convention includes a form of a procedural rule that precludes a party from relying on the expiration of a limitations period unless it has timely raised a corresponding defense in a relevant legal proceeding. *See* Article 24.

THE UNIDROIT PRINCIPLES OF INTERNATIONAL COMMERCIAL CONTRACTS

The UNIDROIT Principles of International Commercial Contracts represent a different approach to unification and harmonization of international commercial law. The CISG and its comparable conventions in other fields attempt to create positive law—*i.e.*, formally binding law issued by a sovereign authority—for specific international transactions. But given the differences among domestic legal systems the success of such efforts requires cooperation, conciliation, and compromise if the final legal product is to have any chance of broad acceptance by national governments. The CISG in fact reflects a great number of such compromises.

With the Principles, in contrast, UNIDROIT has proposed something quite different. Instead of positive law, the Principles are the equivalent of an international "Restatement of Commercial Contracts," and generally apply to all such contracts, whatever the specific type. And because they are not designed for ratification as a formal treaty, the Principles do not need the approval of any national government. Thus, the substantive rules of the Principles are often different from those of the CISG, because the Principles were drafted by independent experts (not official delegations of governments), and the drafters thus could adopt what they considered to be best practices in international commercial contracts.

In transactions to which the CISG is applicable, the courts generally should apply the rules of the CISG. Some scholars have argued, however, that where the CISG is silent or ambiguous or otherwise contains gaps, CISG Art. 7(2)'s instruction to consult the "general principles" of the Convention may permit reference to the UNIDROIT Principles (see above). A more nuanced approach requires a careful appreciation that the Principles do not act of their own force, but rather may serve as a source of guidance on the contemporary meaning of the general principles of the Convention. In other words, in narrow circumstances the Principles may provide a perspective for interpreting and filling gaps in the CISG but only to the extent that they provide an insight into the "general principles" that *already exist* within the CISG.

The more common situation in which the Principles have had influence is in international arbitrations. In this context arbitrators deciding on international commercial disputes sometimes turn to the Principles as a general statement of international contract principles (and available evidence suggests that this has occurred over three hundred times). The parties to an international contract themselves may expressly choose the Principles as the law to govern their contract (although scant evidence of this exists). The more common situation is that arbitrators faced with difficult choice-of-law issues decide not to rely entirely on one body of domestic law and instead resort to the Principles as a more neutral statement of international custom. Finally, the drafters hoped that the Principles might serve as a model law, especially for less developed countries. Note that, in all these uses, the effectiveness of UNIDROIT's Principles depends upon their persuasive value.

To promote maximization of their persuasive value, UNIDROIT assembled subject matter experts and requested that they draft the Principles to reflect current trade practices. These practices could be reflected either in conventions, such as the CISG, or in private contracts, such as general conditions or standard form contracts in use by industry groups. Where no common trade practice existed, the drafters were instructed to formulate solutions best adapted to international commercial transactions, whether they were in fact part of any existing legal regime or not. Thus, they do not necessarily represent the national rule of a majority of states.

The principles initially were drafted over a period of 20 years, and were adopted by UNIDROIT's Governing Council in May, 1994. UNIDROIT intends to update the Principles on a regular basis (and in fact did so in 2004 and again in 2010). The Principles thus are more comprehensive than the CISG. Moreover—and again because broad consensus of national governments was not required—the Principles cover a range of issues deemed too sensitive for inclusion in the CISG, such as validity (*i.e.*, defenses to enforcement), authority of agents, and the rights of third parties. Thus, the Principles include a variety of more modern and innovative concepts such as on negotiations in bad faith; on the duty of confidentiality; on merger clauses; on the use of standard forms; on the battle of the forms; and on "hardship" as a formal basis for excuse of performance. There are provisions on payment, not only by "cheque," but also by funds transfers and other methods, and on the currency to be paid in the absence of specification; on assignment of contract rights; and on multiple parties to a single contractual deal. The 2010 version is structured around one general and ten substantive chapters:

Chapter 1: General Provisions

Chapter 2: Formation and Authority of Agents

Chapter 3: Validity

Chapter 4: Interpretation

Chapter 5: Content, Third Party Rights and Conditions

This Nutshell cannot provide a detailed, comprehensive analysis of the entirety of the Principles. Instead, it will focus on their approach to three of the most significant issues in international commercial contracting: the battle of the forms, the unilateral use of standard form contracts, and excuse of performance by changed circumstances.

Battle of the Forms and Standard Business Terms. As fundamental matter, the Principles follow the familiar scheme of contract formation that requires an offer and its unconditional acceptance. *See* Articles 2.1.1–2.1.10. Where a reply to an offer contains any additions, limitations, or modifications, Article 2.1.11 also endorses essentially the same approach as the CISG: The reply does not operate as an acceptance, but is instead a rejection and a counter-offer, unless the differences do not "materially alter" the terms of the offer. *Compare* CISG Article 19(1), (2).

Unlike the CISG, however, the Principles have express provisions that address the common situation in which one or both parties use standard business terms. Although difficult to pin down in a modern world of computer-generated contract clauses, Article 2.1.19 broadly defines "standard terms" to include all such terms that are prepared in advance and for repeat use, and that in fact are used without negotiation. Even in such a case, Article 2.1.19 states that, in general, its basic contract formation rules apply. But the next few Articles substantially undermine the effectiveness of standard terms in actual transactions.

"Surprising" Terms. Where only one party proposes standard, preformulated terms without negotiation, no formal "battle" of forms arises, but such terms nonetheless may be one-sided. Article 2.1.21 states the obvious principle that an express agreement prevails over any such standard terms. But Article 2.1.20 also states that a standard term is not "effective" if the "other party could not reasonably have expected it," unless (of course) that party "expressly" accepted it. Thus, the Principles relate such terms to the expectations of the non-drafting party, and adopt as a norm the real world assumption that standard terms are rarely read.

The Comments to the Principles indicate that the non-drafting, non-reading party is bound to many, but not all, terms that are standard in an industry. Such a party is not bound, however, by a "surprising" term. One example in the Comments of a "surprising" term relates to a travel agency tour package under which the agency assumes full responsibility for the tour, but the standard terms then state that the agency is merely an agent of the hotelkeeper and is not liable for hotel accommodations. Other examples include a choice of foreign law clause in an insurance contract and a term in a foreign language that requires local arbitration. Thus, unexpected terms can be surprising either because of their "content" or because of their "language or presentation." In some respects, this resembles the unconscionability doctrine of U.S. law, but there is less emphasis on finding both "harsh terms" and "unequal bargaining power" in the contracting process.

The "Battle of the Forms." Where both parties send standard business terms (*i.e.*, in a true "battle of the forms"), Article 2.1.22 eschews the traditional "mirror image" and "last shot" rules. Instead, it provides that if both sides propose standard terms, a contract nonetheless is concluded if the parties have reached an agreement on all terms other than those in the "standard terms." The approach of Article 2.1.22 also should refuse effect to clauses in standard terms that state that no agreement is formed unless the other party accepts all proposed standard terms ("my way or the highway" clauses). If such a clause appears only in the "small print" standard terms, it is ineffective; but if it is raised "clearly" —*i.e.*, in the "non-standard terms" or expressly in negotiation—it would prevent the formation of the contract. Thus, the rationale of this provision is that where the parties agree on those terms that they are willing to raise individually and negotiate, they should be bound to a contract (even if they both have submitted standard terms not included in their express negotiations).

What are the terms of that contract? Instead of adopting the traditional "last shot" doctrine, or even the modified "first shot" doctrine of UCC § 2–207, the Principles adopt the "knock-out" (or perhaps better, "overlap") rule. The terms of the contract include (1) the "agreed terms"; (2) those standard terms that are "common in substance," unless objected to; and (3) the default rules of the Principles. Thus, the rationale of the Principles is that where the parties agree on terms that they are willing to raise individually and negotiate, those agreed terms are the terms of the contract. The typically unread standard terms prepared in advance by the parties' respective lawyers, in contrast, do not become part of the contract unless they agree in substance (a relatively rare occurrence).

Excuse for Non-Performance. The Principles provide two different paths for asserting excuse from performance by changed circumstances. One is labeled "*Force Majeure*" and the other "Hardship." These two paths are not the equivalent of the common law doctrines of impossibility and impracticability. Instead, the concepts in the Principles have civil law foundations.

The *force majeure* provisions in Article 7.1.7 are similar to those in CISG Article 79, and thus are founded on the concept of "impediment." Like the CISG rule, a party asserting an exemption under the Principles must prove three elements: (a) that its failure to perform was "due to an impediment beyond its control"; (b) that it "could not reasonably be expected to have taken the impediment into account" at the time of the conclusion of the contract; and (c) that it could not reasonably have avoided or overcome the impediment or its consequences. The Article nonetheless leaves the precise parameters of the concepts of an "impediment" beyond a party's "control" undefined, and some commentators have asserted that it requires a complete impossibility and not a mere "impracticability." Today, however, the broadly prevailing consensus is that an extreme hardship will suffice, that is, such extreme difficulty in performance as constitutes impossibility as a practical matter under the circumstances. Nonetheless, given the requirement of an "extreme" burden even under the more flexible consensus view the difference between the two interpretations may not be substantial in actual cases. The non-performing party also must give notice of the impediment, and loses its right claim excuse if it fails to do so, but the Principles do not specify when the notice must be given. And in any event, even a valid "force majeure" excuse only relieves the claimant from liability for damages; the other party retains the right to terminate the contract or withhold its own performance.

The "hardship" provisions in Article 6.2 are completely different from any concepts in the CISG or in the common law—but principally as to the remedy. Thus, Article 6.2.1 states that even when performance becomes "onerous," as a basic principle the affected party must perform. Article 6.2.2 then introduces the civil law concept of "hardship." Hardship occurs when "the occurrence of events fundamentally alters the equilibrium" of the contract, either because of increased costs or a decrease in the value of the return performance. Illustrations include a complete disappearance of a market for a product due to change in government and an unexpected 80% decline in the currency of payment. This would be in line with many of the "price unconscionability" cases in the United States. (An original comment to the Principles that a 50% change might be sufficient to trigger the application of the doctrine, however, has since been removed, presumably for substantive reasons.) To rely on such a hardship, Article 6.2.2 requires that the claimant prove that (a) it learned of the relevant events after contract formation, (b) it could not reasonably have taken the events into account at contract formation, (c) the events are beyond its control, and (d) it did not assume the risk that the events would occur.

The novel aspect of "hardship" under the Principles is the remedy. Even if proven, hardship does not by itself excuse performance. Instead, under Article 6.2.3 the effect is merely to entitle the disadvantaged party to "request renegotiations" without "undue delay." This request, however, does not "in itself" entitle the disadvantaged party to withhold performance. If the attempt to renegotiate fails, either party may seek intervention by a court with appropriate jurisdiction. Whether intervention by an arbitral tribunal is available as an alternative is not expressly stated. A court that finds the hardship criteria satisfied has the power to "adapt" the contract so as to "restore its equilibrium," or even to terminate the contract at a time and under terms that it deems appropriate.

CHAPTER 3

STRUCTURING THE INTERNATIONAL SALE OF GOODS TRANSACTION

An international sale of goods transaction raises a whole variety of challenges not present in the typical domestic transaction (*e.g.,* a sale of goods from Wisconsin to Maryland). Chapter 1 highlighted the significant cultural and linguistic challenges. Chapter 2 examined the legal challenges, and in particular how an international treaty can address the potentially significant differences in the sales law of the various domestic legal systems.

But some challenges arise from the very nature of a sale of physical objects between traders in different countries. The first may be the most obvious: An international sale usually involves a greater geographic distance between the seller and the buyer, and this most often necessitates transportation by a third-party carrier. In addition, the respective home countries of the buyer and the seller likely will have different currencies, different banking and payment practices, different trade customs, and different insurance expectations. These differences may make negotiations over the details of delivery and payment substantially more difficult. As a more fundamental matter, it also is more likely that the buyer and the seller will not know each other (or at least not well), such that neither will wish to perform first and then trust that the other will timely and fully perform later.

These challenges increase the importance of carefully structuring an international sales transaction in advance and based on agreed international customs and practices. In this chapter, we address three widely utilized transaction structures that enable distant, unfamiliar buyers and sellers to engage in mutually beneficial international sale of goods transactions—without the need for one side to rely entirely on the good faith of the other.

We first examine the important role of international "commercial terms." These reflect an assortment of international customs that define the seller's delivery obligations and the buyer's reciprocal payment obligations, as well as the allocation of risk while the goods are in transit. The special feature of commercial terms is that they permit the parties, by a simple three-letter reference (*e.g.*, FOB or CIF), to choose the structure that best suits their interests in a given transaction.

Next, we review the "payment against documents" arrangement. This reflects a transaction type that enables the seller to ship the goods against a formal obligation of the buyer to pay when the seller presents documents proving that the contract goods are in transit. (A more elaborate form of payment is an international letter of credit, a subject we take up in Chapter 4.)

Finally, we explore the special role of bills of lading in international sales transactions. A bill of lading serves the important triple function of a contract of carriage with the carrier, a receipt for the delivered goods, and (most important) a document of title that defines who has title to the goods and thus to whom the carrier may and must deliver them. We conclude this chapter with some comments on the broader issue of international electronic commerce.

COMMERCIAL TERMS AND THEIR ROLE IN INTERNATIONAL SALES TRANSACTIONS

Where the goods are to be carried from one location to another as part of the sale transaction, the parties often will agree on a "commercial term" to define the delivery obligations of the seller and the payment obligations of the buyer. The most common of such terms are FOB (Free on Board), FAS (Free Alongside Ship), CIF (Cost, Insurance and Freight), and CFR (Cost and Freight)—but many other variants also exist. The UCC includes definitions of these four most common terms (*see* §§ 2–319, 2–320), but international traders rarely use these potentially idiosyncratic notions of domestic law. In fact, the UCC definitions are increasingly obsolescent because they do not include the modern terminology associated with air freight, containerization, or multimodal transportation practices.

In international commerce the dominant source of definitions for commercial delivery terms are

"Incoterms," a set of copyrighted rules published by the International Chamber of Commerce (ICC). The Incoterms, an acronym for International Commercial Terms, provide rules for determining the obligations of both the seller and the buyer under defined commercial terms (such as FOB or CIF). The Incoterms state what acts the seller must do to deliver, what acts the buyer must do to accommodate delivery, what costs each party must bear, and at what point in the delivery process the risk of loss passes from the seller to the buyer. Each of these obligations may be different for different commercial terms. Thus, for example, the obligations, costs, and risks of the seller and the buyer are different under FOB than they are under CIF.

Because the ICC is a non-governmental entity, the Incoterms do not have the formal force of law of either national legislation or an international treaty. Thus, they cannot be the governing *law* of any contract. Instead, they are a written form of custom and usage in the trade, which the parties can, and often do, expressly incorporate in their international contracts for the sale of goods. Alternatively, if the Incoterms are not expressly incorporated in the contract, they nonetheless may have effect as an international trade usage. Courts in the United States, France, Germany, and elsewhere have so ruled, describing the Incoterms as a widely observed usage for commercial terms. This description has allowed the Incoterms to qualify under CISG Article 9(2) as a "usage . . . which in international trade is widely known to, and regularly observed by, parties to" international sales contracts.

Although (as noted) the UCC has definitions for some commercial terms (*e.g.*, F.O.B., F.A.S., C.I.F.), these definitions are expressly subject to "agreement otherwise." *See* §§ 2–319(1)-(4), 2–320(2). Thus, an express reference to the Incoterms will supersede the UCC provisions, and U.S. courts have so held. Even if the UCC (rather than the CISG) governs a particular contract, the UCC leaves open the serious possibility that the Incoterms would apply as a "usage of trade." Under UCC § 1–303(c), such a usage is "a practice or method of dealing having such regularity of observance . . . as to justify an expectation that it will be observed with respect to the transaction in question." A usage need not be "universal" nor "ancient," just "currently observed by the great majority of decent dealers." *See* § 1–303, comment 4. Moreover, as revised in 2010, the Incoterms now expressly recognize that they may be used in "both domestic and international trade."

The 2010 Revisions of Incoterms. The 2010 revisions of the Incoterms were designed principally to respond to general developments in international trade and transport practices. The revisions had two principal purposes. First, they distilled and organized the eleven defined commercial terms into two general categories: those limited to sea and inland waterway transport, and those permitted for any mode of transport. The former category includes the most frequently used terms in large international transactions, CIF and FOB, as well as their more specific versions, CFR (Cost and Freight) and FAS (Free Alongside Ship). The latter category includes the seven other terms that are also occasionally used in water transport, but are more common for air, land, and rail transportation (see below).

The second principal purpose of Incoterms 2010 was to address specific legal and factual developments relating to the transportation of goods, and in particular electronic communication. Thus, the new rules endorse the substitution of paper communications with an "equivalent electronic record or procedure." Moreover, they broadly embrace such electronic communications where either the parties so agree or such is "customary" in the trade. This reference to trade custom should increasingly authorize buyers and sellers to fulfill communication and documentation requirements with electronic equivalents. Moreover, the new Incoterms adopt an open-ended definition of "electronic records" to permit adaptation to new technologies in the future.

Incoterms 2010 give the parties a menu of eleven (formerly, thirteen) different commercial terms to describe the delivery obligations of the seller and the reciprocal obligations of the buyer to accommodate delivery. Each defines ten specific obligations for the seller and for the buyer. The eleven Incoterms rules—listed alphabetically—are as follows:

1) CFR (Cost and Freight)

2) CIF (Cost, Insurance and Freight)

3) CIP (Carriage and Insurance Paid)

4) CPT (Carriage Paid To)

5) DAP (Delivered at Place)

6) DAT (Delivered at Terminal)

7) DDP (Delivered Duty Paid)

8) EXW (Ex Works)

9) FAS (Free Alongside Ship)

10) FCA (Free Carrier)

11) FOB (Free On Board)

One may organize these eleven different terms in a variety of ways. One is along a spectrum according to the respective responsibilities of the seller and the buyer. At one end of the spectrum would be EXW (Ex Works), under which the seller must merely make the goods available at its own place of business (or other named place); at the other end would be DDP (Delivered Duty Paid), which obligates the seller to deliver the goods all the way to the buyer's location and to assume even the responsibility and cost of import customs clearance in the buyer's home country. The others fall along the spectrum and thus permit the parties to choose the term that best fits their specific commercial transaction. Another way to organize the eleven terms is a division between the one that does not assume that a carrier will be involved (EXW), and all the other ten. A third, suggested above, is between those four terms that require water-borne transportation (FAS, FOB, CFR, CIF) and the other seven, which are applicable to any mode of transportation, including multimodal transportation (CIP, CPT, DAP, DAT, DDP, EXW, and FCA). The UCC has none of the latter seven terms, although the types of transactions they cover arise routinely, and although the parties may be able to achieve the same results with careful adjustments to the UCC designations "F.O.B. place of shipment," "C. & F.", "C.I.F.," and "F.O.B. named place of destination." *See again* §§ 2–319 through 2–322.

One also might divide the ten terms requiring transportation into "shipment contract" terms (FCA, FAS, FOB, CFR, CIF, CPT, and CIP) and "destination contract" terms (DAP, DAT, and DDP). The UCC and the CISG each use a form of these concepts. *Compare* UCC §§ 2–503, 2–504, and CISG Art. 31. The underlying notion is that in shipment contracts the seller need merely put the goods in the hands of a carrier and arrange for their transportation, but transportation is at the buyer's risk and expense. *Compare* UCC § 2–504. In destination contracts, in contrast, the seller must put the goods in the hands of the carrier, arrange their transportation, and bear the cost and risk of transportation to the named location. Unfortunately, many aspects of transportation usages have changed since the UCC was first drafted in the 1950s, and the UCC concepts do not always fit the practices that the newly updated Incoterms are able to address.

The following is a brief discussion of each of the Incoterms rules. They are addressed in the two principal groupings identified by the ICC: the rules for sea and inland waterway transport, and the rules for any mode or modes of transport:

Rules for Sea and Inland Waterway Transport

FAS. Under the Incoterms Free Alongside Ship (FAS) commercial term, the seller is obligated to deliver the goods alongside a ship that the buyer must arrange and identify at a named port of shipment. (The seller instead may "procure" goods already on a ship in transit by purchasing a negotiable bill of lading or similar document that controls delivery of the goods.) The seller thus must bear the costs and risks of inland transportation to the named port of shipment. The risk that the goods will be damaged or lost in transit (the "risk of loss") will transfer to the buyer at the time the goods are delivered alongside the ship. The seller has no obligation to arrange transportation or insurance for the "main" (or water-borne) part of the carriage, but does have a duty to notify the buyer that the goods have been delivered alongside the ship. The seller must provide a commercial invoice and the "usual proof" that the goods have been so delivered (or an equivalent electronic record for either). The seller is obligated to obtain any licenses or other approvals for export clearance, and the buyer has the same obligations for import clearance.

The Incoterms definition has no provisions on either payment or post-shipment inspection by the buyer; otherwise-applicable domestic law or the

CISG will apply to fill these gaps. Under the UCC "F.A.S. vessel" term (§ 2–319(2)), the buyer must pay against a tender of documents, such as a negotiable bill of lading, before the goods arrive at their destination and before the buyer has any post-shipment opportunity to inspect the goods. UCC § 2–319(4). Otherwise, the UCC "F.A.S." term is similar to the Incoterms "FAS" term, including obligating the seller only to deliver the goods alongside a named vessel and not obligating the seller to arrange transportation to a final destination. The Incoterms FAS term does not require that the seller obtain a negotiable bill of lading or that buyer pay against documents, but also does not restrict the buyer's right of inspection before payment.

FOB. The Incoterms Free on Board (FOB) commercial term is similar to the FAS term, except that the seller is obligated to deliver the goods *on board* the ship arranged by the buyer at a named port of shipment. Thus, this term also is appropriate only for water-borne transportation. The seller must bear the costs and risks not only of inland transportation to the named port of shipment, but also until it has placed the goods "on board the vessel nominated by the buyer" (or has "procured" rights to goods already in transit). The seller has no obligation to arrange transportation or insurance, but does have a duty to notify the buyer that the goods have been delivered on board the ship. The seller "may" arrange carriage at the buyer's expense if requested by the buyer, or if it is "commercial practice" for the seller to do so and the buyer does not timely object. But even under such circumstances, the seller may refuse to make such arrangements as long as it so notifies the buyer. The risk of loss will transfer to the buyer at the time the goods are "on board the vessel." The seller must provide a commercial invoice and the "usual proof" that the goods have been so delivered (or an equivalent electronic record for either), as well as an export license for the goods. Again, the buyer is responsible for import clearance.

The Incoterms FOB definition also has no provisions on either payment or post-shipment inspection by the buyer. The nature of an FOB term nonetheless generally does not reflect an agreement on "payment against documents" (see CIF below) or restrict the buyer's right to inspect the goods before payment, unless such a term is expressly added or there is a known custom in a particular trade. In addition, it is more likely that an FOB term does not reflect an agreement that the seller must obtain and tender a negotiable bill of lading.

The UCC also defines "F.O.B.," but it is not a term requiring water-borne transportation and otherwise has certain aspects that do not work well with the Incoterms conception of FOB. Instead, the UCC "F.O.B." is more closely aligned with the Incoterms FCA term (see below). But the UCC also has a term "F.O.B. vessel" (§ 2–319(1)(c)), which relates only to water-borne transportation, and therefore is most closely linked to the Incoterms FOB term. Under the UCC, however, the term "F.O.B. vessel" requires the buyer to pay against a tender of documents, such as a negotiable bill of lading, before the goods arrive at their destination and before the buyer has any post-shipment opportunity to inspect the goods. UCC § 2–319(4). Otherwise, the UCC "F.O.B. vessel" term is similar to the Incoterms FOB term, including obligating the seller only to deliver the goods on board the ship and not obligating the seller to arrange transportation to the final destination.

CIF. The Incoterms Cost, Insurance and Freight (CIF) commercial term differs in fundamental respects from the FAS and FOB terms. With a CIF term, the seller is obligated to arrange for both transportation and insurance to the named destination port and to deliver the goods on board the ship that it—not the buyer—is obligated to arrange (or to "procure" rights to the goods already in transit). Thus, the term also is appropriate only for water-borne transportation.

In contrast to FAS and FOB, the CIF term separates the cost point from the delivery and risk point: The seller must arrange the transportation and pay the freight costs to the *destination port*, but has completed its delivery obligations when the goods are placed "on board the vessel" at the (outbound) *port of shipment*. Similarly, the seller must arrange and pay for insurance (with a "company of good repute" and for 110% of the contract price) during transportation to the *port of destination*, but the risk of loss transfers to the buyer at the time the goods are on board the vessel at the *port of shipment*. The seller must merely give the buyer any notice normally needed "to enable the buyer to take the goods." The seller must provide a commercial invoice and "the usual transport document" for the destination port (or an equivalent electronic record for either). The seller also must obtain any necessary export license, with the buyer responsible for any import formalities.

Perhaps the most important aspect of the CIF term is a requirement that the seller provide a transport document that will enable the buyer "to claim the goods from the carrier" and, unless otherwise agreed, "to sell the goods in transit by the transfer of the document to a subsequent buyer or by notification to the carrier." The traditional manner of enabling the buyer to do this—in either a "payment against documents" transaction (see below) or a letter of credit transaction (see Chapter 4)—is for the seller to obtain a *negotiable* bill of lading from the carrier and to tender that negotiable document to the buyer through a series of banks. Modern commercial practices also permit use of a nonnegotiable "waybill" to fulfill the alternative ("to sell the goods in transit ... by notification to the carrier"); but most legal systems do not have rules to support this arrangement. Thus, to avoid uncertainty a seller wishing to rely on this alternative should include in the contract of carriage a clear definition of the buyer's corresponding rights *against the carrier* (such as through incorporation of the Comité Maritime International's "Uniform Rules for Sea Waybills" (1990), see Rule 6(ii)).

A closely related issue is the identification of the point at which the buyer must pay the seller and whether the buyer has a right to inspect the goods prior to such payment. The Incoterms 2010 CIF definition has no express provisions on either subject. Traditionally, however, a CIF term has been understood to reflect an agreement between the buyer and the seller on a "payment against documents" arrangement. Under such an arrangement, the buyer must pay when the seller presents the negotiable bill of lading (and any other required documents confirming shipment). As noted, the seller tenders those documents through the banking system. The banks allow the buyer to obtain possession of the bill of lading (and thus rights to the goods) only after the buyer pays the price due the seller under the sale of goods contract. Thus, the buyer "pays against documents," most often while the goods are at sea, and before any post-shipment inspection of the goods is possible. The buyer's rights in this regard are limited to an inspection of the bill of lading to ensure that it describes the goods as provided in the parties' sale contract.

The common law has long recognized this presumption underlying the CIF term (although of course other terms in the parties' contract may indicate otherwise). In the United States, the UCC's definition of "C.I.F." *formally* requires the buyer to "make payment against tender of the required documents." UCC § 2–320(4). Courts in England and elsewhere in the common law world have held likewise. However, the force of the interpretive presumption in favor of a "payment against documents" agreement under a CIF term is less clear in civil law systems, and as noted the 2010 version of the Incoterms definition for CIF (and for CFR, see below) does not provide express guidance on the subject.

The UCC "C.I.F." term otherwise is similar to Incoterms CIF. Section 2–320(4) likewise requires the seller to (a) deliver the goods to the carrier at the port of shipment and bear the risk of loss only to that port, (b) arrange and pay for freight and insurance to the port of destination, and (c) obtain and forward to the buyer a negotiable bill of lading covering the transport to the destination port.

CFR. The Incoterms Cost and Freight (CFR) commercial term is similar to the CIF term, except that the seller has no obligations with respect to either arranging or paying for insurance coverage of the goods during transportation. Under the CFR term, the seller is obligated to arrange and pay for transportation to the named destination port and then to deliver the goods on board the ship that it must arrange for the transportation (or to "procure" rights to the goods already in transit). Thus, the term again is appropriate only for water-borne transportation.

Like CIF, the seller must arrange the transportation and pay the freight costs to the *destination port*, but has completed its delivery obligations when the goods are placed "on board the vessel" at the *port of shipment*. But in contrast with CIF, the seller has no express obligation to arrange or pay for insurance on the goods during transportation, although again the risk of loss transfers to the buyer at the time the goods are on board the vessel at the *port of shipment*. Under CFR as well, the seller must give the buyer any notice needed to enable the buyer to take the goods. The seller also must provide a commercial invoice as well as "the usual transport document" for the destination port (or an equivalent electronic record for either), and obtain any necessary export license (with the buyer responsible for any import formalities).

As with CIF, the Incoterms CFR definition has no provisions on either payment or post-shipment inspection. However, like CIF it requires that the seller obtain a transport document that will enable the buyer "to sell the goods in transit by the transfer of the document to a subsequent buyer or by notification to the carrier." Under traditional commercial practices, this again commonly is understood to require a negotiable bill of lading (see above for CIF). In addition, the UCC (§ 2–320(4)) and courts in the common law world hold that the CFR term presumes an agreement that the buyer must pay upon the seller's tender of such a bill of lading (and any other required shipment documents). Most often, this means that the buyer must pay while the goods are still at sea, thus precluding post-shipment inspection of the goods before payment. But again, whether this presumption obtains in the civil law world is less clear, and the Incoterms CFR definition has no express language on the subject.

Rules for Any Mode or Modes of Transport

EXW. Under the Incoterms Ex Works (EXW) commercial term, the seller must only tender the goods by placing them "at the disposal of the buyer" at an agreed point. But if there is no agreed point, the seller "may select the point that best suits its purpose," and this most often will be its own premises. Thus, the seller has no obligation to deliver the goods to a carrier or to load the goods on any vehicle. In short, as the Incoterms state, the EXW term "represents the minimum obligation of the seller." This term is best suited for those sellers who are new to international export transactions or where the buyer has substantial expertise in international transportation of goods.

The seller also must give the buyer any notice necessary for the latter to take delivery of the goods, but the seller has no obligation to arrange for transportation or insurance. The seller must provide a commercial invoice, or an equivalent electronic record, but has no obligation to obtain a document of title (or any other transport document) or an export license.

The Incoterms EXW definition has no effect upon either payment or inspection rights under the contract (although of course the buyer must assume any costs of pre-shipment inspection). The risk of loss transfers to the buyer at the time the goods are placed at buyer's disposal. This rule is contrary to the default rules of both the UCC (§ 2–509) and the CISG (Art. 69), which postpone passing the risk in a non-delivery transaction until the buyer's actual receipt of the goods (based on the assumption that the seller is more likely to have insurance and to be able to protect the goods until actual delivery to the buyer).

FCA. Under the Incoterms Free Carrier (FCA) commercial term, the seller is obligated to deliver the goods, cleared for export, into the custody of a carrier nominated by the buyer, usually the first carrier in a multimodal transportation scheme. Indeed, with the growing use of "containerized" shipments in recent decades—under which goods are shipped in standard-sized, sealed containers for easy loading and unloading across different modes of transport—FCA is the preferred term for multimodal transportation. The seller has no obligation to pay for transportation costs or insurance. However, the seller "may" arrange transportation at the buyer's expense if requested by the buyer, or if it is "commercial practice" for the seller to do so and the buyer does not timely object. But even under such circumstances, the seller may refuse to make such arrangements as long as it so notifies the buyer. Even if the seller does arrange transportation, it has no obligation to arrange for insurance coverage during transportation.

The seller's delivery obligation under an FCA term consists of merely loading the goods on the transport arranged by the buyer (or delivering them into the custody of a person otherwise nominated by the buyer) and then notifying the buyer that this has occurred. The risk of loss transfers to the buyer upon such delivery, although the buyer may not receive notice until after that time. The seller must provide a commercial invoice or an equivalent electronic record, any necessary export license, and "the usual proof that the goods have been delivered" (or, again, an equivalent electronic record). The Incoterms FCA definition has no provisions on either payment or post-shipment inspection.

The Incoterms FCA term is the one most comparable to the UCC's "F.O.B. place of shipment" term under § 2–319(1)(a). However, there are two sources of potential confusion in such a comparison. One is that Incoterms has its own "FOB" term, which is different; this creates a risk of a false comparison between the UCC "F.O.B." term and the Incoterms "FOB" term. The other is that the obligations under FCA and the UCC "F.O.B. place of shipment" term are, in fact, different. Under the UCC's "F.O.B. place of shipment" term, the seller must arrange transportation (UCC §§ 2–319, 2–504), while the seller must do so under Incoterms FCA only by special agreement. Further, under UCC § 2–504, the seller under an F.O.B. place of shipment term must also "obtain and promptly deliver . . . any document necessary to enable the buyer to obtain possession of the goods." Under Incoterms FCA, the seller need merely provide, at buyer's request, "assistance" to the buyer in obtaining a transport document.

CIP and CPT. The Incoterms Carriage and Insurance To Paid (CIP) and Carriage Paid To (CPT) commercial terms parallel its CIF and CFR terms, except that the former two may be used for any type of transportation (including multimodal transportation) and thus are not just for waterborne transportation. The CIP term is the analog to the CIF term. Under the CIP term, the seller is obligated to arrange and pay for both transportation and insurance to a named *destination* place. However, like CIF the seller completes its delivery obligations, and the risk of loss passes to the buyer, upon delivery to the first carrier at the place of *shipment*. But, because the CIP definition does not refer to loading on a "vessel," the term also is appropriate for multimodal transportation. The CPT commercial term is the analog to the CFR term, in that the seller has no duty to arrange or pay for insurance coverage of the goods during transportation.

Under both CIP and CPT, the seller must notify the buyer that the goods have been delivered to the first carrier, and also give any other notice required to enable the buyer "to take the goods." Under both, the seller also must provide a commercial invoice, or an equivalent electronic record, any necessary export license, and "the usual transport document." But—unlike CIF and CFR—the seller is obligated to obtain a document that would "enable the buyer to sell the goods in transit" (such as a negotiable bill of lading) *only if* this is "agreed or customary." Thus, unless the parties expressly agree to a "payment against documents" term or a special trade usage exists, the CIP or CPT commercial term does not require payment against documents or restrict inspection rights before payment. These Incoterms definitions contain no other payment or post-shipment inspection provisions. As with all of the other seven Incoterms rules for any mode of transport, the UCC has no definition for a CIP or CPT term.

DAP and DAT. The Incoterms 2010 have two new terms, DAP (Delivered at Place) and DAT (Delivered at Terminal), which replace four former terms (DES, DEQ, DAF, and DDU). Both again can be used with any type of transportation, including multimodal transport. In both, the seller is required to arrange transportation, pay the freight costs, and bear the risk of loss to a named destination point. Although these definitions have no provisions on insurance during transportation, because the seller bears the risk of loss during transport, it is well-advised to arrange and pay for insurance or it otherwise will act as a self-insurer. There are also no provisions on payment or post-shipment inspection, but there is no requirement for use of a negotiable bill of lading, and delivery occurs only after arrival of the goods. Thus, there is no reason to imply a "payment against documents" requirement if none is expressly stated. On the other hand, the parties (as always) are free to agree expressly on both a destination commercial term and a payment against documents term.

Under the Incoterms DAP rule, the seller bears the responsibility, costs, and risks of delivering the goods at the destination specified in the contract. The seller completes its delivery obligations under DAP when the goods reach the named place and are placed at the disposal of the buyer on the arriving means of transport ready for unloading by the buyer. Thus, the seller is obligated to arrange and pay for transportation to the named destination port. The risk of loss also transfers to the buyer when the seller completes its delivery obligation there. The seller (obviously) must clear the goods for export, but is not responsible for import duties or other import formalities.

The Incoterms DAT rule is similar to DAP, for the seller again bears the responsibility, costs, and risks of delivering the goods to the terminal at the location specified in the contract. Terminal includes all forms of terminals (whether quay, container or rail yard, or road, rail, or air terminal). Unlike DAP, however, the seller also is responsible for *unloading* the goods from the arriving means of transport. The seller completes its delivery obligations, and the risk of loss passes to the buyer, when the goods are unloaded from the arriving means of transport and are placed at the disposal of the buyer at the named terminal at the place of destination. Like DAP, the seller is responsible for export clearance, but is not responsible for import clearance.

Under both DAP and DAT, the seller must give the buyer any notice necessary to allow it "to take measures that are normally necessary to enable the buyer to take delivery of the goods." Under each, the seller also must provide a commercial invoice or an equivalent electronic record and must provide the buyer with a document "enabling the buyer to take delivery of the goods" at the defined point.

DDP. The final Incoterms rule, DDP (Delivered Duty Paid), places the highest level of responsibility on the seller (and thus the lowest responsibility on the buyer). Under the DDP commercial term, delivery occurs and the risk of loss passes when the goods are placed at the buyer's disposal at the named place in the country of destination, *cleared for importation* into that country. The buyer is responsible for unloading the goods from the arriving means of transport, but the seller must obtain the import license, pay all import duties and terminal charges, and complete all customs formalities at its risk and expense. The closest UCC commercial term is "F.O.B. destination," § 2–319(1)(b), but it lacks substantial detail as compared to the Incoterms DDP term.

Under DDP, the seller again must give the buyer any notice necessary to allow the latter to take measures necessary to accept delivery. The seller also must provide a commercial invoice or an equivalent electronic record as well as a document that enables the buyer to take delivery of the goods at the named place.

THE "PAYMENT AGAINST DOCUMENTS" TRANSACTION

The "payment against documents" transaction is an essential arrangement in international business because it addresses a fundamental trust problem between a seller and an unfamiliar, distant buyer: either the seller must ship the goods first and hope that the buyer accepts and pays for them, or the buyer must pay first and hope that the goods arrive and conform to the contract. The problem is especially serious for the seller, because most legal systems grant the buyer a right to inspect the goods before payment. *See, e.g.,* CISG Art. 58(3); UCC § 2–513(1). Thus, if the seller ships the goods and the buyer rejects them after inspection, the seller is left with goods at a foreign location and no payment. Its options are then limited to assuming the expense and hassle of a return shipment or a distress sale at the foreign port.

What is a "payment against documents"—aka "cash against documents" (CAD)—transaction and how does it solve this fundamental trust problem? Such a transaction arises if, upon the conclusion of the parties' contract for the sale of the goods, the seller insists on an agreement that the buyer pay upon presentation of the shipment documents, rather than after delivery and inspection of the goods. The seller must bargain for such a payment term and ensure that it is expressed in the sales contract. As noted above, an agreement on payment against documents also may arise by implication from the nature of certain commercial terms (such as, in the common law world at least, CIF and CFR). But it otherwise normally will not be implied.

In a payment against documents transaction, the seller will pack the goods and prepare a commercial invoice. If the commercial term so requires (*e.g.,* under a CIF term), the seller also will procure an insurance certificate (another form of contract) covering the goods during transit. The seller then will deliver the goods to the carrier, which issues a "bill of lading" as a combination receipt and contract to carry the goods to the named destination. The carrier also will describe on the bill of lading itself— almost always from information provided by the seller—the goods it has received. And, most important, the carrier then will be liable to deliver ("turn out") goods in accordance with this description.

As a general matter, the bill of lading contract will require that the carrier, in return for payment of the freight charge, deliver the goods *either* (a) to the named "consignee" in a "straight," or non-negotiable, bill of lading, or (b) to the person in possession ("holder") of a properly indorsed "order," or negotiable, bill of lading (*e.g.*, "to seller or order"). But for a payment against documents transaction, only an order (negotiable) bill of lading is appropriate, because it will permit the buyer to obtain delivery of the goods *only if* (a) the buyer has physical possession of the bill of lading and (b) the seller has properly indorsed the bill over to the buyer. (For more on "order" bills of lading, see the "The Role of Bills of Lading in International Sales Transactions," below.)

The fundamental function of a negotiable bill of lading lies in its status as an embodiment of the legal rights to the goods as described therein. From its nature a negotiable bill of lading thus controls the right to obtain the goods from carrier, and also provides valuable assurances to both the buyer and the seller. To the buyer, it provides assurance that the goods—as described therein—have been delivered to the carrier and are destined for the buyer and not some third party. To the seller, and any collecting banks acting on seller's behalf, it provides assurance that the carrier will deliver the goods to the buyer only if the buyer has obtained possession of the bill of lading. And of course, the seller and its collecting banks will deliver the negotiable bill of lading to the buyer only after it has paid the purchase price for the goods.

Thus, when a bank undertakes to collect funds from the buyer for the seller, it receives from the seller a document of title (the negotiable bill of lading) issued by the carrier. This document gives the bank control over the carrier's delivery of the goods—because the buyer cannot obtain possession of the goods from the carrier without possession of the negotiable bill of lading. And because the banks receive this document of title from the seller only on the condition of payment, they will demand payment (or a legally binding assurance of payment) from the buyer before the buyer receives the ability to obtain the goods from carrier.

Once the seller has obtained a negotiable bill of lading made out to its "order," how does this payment arrangement actually work? First, it prepares and forwards along with the bill of lading a "draft," together with an invoice and any other documents required by the sales contract. Like a check drawn on a bank, the draft functions as a legal vehicle for "withdrawing" from the buyer the amount owed to the seller under the sales contract in exchange for the seller's delivery of the goods. The seller uses the banking system as a collection agent for the draft. The draft usually will be a "sight draft," which is payable on demand ("on sight") when presented to the buyer. The draft is drawn for the amount due under the sales contract, and it is payable to the seller's "order." Thus, the draft also is a "negotiable" instrument in the sense that the seller may sell the right to payment to another person—such as a bank—before the draft is presented to the buyer.

The seller then indorses both the negotiable draft and the negotiable bill of lading and delivers them (along with any other required documents) to its local bank (which for ease of reference we will refer to as "Seller's Bank"). If no letter of credit is involved in the transaction, Seller's Bank usually will take these documents only "for collection." In this typical case, the seller also will provide a "collection instructions" form that describes the conditions for release of the bill of lading to the buyer (typically, full payment). Seller's Bank deals with such "for collection" items individually, without assuming that they will be honored, and therefore without giving the seller a provisional credit in the seller's bank account prior to payment by the buyer. But Seller's Bank instead may decide to "discount" (*i.e.*, buy) the bill of lading and draft outright, and thereby both become the owner of the goods and acquire the right to payment from the buyer (see the last sentence of the previous paragraph).

With the standard collection arrangement, Seller's Bank then is required to send the draft, the bill of lading, and the other accompanying documents for presentment to the buyer through "customary banking channels." If no other intermediary banks are involved, Seller's Bank will deliver the documents to a bank at the buyer's location ("Buyer's Bank"), which will notify the buyer of their arrival. Buyer's Bank then will demand that the buyer "honor" the sight draft, which means to pay the stated amount promptly. (In the case of a "time draft," the buyer must "accept" it, which means to assume a binding legal obligation to pay at the later defined time.) The buyer may require the bank to "exhibit" the documents to allow the buyer to determine whether they conform to the contract. The most important document at this point is again the negotiable bill of lading, for the buyer may inspect the description of the goods on the bill to ensure that it conforms to the seller's obligations under the sales contract.

In short, the buyer must "pay against the documents" and not upon delivery of the goods themselves. Once the buyer has paid, or arranged to pay, Buyer's Bank will give possession of the negotiable bill of lading to the buyer. Only then will the buyer be able to obtain the goods from carrier. The buyer never sees the goods, only the documents—so it inspects the documents rigorously to determine that they comply exactly with the requirements of the sales contract. Substantial performance by the seller in the tender of documents is not acceptable.

The following diagram illustrates an international sale of goods transaction involving payment against documents arrangement:

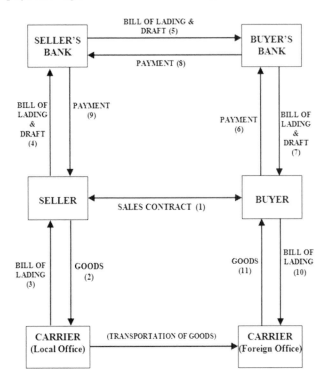

Note the risks to each party. We will begin with the seller: If it ships conforming goods as described on the bill of lading, it will be paid before the documents (and of course the goods) are released to the buyer. Thus, the seller will not lose control of the goods without being paid for them. If the buyer pays Buyer's Bank, the proceeds are remitted immediately and automatically to the seller's bank account in the seller's home country.

What can go wrong from the seller's point of view? The seller has shipped the goods to a foreign buyer without advance payment, and with no absolute guarantee of payment from anyone other than the buyer. The buyer may refuse to pay the sight draft when it arrives. This would give the seller a cause of action, but often that requires a lawsuit at the buyer's home jurisdiction, with its extra expense, delay, and uncertainty. In particular, the seller could feel that it will be the target of discrimination in the courts of the foreign country.

The seller would still have control of the goods, because after dishonor of the draft, the collecting banks will return the bill of lading to the seller. However, the goods would now be at a foreign destination—one at which the seller may have no agents, and no particular prospects for resale. In addition, if the seller wishes to bring the goods back to its base of operations (and normal sales territory), it would have to arrange and pay a second transportation charge, and this may be substantial in relation to the value of the goods. The payment against documents arrangement will leave the seller somewhat better situated, because the buyer may review only the documents (especially, the bill of lading) in deciding whether it will pay. But a dishonor of the draft by the buyer also can create economic circumstances in which the seller's only rational option is a distress sale at a foreign location. This risk to the seller is inherent in the payment against documents transaction, unless the seller requires that the buyer also arrange for the issuance of a letter of credit. (*See* Chapter 4 for a complete description and discussion of the letter of credit transaction.)

The buyer, of course, also bears some risks in a payment against documents transaction. To be sure, its payment of the price will give it a document from the carrier entitling it to delivery of the goods. It also likely will have an insurance certificate protecting against casualty loss in transit, and—if it had the foresight to arrange this in advance (see below)—perhaps even a third-party inspection certificate confirming that the goods conform to the sale contract. In other words, the buyer should receive what it bargained for: delivery of conforming goods or insurance proceeds sufficient to cover any loss.

However, without the ability to inspect the actual goods before payment, the buyer cannot be absolutely assured that they conform to the contract. What can go wrong from the buyer's point of view? At least six distinct problems could arise:

(a) The goods could be lost or stolen after title has passed to the buyer;

(b) The seller could ship goods that do not conform to the contract. The non-conformity could range from (i) the seller fraudulently shipping scrap paper to (ii) incorrect labeling on the packaging, which can cause problems with customs agents in both countries to (iii) different quality standards in the seller's and buyer's home countries.

(c) The carrier could stow the goods improperly or operate so negligently that they are damaged in transit, something that may be difficult to prove.

(d) A fraudster could forge a bill of lading, such that the carrier in fact never issued a bill covering the goods at all.

(e) A bad actor could steal the bill of lading and attached draft after issuance, forge the seller's indorsements, and then present the documents to the buyer (or the carrier).

or

(f) The bill of lading may "misdescribe" the goods such that it upon arrival they do not conform to what is stated on the bill.

Some of these problems are recognized and dealt with in the standard handling of the payment against documents transaction. For example, under a CIF term the seller must arrange and pay for insurance covering the goods against loss or damage in transit. Other problems, such as payment before inspection, make buyers feel unprotected, and they have searched for devices within the transaction that can afford them more protection. Such a device, in common use in modern transactions, is the Inspection Certificate. This involves the buyer contracting with an independent third party to inspect the goods before the seller delivers them to the carrier. The buyer then has the inspection certificate as a separate verification—beyond that of the seller and of the carrier in the bill of lading—of what goods the seller actually shipped.

Three problems nonetheless may remain that are uniquely related to any transaction using a bill of lading:

(a) The loss or theft of the bill of lading, followed by a forgery of a necessary indorsement and carrier's misdelivery (delivery of the goods to the wrong person under a bill of lading).

(b) The misdescription of the goods by the seller/shipper and in the bill of lading, followed by carrier's delivery of goods that do not conform to the description in the bill of lading.

(c) The forgery of a complete bill of lading by a malevolent shipper without carrier's knowledge or approval.

These risks highlight the importance of the bill of lading in an international sales transaction, a subject we take up in the next section.

THE ROLE OF BILLS OF LADING IN INTERNATIONAL SALES TRANSACTIONS

Bills of lading play a significant, indeed essential, role in international sales transactions. A bill of lading is a document issued by a carrier upon receipt of goods from a shipper (commonly, the seller in a sales transaction). Such a document serves three independent, but related functions: (1) First, it is a contract of carriage under which the carrier undertakes to transport the goods to the defined destination for the defined fee; (2) second, it is a contract of bailment, including a description of the goods by the carrier as received from the shipper; and (3) it is a "document of title" covering the goods in that it embodies the legal rights to the goods and defines who is legally entitled to their possession (*i.e.*, to whom the carrier may and must deliver them).

State, federal, and international law all have rules governing bills of lading. A separate article of the UCC, Article 7, broadly regulates "Documents of Title," including bills of lading. But the regulation of bills of lading, and in particular the relationship of the carrier to its customers, also is the subject of three international conventions and three U.S. federal statutes. The three conventions—the so-called Hague Rules, Hague/Visby Rules, and Hamburg Rules—all cover the same subject matter, but are progressively more customer-oriented. With this multiplicity of treaties governing the terms of the bill of lading and its use, conflicting concepts should be expected. Such concerns led to the negotiation and conclusion of an entirely new treaty, the UN Convention on Contracts for the International Carriage of Goods Wholly or Partly by Sea (2009). These so-called "Rotterdam Rules"— which the United States has signed but not yet ratified as of 2016—may well be acceptable to a noteworthy majority of maritime states, whether principally supportive of buyers, sellers, or carriers.

As of 2016, however, the United States has accepted only the Hague Rules, which it enacted into its domestic law as the Carriage of Goods by Sea Act (COGSA) (now in a statutory note to 46 U.S.C. § 30701). (The United States also has in force a more limited pre-COGSA statute, the Harter Act, 46 U.S.C. § 30701 *et seq.*, which governs certain narrow aspects of the domestic transport of goods.) COSGA defines the basic obligations of the carrier regarding the care for and transportation of the goods. It also establishes the fundamental rule that the bill of lading is "prima facie evidence of the receipt by the carrier of the goods as therein described." COGSA, § 3(4).

The most important federal law regulating bills of lading, however, is the Federal Bill of Lading Act (FBLA, also known by its earlier name, the Pomerene Act). 49 U.S.C. § 80101 *et seq.* The FBLA governs all interstate and all *outbound* international shipments that involve a bill of lading issued by a common carrier and to that extent it entirely preempts contrary state law (such as the UCC). UCC Article 7 continues to apply, however, for bills of lading covering *inbound* international shipments.

UCC Article 7 and the FBLA recognize both of the two different types of bills of lading noted above—a non-negotiable (or a "straight") bill of lading, and a negotiable (or "order") bill of lading. Each represents the contract between the carrier and the shipper, and will set forth the terms of that contract expressly or incorporate the carrier's terms and tariffs by reference. Nonetheless, for the reasons explored in more detail below, the typical, large international sale of goods transaction between unrelated parties of its nature will require a negotiable bill of lading.

Shippers and carriers also use a variety of specialized terms to describe specific aspects of bills of lading. Thus, for example, they often refer to an "on board" bill of lading. An "on board" bill of lading is issued once the goods have been loaded on board the vessel bound for the stated destination. A "clean" bill of lading is one that has no clause or notation on its face indicating visible or possible defects in the packaging or condition of the goods. Simple comments regarding amount, weight, or other descriptions provided by the shipper will not, however, "foul" the bill of lading, provided that they do not incorporate other documents indicating defects in the cargo.

In addition, the parties can arrange the transport on the basis of a "multimodal" (or "combined transport") bill of lading. This involves an agreement by the carrier to transport and deliver the goods to their final destination using any required connecting carriers (such as railroads, trucks, and air carriers). In such a case, a single bill of lading will govern all of the links in the transportation chain. A "through" bill of lading arrangement covers the same basic idea, except that each involved carrier may issue a separate bill for its specific segment in the chain. Both forms are increasingly common because they are well suited for goods delivered in standardized containers.

Negotiable and Nonnegotiable Bills. A nonnegotiable bill of lading differs in fundamental respects from a negotiable one. Under a non-negotiable bill of lading, the carrier obligates itself to deliver the goods at the destination point *only* to the "consignee" named in the bill of lading. 49 U.S.C. § 80110(a). Physical possession of such a bill of lading does not confer rights over the goods or against the carrier. Thus, transfer of the physical bill (even with an indorsement) will not transfer any rights over the goods, because again with a nonnegotiable bill the carrier is obligated to deliver the goods *only* to the one, named consignee. This typically will be shipper/seller, because if the nonnegotiable bill names the buyer as consignee, the latter will have a right to claim the goods from the carrier whether it has already paid the seller or not. For this reason, nonnegotiable bills of lading are not appropriate for a "payment against documents" transaction, and the case reporters are full of litigation where an attorney tried a shortcut using a straight bill of lading as the "easy" way to do this transaction—and sacrificed the client's interests in the process. Nonnegotiable bills of lading also are called "air waybills," "sea waybills," and "freight receipts" (among other names) depending upon the principal method of transportation for the goods.

For a negotiable bill of lading, in contrast, physical possession is essential to determining the rights to the goods and the delivery obligations of the carrier. Under a negotiable bill of lading, the carrier obligates itself to deliver the goods to the "holder" of the bill at the destination point. 46 U.S.C. § 80110(a). A negotiable bill of lading may be issued either to "bearer" or to the "order" of a named person. A bearer bill of lading is transferred by physical delivery alone, and anyone in possession becomes the "holder" and thus may demand delivery of the goods from the carrier. Because of the inherent risks of such a practice, negotiable bills of lading issued to bearer are substantially less common in international transactions.

An "order" bill of lading on the other hand is issued to a named person (the consignee, usually the original shipper/seller). But again because the bill is negotiable, that consignee has the power to "order" delivery of the goods to someone else. It does this by indorsing (*i.e.*, signing) the bill over to a third person along with a transfer of physical possession of the bill itself. The named transferee then becomes the "holder" of the bill. This is the essential feature of a negotiable bill of lading: By transferring physical possession along with any required indorsement, the original consignee may transfer rights in and control over the goods.

The original consignee may indorse the negotiable bill of lading two ways: (1) "in blank," that is, with a bare signature ("*Michael Van Alstine*"); or (2) by a "special indorsement," which identifies the next intended holder by name ("Deliver the goods to Ralph Folsom, or order. *Michael Van Alstine*"). *See* 46 U.S.C. § 80104(a). Under a blank indorsement, any person in possession becomes a holder, and is thus entitled to demand delivery from the carrier. Under a special indorsement, in contrast, only the named indorsee can become a holder, and only that person can demand delivery from the carrier (or indorse the bill of lading to still another party so as to make it the holder). Thus, the special indorsement protects the interests of the parties from thieves and forgers much better than a blank indorsement.

The important role of bills of lading in international sale of goods transactions—as well as the fundamental differences between negotiable and nonnegotiable bills—may be illustrated by an examination of three of the most common forms of bill of lading disputes: (a) misdelivery of the goods by the carrier; (b) misdescription of the goods in the bill of lading; and (c) forgery of the bill of lading in the first place. The following materials will analyze these three issues in turn.

Misdelivery. As the above materials indicate, the carrier's delivery obligation differs fundamentally as between a nonnegotiable and a negotiable bill of lading. This in turn defines the carrier's potential liability for "misdelivery." With a nonnegotiable bill, the carrier's obligation is clear: It must deliver *only* to the named consignee. As a result, the carrier is liable to that consignee if it delivers the goods to anyone other than the consignee (or according to the consignee's direct instructions). 49 U.S.C. § 80110(b)(2).

For a negotiable bill, in contrast, possession of the actual bill is crucial. By obtaining possession of the actual negotiable bill of lading, properly indorsed over to him, a person becomes a "holder" and acquires title to the goods and thus the right to delivery from the carrier. *See* 49 U.S.C. § 80105(a)(providing that a person to whom a negotiable bill of lading is negotiated "acquires the title to the goods"). Thus, the carrier must see the actual bill of lading to confirm that the person demanding the goods has possession of the bill and that it has the proper chain of indorsements over to that person. 49 U.S.C. § 80110(b)(3).

The carrier then will be liable to the holder of a negotiable bill of lading for misdelivery if it delivers the goods to anyone but that person. In this sense the negotiable bill of lading is an especially secure document of title, because possession of it, properly indorsed to the possessor, controls title to the document, title to the goods, and the direct obligation of the carrier to deliver the goods only to the holder. For this reason, the negotiable bill of lading is appropriate for a "payment against documents" transaction. The collecting banks can use their possession of such a bill to control title to both the goods and the document until they have secured payment of the agreed purchase price from the buyer. Some countries, for regulatory reasons, recognize only "straight" bills of lading and not negotiable bills of lading; but as this brief review illustrates, the negotiable bill of lading provides important security to an international sale of goods transaction.

The holder of the bill of lading does not have absolute title to the goods in all cases, but nearly so. If the shipper was not the owner of the goods in the first place—for example if a thief stole the goods from the true owner at gunpoint—then no holder of the bill of lading will have title to the goods because the shipper's claim of title was "void" from the beginning. 49 U.S.C. § 80105(a); UCC § 7–503(a). However, if the owner voluntarily parted with the goods but was defrauded by the shipper (*e.g.*, a "cash sale" in which the check later bounces), then the shipper obtains "voidable" title and can pass good title to a holder of the document who purchases it in good faith for value without notice. 49 U.S.C. § 80105(a)(providing that the transferee of a negotiable bill of lading acquires title that "the person negotiating the bill had the ability to convey to a purchaser in good faith for value"); UCC §§ 7–501(a), 7–502(a), 7–503(a)(same, with reference to § 2–403). The rights of such a good faith holder for value are also superior to any seller's lien or right to stop delivery of the goods in transit. 49 U.S.C. § 80105(b).

Under the Federal Bill of Lading Act, as under the UCC, any forgery of a necessary indorsement is not effective to create or transfer rights, whether the forgery is perfect or inept. Further, any unauthorized signature by an agent is treated as a forgery, if it was made without actual, implied, or apparent authority.

The protection is illustrated in the situation where a thief steals a negotiable bill of lading from the holder who was in possession of the document under a special indorsement. As described above, the holder's indorsement is necessary to transfer rights to the document and the goods to any other party. Without that indorsement, the thief is not a holder and has no rights to the document or goods. If the thief forges the holder's signature (even perfectly), that forgery is ineffective, and the thief is still not a holder and still has no rights. If the thief transfers the document to another party, that party also is not a holder and cannot obtain rights under the document without the original holder's signature. *See Adel Precision Products Corp. v. Grand Trunk Western R. Co.*, 51 N.W.2d 922 (Mich. 1952) (a famous case in which a buyer of goods obtained possession of a negotiable bill of lading and forged the indorsement of the seller/consignee). The carrier is still obligated to deliver the goods only to the holder, the victim of theft.

If the carrier nonetheless delivers to the forger, or to someone who received the document from the forger without the holder's indorsement, the carrier is liable for misdelivery under 49 U.S.C. § 80111. (The forger of course is also liable, if he can be found.) The concept is that each person who takes the bill of lading should "know its indorser." If the goods are misdelivered, the person who wrongfully received the goods is liable. Such a person, as well as all other transferees after the forger, all made warranties under 49 U.S.C. § 80107 that they had "a right to transfer the bill and title to the goods described in the bill." In the case of a forgery, each person in the chain is liable for breach of this statutory warranty because in fact it had no such right or title. Each person has a warranty action against its transferor and each transferor, in turn, has a warranty action against its transferor—and so on back up the chain of transfers. The purpose is to push liability back up the chain of transfers to the person who took from the forger (and, if he can be found, to the forger himself).

Collecting banks, if they transfer the document for value, also can be subject to this warranty liability. If the buyer pays, and those funds are transmitted to the forger, then the collecting banks have received value. However, such banks have several potential escape valves. One is to disclaim such warranty liability when indorsing or transferring the bill of lading. The FBLA provides that its transfer warranties do not arise if "a contrary intention appears." 49 U.S.C. § 80107(a). Thus, an indorsement "XYZ Bank—no warranties" would clearly disclaim liability for such a warranty. Banks may similarly argue that banking custom relieves them from any duty to examine documents, with the result that an implicit blanket statutory "contrary intention" exists as a matter of custom. A second avenue is to claim that the bank is only holding the document "as security for a debt," because the statute exempts such holders from warranty liability. The difficulty with this avenue is that a collecting bank does not pay the seller until after it receives payment, so it never becomes a creditor, secured or otherwise. Finally, if a bank incorporates by reference the ICC's Uniform Rules for Collections (1995) when it forwards the documents, it may effectively avoid liability for problems not apparent on the face of the documents. Each of these approaches has analytical difficulties, but they may indicate a blanket intention to disclaim the statutory warranties by implication. In any event, any bank found to have warranty liability can pass this liability back to its transferor, as long as it can identify and find that transferor.

The principal party subject to liability in the case of a misdelivery, however, will be the carrier. As noted, in the case of a non-negotiable bill of lading the carrier will be liable if it delivers the goods to anyone other than the named consignee (or its designee); and in the case of a negotiable bill of lading the carrier will be liable if it delivers the goods to anyone other than the holder. In the case of such a misdelivery, the FBLA provides that the carrier is liable to "a person having title to, or right to possession of," the goods. 49 U.S.C. § 80111. For a negotiable bill of lading that already has been negotiated to a third party holder, this of course will be that holder. Indeed, as noted FBLA § 80105(a) expressly states that a person to whom a bill of lading is negotiated "acquires title to the goods."

If the thief forged the indorsement of the original consignee *before* the seller/shipper/consignee could negotiate the bill to a third party holder, then the competing claimants will be the seller and the buyer. In such a case, the proper plaintiff commonly will be the buyer because under the UCC, "title" to the goods generally will pass from the seller to the buyer at the time of physical shipment of the goods (unless seller was obligated to deliver at the buyer's location). *See* § 2–401(2)(so providing "even though a document of title is to be delivered at a different time or place"). But if the buyer has already wrongfully refused to pay, the seller may be able to rescind the sales contract, obtain a right to repossess the goods, and thus have the rights against the liable carrier. (This obviously will not be the case in a "payment against documents" transaction, because the theft and forgery will mean that the bill of lading was not presented to the buyer at all, and thus that the buyer would not yet have had an obligation to pay the seller.)

Misdescription. The carrier responsible for transporting the goods is not a party to the contract between (*i.e.*, is not in "privity" with) the seller and the buyer in the sale of goods transaction. Therefore, the carrier has no obligation to deliver goods that conform to the sale contract. However, when the seller/shipper delivers the goods to the carrier, the bill of lading issued by the carrier will contain a description of the goods. As noted above, COSGA declares that the bill of lading is "prima facie evidence of the receipt by the carrier of the goods as therein described." COGSA, § 3(4). COGSA in fact requires the carrier to issue a bill of lading with information on "[e]ither the number of packages or pieces, or the quantity, or weight, as the case may be, as furnished in writing by the shipper." COGSA § 3(3). But if the shipper provides a description of the goods, COGSA § 3(3)(c) permits the carrier to exclude from the bill of lading any information that it "has had no reasonable means of checking."

In any event, the carrier has an obligation to deliver goods that conform to the description in the bill of lading. In specific, the Federal Bill of Lading Act declares that the carrier is liable for a failure to deliver goods that "correspond to the description contained in the bill." 49 U.S.C. § 80113(a). This obligation is owed to the owner of the goods under a nonnegotiable bill of lading or to the holder of a negotiable bill of lading, provided the owner or holder "gave value in good faith relying on the description."

The problem with this obligation is that the carrier usually does not know what it is carrying, because the goods are often in containers. Thus, the carrier knows that it received a *container* labeled "100 Apple iPads." But it will not, and is not expected to, open the container to check whether it contains iPads, or to count how many items actually are in it. Even if it opened the container, the carrier would not be expected to check whether each iPad is in working order. Even if it did so check, it is not likely to have the expertise to determine whether each can perform as expected or is otherwise are defective in some way. Thus, the carrier is not expected to warrant the description and capability of packaged goods delivered to it for transport.

To solve this problem, the FBLA allows carriers to limit their liability for unknown misdescriptions on the bill of lading through what are generally known as "Shipper's weight, load, and count" or "SLC" clauses. 49 U.S.C. § 80113(b). The FBLA defines three requirements for effective SLC clauses.

First, the bill must have appropriately clear disclaimer language. The Act itself provides the following examples:

- "contents or condition of contents of packages unknown";

- "said to contain"; and

- "shipper's weight, load, and count."

These exact linguistic formulations, however, are not required. Rather, the FBLA expressly provides that "words of the same meaning" will suffice.

Second, a disclaimer is effective only to the extent that the carrier "does not know whether any part of the goods were received or conform to the description." 49 U.S.C. § 80113(b)(3). If the carrier has actual knowledge of a problem, it may not passively allow the shipper to provide a misdescription in the bill of lading.

Third, it must actually be true that the shipper loaded the goods on the vessel. When the carrier itself loads the goods, it is obligated to count the number of packages, note the condition of the packages, and, for bulk goods, "determine the kind and quantity" (although not the quality) of the goods. For bulk freight, even where it is loaded by the shipper, the carrier also must determine the kind and quantity of the freight if the shipper so requests and provides adequate facilities for the carrier to weigh the freight. In situations where the carrier must count packages or weigh the goods, disclaimers such as "shipper's weight, load, and count" will not be effective. 49 U.S.C. § 80113(d).

The requirement that the shipper—or its designee—actually load the goods seems appropriate for disclaimers of the "shipper's weight, load, and count" variety; but it seems inapposite for disclaimers of the "said to contain" or "contents or condition of contents of packages unknown" variety. Nonetheless, the carrier will be liable for a misdescription even with an otherwise clear "SLC" disclaimer if it issues a bill of lading and the shipper, for example, in fact never loaded anything on board the carrier's vessels.

More generally, the carrier must make at least a "reasonable inspection" of the goods under the circumstances. Thus, the carrier is responsible for checking readily observable facts—quantity, the number of cartons, obvious information about the weight of a shipment, and the like. These are items that the carrier is likely to check in any event, to be certain that cartons are not inadvertently left behind, and to determine the appropriate freight charge.

However, this minimal obligation of a "reasonable" inspection does not include most quality terms (such as whether the goods are in operating condition) or information that the carrier does not have the ability to confirm (such as what goods are in a sealed container). Thus, it can truthfully say that it has received 100 cartons "said to contain" Apple iPads, without opening the cartons; but it does need to count the number of cartons. The intersection of these rules arises when the carrier accepts a sealed container supposed to contain 2000 tin ingots weighing 35 tons, and issues a bill of lading for a container "said to contain 2000 tin ingots." If the container is empty and weighs less than a ton, and this information is readily apparent to the carrier, the carrier's disclaimer is not likely to provide protection. *Berisford Metals Corp. v. S/S Salvador*, 779 F.2d 841 (2nd Cir. 1985) (also addressing the separate limitation in COGSA on the *amount* of carrier liability).

Forged Bill of Lading. If the carrier issues a bill of lading for which it received no goods at all, the carrier is likely to be liable, as is described above. However, suppose the carrier never issued a bill of lading in the first place. Instead, a person unrelated to the carrier created (and then forged) the bill of lading in the name of the carrier, with no authority from the carrier. The buyer who pays upon receipt of such a bill of lading (such as in a "payment against documents" transaction) or otherwise purchases such a forged bill of lading has paid funds, probably through a series of banks, but finds that the carrier has no goods to deliver. There is no misdelivery or misdescription claim against the carrier, for the carrier never issued a bill of lading covering goods at all. If the carrier did not issue the bill of lading and its "signature" is a forgery or otherwise unauthorized, that signature is not effective, and carrier will not be liable on the bill (absent some sort of actionable negligence).

The forger of course is liable for the fraud, if found. But unlike the forged indorsement situation, the carrier never received any goods, and thus cannot be liable for failing to deliver. Nonetheless, like the forged indorsement situation, each party that transferred the bill of lading for value makes warranties to later parties, and the first warranty is that "the bill is genuine." 49 U.S.C. § 80107(a)(1). If the bill of lading itself is forged, that warranty is breached. Thus, all parties that transferred the bill and received payment may be liable in a breach of warranty action by later transferees. The concept is that the last person to purchase the bill will "know its transferor," and be able to recover against that transferor. That transferor can, in turn, recover against *its* transferor, and so on up the chain of transfers, until the loss falls either on the forger or on the person who took the bill from the forger.

Again, collecting banks that have transferred the document for value can be subject to this warranty liability. But again, such banks will have the same three potential escape valves discussed under forged indorsements above: (1) an express disclaimer of warranty that indicates "a contrary intention"; (2) a claim that the bank is holding the document only "as security for a debt"; and (3) the limitation in the ICC Collection Rules that banks need examine only the appearance of the documents. Again, each of these approaches may have analytical difficulties, but they also may reflect a blanket, implicit indication to disclaim the statutory warranties for banks that merely act as collection agents. In any event, any bank found to have warranty liability can pass this liability back to its transferor, as long as it can identify and find that transferor. Finally, if UCC Article 7 applies, such as for an inbound shipment, "a collecting bank or other intermediary" warrants *only* its good faith and authority in transferring the bill of lading (*i.e.*, not the bill's genuineness). § 7–508.

ELECTRONIC BILLS OF LADING

The Federal Bills of Lading Act does not define "bill of lading" and does not require that it be written on a piece of paper or have a physical signature by anyone. Thus, use of electronic bills of lading would seem to be a technical possibility. However, all of the primary rules of this federal law are founded on an implicit assumption that the bill of lading—at least a negotiable one—is a paper document. The references to indorsement (in blank or to a specified person), transfer by delivery, and "person in possession" make sense only for a paper document.

Nonetheless, telecommunications technology can provide electronic messages that perform the main functions of the bill of lading: as a receipt, a transport contract, and a document of title. Thus, several types of bill of lading equivalents are currently in use; but most of them are used only as receipts for the goods generated by the carrier. This is especially true for nonnegotiable bills of lading (also known as waybills), which do not need to be presented to a carrier to obtain possession of the goods. As a federal court recently observed, "[s]ince the physical document is no longer necessary to the transaction, [a] waybill may be transmitted electronically or telexed between the parties." *Quanzhou Joerga Fashion Co., Inc. v. Brooks Fitch Apparel Group, LLC*, 2012 WL 4767180 (S.D.N.Y. 2012).

With this foundation, several efforts have been made to facilitate the use of electronic carrier-issued international receipts for goods. For example, the U.S. Interstate Commerce Commission now authorizes the use of uniform electronic bills of lading, both negotiable and non-negotiable, for both motor carrier and rail carrier use. *See* 49 CFR Part 1035. More generally, at least two federal courts also have recognized the effectiveness of electronic bills of lading, at least in certain respects. These developments, however, relate to the role of bills of lading merely in evidencing a carriage contract and in communicating information about the goods, the shipper, and the consignee. The recognition by the Interstate Commerce Commission and the court cases do not address issues relating to defining the rights and obligations of the parties to the electronic bill.

Thus, these electronic bills do not allow for further sale or rerouting of the goods in transit, or for using the bills of lading to finance the transaction. Under the U.S. I.C.C. regulations, for example, negotiable uniform electronic bills of lading must "provide for indorsement on the back portion" (49 CFR § 1035.1), but there is no explanation of how an electronic message has a "back portion," or how "indorsement" is to be effected.

Industry groups and private companies also have attempted to create programs that utilize electronic carrier-issued international receipts for goods. Most of these efforts relate to nonnegotiable electronic waybills under which shippers provide relevant information through the carrier's website and the shipper or consignee then prints out a waybill document at either the origin or destination. A notable example is the e-Air Waybill (e-AWB) jointly sponsored by the International Air Transport Association (IATA) and the International Federation of Freight Forwarders Association (FIATA).

The Comité Maritime International has adopted Rules for Electronic Bills of Lading (the "CMI Rules"). Under these rules, any carrier can issue an electronic bill of lading as long as it will act as a clearinghouse for subsequent transfers. Upon receiving goods, the carrier sends an electronic message to the shipper describing the goods, the contract terms and a "private key." The shipper then has the "right of control and transfer" over the goods, and is called a "holder." An electronic message from the shipper that includes the private key can be used to transfer the shipper's rights to a third party, who then becomes a new holder. The carrier then cancels the shipper's "private key" and issues a different private key to the new holder. Upon arrival, the carrier delivers the goods to then-current holder or a consignee designated by the holder.

To take advantage of the CMI Rules, the original parties to the transaction must agree that the CMI Rules will govern the "communications" aspects of the transaction—the rules are voluntary and do not automatically have the force of law. But such an agreement may come merely through a reference in the carriage contract.

The CMI Rules are not intended to govern the substantive laws of bills of lading provisions, only the electronic transfers of the electronic bill of lading. The Rules thus reflect an attempt to create an "electronic" writing that functions as a negotiable document of title by contract and estoppel. This system has not received broad acceptance, however, because it does not create a foundation for defining clear property rights or for a transfer of such rights to independent third parties (the essential function of a negotiable bill of lading). In addition, there is some concern that the CMI Rules do not address certain important issues, such as what happens when the system fails.

The Commission of the European Committees has sponsored the BOLERO electronic bill of lading initiative, which is based on the CMI Rules, and is now a separate enterprise. However, under the BOLERO system neither a bank nor a carrier is the repository of the sensitive information regarding who has bought and sold the cargo covered by the electronic bills of lading. Instead, BOLERO establishes a "cloud-based" central registry that is independent of the shipper, the carrier, the ultimate buyer, and all intermediate parties.

More recently, the BOLERO system operators have teamed with the Society for Worldwide Interbank Financial Telecommunication (SWIFT) to create a "Core Messaging Platform" for the presentation of formal electronic documents such as bills of lading ("eBL"). Like other such efforts, the system depends on all parties to the transportation chain agreeing to a comprehensive Rulebook, which provides for the dispatch and receipt of legally binding electronic bills of lading and, most important, a formal "fingerprinting" to ensure recognition of only one "original" bill. Thus far, however, this system also has not been able to establish a secure foundation for broad use of electronic bills of lading.

The most significant challenge in all of these efforts has been in making an electronic bill of lading negotiable so that it remains authentic, unique, confidential, and transferrable in a way to bind third parties. Most bankers have been skeptical of the device created by the CMI Rules, including as clarified in the BOLERO system. In addition to fraudulent transactions, there is a risk of misdirected messages. Thus, a bank could find itself relying on non-existent rights from a fraudulent actor impersonating the carrier. Although the new BOLERO system seeks to minimize these risks, the banks are concerned as to whether carriers will accept liability for losses due to such fraudulent practices. The banks also are concerned that the full terms and conditions of the CMI and BOLERO Rules are not available to or perhaps binding on subsequent "holders." Thus, the CMI and BOLERO Rules have not yet seemed to find wide acceptance and bills of lading are still primarily paper-based in both the payment against documents and letter of credit transactions—although some early seeds to the contrary can been seen in bulk transactions (iron ore, etc.). The two *generalized* exceptions may be, first, for shipments entirely internal to a single company (*e.g.*, from one branch office to another) and, second, for direct sales to long-term, dedicated customers, where no financial arrangements are involved or contemplated.

Other systems also have been tried. The "Trade Card System" is an Internet-based, paper-less system that allowed electronic settlement of payments for purchases of goods and related services. A private enterprise, essDocs, offers "CargoDocs" electronic bills of lading, but—like the BOLERO system— their reach is limited to a closed group of those shippers, carriers, etc. that agree to a comprehensive contractual framework. All such systems, however, have difficulties in providing bills of lading that could be used as collateral—as least (again) beyond the closed group of participants in the system.

Two legal developments nonetheless may facilitate and promote the future development of secure and commercially viable electronic bills of lading. First, recent revisions to the UCC expressly contemplate "electronic documents of title," including electronic bills of lading. UCC Article 1 defines an electronic document of title as one "evidenced by a record consisting of information stored in an electronic medium" (§ 1–201(b)(16)) and then broadly defines a "record" to include information that is "stored in an electronic medium and is retrievable in perceivable form" (§ 1–201(b)(31)). The most recent revisions to UCC Article 7 then address issues concerning the security of electronic bills of lading through the concept of "control" (§ 7–106(b)). At the core of this concept is a requirement that "a single authoritative copy of the document exists which is unique, identifiable, and … unalterable." § 7–106(b)(1)(with certain defined exceptions). Article 7 then has specifically tailored rules for the "negotiation" of an electronic document of title. *See* § 7–501(b).

Second, the recently concluded Rotterdam Rules create an explicit legal framework for the creation, transfer, and enforcement of "negotiable electronic transport records." Deliberately medium and technology neutral, these rules should both accommodate and foster future technological innovations. Thus, the only requirements for the use of a "negotiable electronic transport record" are functional: it must arise subject to procedures that provide for (a) a method for the issuance and the transfer of the record to an intended holder, (b) an assurance that the record "retains its integrity," (c) the manner by which the holder can "demonstrate that it is the holder," and (d) the manner of confirming the delivery to the holder or of terminating the record. *See* Articles 9, 51(4), and 57. Although only three countries have ratified the Rotterdam Rules as of 2016, there are positive indications that many countries will do so, including the United States. (For the use of electronic bills of lading under letters of credit, *see* Electronic Aspects of Letter of Credit Transactions in Chapter 4.)

INTERNATIONAL ELECTRONIC COMMERCE IN GENERAL

The rapid and phenomenal growth of e-commerce in the modern economy caught the legal regimes of the world unprepared. None was ready for the legal problems caused by the new forms of contract-making, payment, performance, and information exchange. They have done their best to adapt traditional rules to new transaction patterns, but each legal regime has adapted in a different manner. Thus, although some fundamental principles are the same, there is little consistency in the rules applicable to e-commerce transactions which cross national borders.

Such a lack of consistency is not new, but the problems are magnified by another aspect of e-commerce: The parties often do not know when an e-commerce transaction is in fact across jurisdictional boundaries. A website with a ".com" address may literally be located anywhere in the world. Thus, the website address of each party, which may be the only information each about of the other, may not reveal the transborder nature of the transaction.

E-commerce also raises a number of important challenges for the traditional rules of contract law. These include how to satisfy writing and signature requirements, authentication and attribution without personal contact, security and integrity of electronic messages, and express and implied terms for both commercial and consumer contracts. It also raises jurisdiction issues, ranging from choice of law to sufficient contacts for the exercise of personal jurisdiction, to "presence" in a jurisdiction for purposes of regulation by public authorities. The public authorities not only wish to prevent fraud and deception by "e-merchants," but also to regulate privacy, intellectual property, and taxation issues, among others. In all these areas, there are very few statutory rules or decided cases; and, where there are, the existing rules and approaches to e-commerce differ from one legal regime to another.

Domestic U.S. Legislation: E-SIGN. In the United States, a federal statute from 2000, the Electronic Signatures in Global and National Commerce Act ("E-SIGN"), served as a significant impetus to the legal enforceability of e-commerce transactions. E-SIGN was not adopted to displace the substantive rules of contract law, but rather to facilitate the use of electronic records and signatures in interstate and foreign commerce.

E-SIGN establishes two fundamental principles, "notwithstanding any statute, regulation, or other rule of law": (1) "a signature, contract, or other record . . . may not be denied legal effect, validity, or enforceability solely because it is in electronic form"; and (2) "a contract . . . may not be denied legal effect, validity, or enforceability solely because an electronic signature or electronic record was used in its formation." *See* 15 US.C. § 7001. Moreover, even under E-SIGN, a party may give notice that it will not be bound by electronic messages, and thus negate E-SIGN's rules. In addition, E-SIGN does not apply at all for transactions governed by the UCC (but this exclusion does not extend to UCC Article 2 (on sales of goods) or Article 2A (on leases of goods)). The Act also has more specific rules relating to the accuracy and ability to retain contracts and other records as well as transactions with consumers.

The most important aspect of E-SIGN for present purposes, however, is that it allows the individual states to adopt their own statutes on the same subject. Indeed, the Act explicitly declares that a state may "modify, limit, or supersede" its provisions if the state either (a) enacts a specific uniform act, the Uniform Electronic Transactions Act (UETA), as adopted by the Uniform Law Commissions (see immediately below), or (b) otherwise specifies rules and procedures that are consistent with E-SIGN. All states save three have taken advantage of this authorization to adopt UETA, and the three that have not (Illinois, New York, and Washington) have adopted other, conforming legislation.

UETA. Because of E-SIGN's express exception for states that adopt UETA, that uniform state law Act has had a much more significant practical impact in promoting and facilitating electronic commerce. UETA declares four fundamental principles in its Section 7 mandating equal recognition of electronic contracts and communications with paper documents: (1) a record or signature "may not be denied legal effect or enforceability solely because it is in electronic form"; (2) a contract "may not be denied legal effect or enforceability solely because it is in electronic form"; (3) if a law requires a record to be in writing, "an electronic record satisfies the law"; and (4) if a law requires a signature, "an electronic signature satisfies the law." To advance these goals, UETA also has very broad definitions of the key terms "electronic records" and "electronic signatures."

UCITA. The Uniform Law Commissioners also once supported another, much more comprehensive uniform act on the subject of electronic transactions, the Uniform Computer Information Transactions Act (UCITA). UCITA's goal was to provide a comprehensive regulatory regime for contracting via computers (especially, of course, over the internet). The Act thus applies to all transactions involving the transfer of computer information, but primarily governs software licensing transactions (such as, again, downloads over the internet). It then broadly addresses, in quite detailed provisions, nearly every significant aspect of transactions effected solely through computers.

UCITA's format is similar to UCC Article 2 on sales of goods, and at one time was intended to be UCC Article 2B. Ultimately, however, it was rejected by the American Law Institute as not sufficiently balanced. The Uniform Commissioners then proposed UCITA as their own, separate uniform act. But the Act has not received broad acceptance, with only two state adoptions (Maryland and Virginia), and even the Uniform Law Commissioners subsequently withdrew their endorsement. Although it too embraces the core principle of the validity of electronic contracts and communications, UCITA has much more detailed (and controversial) provisions on a variety of issues and departs in important particulars from the concepts in UETA.

International Solutions. Electronic commerce of course is a world-wide phenomenon. Indeed, transacting business over the internet is substantially easier and cheaper than the face-to-face (or even telephonic) model on which the law of most domestic legal systems is based. Thus, there is a growing need not only for statutory rules to facilitate e-commerce, but also for uniform rules across jurisdictional borders (because, again, it is not usually clear where the parties are located). Promoting similar rules could be accomplished by either an international multilateral treaty or proposed model legislation.

The UNCITRAL Model Law. A first international effort in the latter direction was a Model Law on Electronic Commerce adopted in 1996 by UNCITRAL (the organization that developed the CISG). The Model Law is a minimalist approach to legislation, seeking to facilitate e-commerce transactions and not to regulate them. This Model Law thus is available as a guide for domestic lawmakers in the enactment of a legal infrastructure to regulate the basic principles of, and facilitate the development of commerce conducted on the basis of, electronic communications and through electronic media.

In its general provisions, the UNCITRAL Model Law provides equality of treatment for paper documents and electronic messages. It provides that "data messages" are not to be denied legal effect because they are electronic, and that any "writing" requirement is satisfied by a data message which is accessible for subsequent reference. A data message meets the legal requirements for a "signature" if there is a method that is "reasonable for the circumstances" both to identify the person sending the message and to indicate that person's approval of the message. (A separate UNCITRAL Model Law on Electronic Signatures (2001) provides more detail on this point.)

An electronic data message also will satisfy any evidentiary requirements, including for "an original document" if "there exists a reliable assurance as to the integrity of the information" and "that information is capable of being displayed to the person to whom it is to be presented." Finally, record retention requirements may be satisfied by retaining data messages if the information therein is "accessible so as to be usable for subsequent reference," is retained in its original format and "can be demonstrated" to be accurate, and permits "identification of the origin and destination of a data message and the date and time when it was sent or received."

The UNCITRAL Model Law also contains more specialized rules that may be varied by agreement between the parties. These rules concern contract formation, attribution of messages, and acknowledgment and time of receipt of data messages. As to attribution, a message is deemed to be sent by a designated originator if it is sent either by an authorized person or by a machine that is programmed by the originator to operate automatically. The addressee of the data message is authorized to rely on it as being from the originator if either an agreed-upon security procedure has been used or the originator enabled the actual sender to gain access to a message identification method.

A major problem with electronic data messages is that they get lost—or are caught in spam or similar computer filters—much more often than messages sent in paper form. Thus, acknowledgment of receipt of electronic messages is much more important to the parties than is acknowledgment of paper-based messages, and the parties often stipulate in their agreements that data messages must be acknowledged. If they so agree, under the UNCITRAL Model Law, such an acknowledgment can be accomplished either by the method agreed upon or, in absence of such an agreement, any sufficiently clear communication or conduct. Even where the parties have not agreed to require acknowledgment, the originator of a data message may unilaterally require it by stating in the body of the message that it is conditional on acknowledgment. In such a case, the data message "is treated as though it has never been sent, until the acknowledgement is received." Receipt of a message generally requires that the message enter an information system outside the control of the originator or its agents.

Other provisions in the UNCITRAL Model Law are specific to the contracts for the carriage of goods and to transportation documents. These provisions generally permit electronic data messages to replace bills of lading and waybills, even where local statutes require a paper document. They also provide that legal rules that require the use of paper documents in carriage contracts are satisfied by such data messages.

The UNCITRAL Model Law on Electronic Commerce has had a significant influence on domestic legislation. As of 2016, more than forty national laws, various EU Directives, and uniform acts in nearly every state of the U.S. (*i.e.*, UETA) and nearly every province of Canada have incorporated some or all of its provisions and concepts.

The UNCITRAL Convention. Building on the success of its model law on electronic commerce, UNCITRAL in the early 2000s turned to a formal treaty to advance the goal of international uniformity, the UN Convention on the Use of Electronic Communications in International Contracts (2005). Like the Model Law on Electronic Commerce, the fundamental purpose of this treaty is to validate communications or contracts in electronic form. But unlike the Model Law, UNICTRAL has proposed this legal product as a treaty, which, like the CISG, would take effect as formal, positive law in the ratifying countries.

By its terms, the Convention applies to electronic communications between parties whose "places of business" are in different states, provided at least one party has its place of business in a Contracting State. Article 1(1). The parties may "opt into" the Convention, but may also "opt out" or otherwise vary the effect of the Convention. Article 3. The Convention does not apply, however, to communications concerning transactions with consumers nor those involving negotiable instruments, documents of title, wills or trusts, or certain types of financial matters. Article 2.

The core principles of the Convention parallel those of the Model Law on Electronic Commerce. First, the Convention declares that a communication or a contract may not be "denied validity or enforceability on the sole ground that it is in the form of an electronic communication." Article 8(1). Second, it emphasizes that nothing in its rules "requires that a communication or a contract be made or evidenced in any particular form." Article 9(1) Third, it expressly validates contracts concluded on an entirely automated basis (Article 12), but defines specific remedies for input errors by natural persons relating to automated message systems. Article 14. Finally, to further its general goal of ensuring functional equivalence between paper documents and electronic communications and contracts, it states that the electronic forms must be "accessible so as to be usable for subsequent reference" (Article 9(2)) and that electronic signatures must identify the person and indicate assent by sufficiently reliable methods. Article 9(3).

Although this Convention formally entered into force on March 1, 2013, thus far only seven countries have ratified it (although some seeds of future success may be seen in the four new ratifications in 2014 and 2015). The extent of its future influence thus remains unclear. A principal reason for this is that many advanced countries, including the United States (through E-SIGN and UETA) and the member states of the European Union (through specific directives on electronic commerce and electronic signatures), already have in place comprehensive legislative schemes that regulate the same subject as the UNCITRAL's Convention.

The as-yet-unrealized goal of the UNCITRAL Convention to achieve formal uniformity in positive law on the subject of international electronic transactions has left an uncertain legal terrain. To be sure, the many efforts to create a foundation for electronic commercial transactions have many similarities in their goals and basic principles. But many differences remain. Moreover, many countries have not at all adapted their local legal rules to address the subject, and thus have left the matter to traditional principles of uncertain relevance. These differences in state, national, and international legal rules on e-commerce are likely to continue to cause difficulties for the participants in international transactions, especially where the location of the parties is unknown even to them. And the challenges and potential conflicts are likely to increase as the exponential growth of electronic, and especially internet-based, contracting continues.

CHAPTER 4

FINANCING THE INTERNATIONAL SALE OF GOODS

THE INTERNATIONAL DOCUMENTARY SALE AND DOCUMENTARY LETTER OF CREDIT

THE PROBLEM

Unlike most domestic sales transactions, in a sale of goods across national borders the exporter-seller and the importer-buyer may not have previously dealt with one another; or each may know little about the other; or each may be unfamiliar with the other's domestic legal system. The seller may not know, for example, (1) whether the buyer is creditworthy or trustworthy; (2) whether information received on these subjects from third parties is reliable; (3) whether exchange controls will hinder or delay payment by the buyer (especially if the buyer's country has a soft currency, but payment is in a hard currency); (4) how great the exchange risk is if the buyer may pay in its home currency; and (5) what delays may be involved in receiving unencumbered funds from buyer.

For its part, the buyer may not know (1) whether the seller can be trusted to ship the goods if the buyer prepays; (2) whether the goods shipped will be of the quantity and quality required by the parties' contract; (3) whether the seller will ship the goods with a reliable carrier and will properly insure them in transit; (4) whether the goods might be damaged in transit; (5) whether the seller will furnish to the buyer sufficient ownership documentation covering the goods to allow the buyer to claim them from the carrier or to respond to possible questions by customs officials; (6) whether the seller will provide the documentation necessary to satisfy export control regulations as well as import customs and valuation regulations (*e.g.*, country of origin certificates, health and other inspection certificates, etc.); and (7) what delays may be involved in receiving unencumbered possession and use of the goods at the buyer's location.

Where the parties are strangers, these risks are significant, and may derail the entire deal. The principal problem is that, because they operate at a distance from each other, the seller and the buyer cannot concurrently exchange the seller's goods for the buyer's payment. The solution is to engage reliable, third-party intermediaries. This is where an international letter of credit comes in, for it can bridge this and similar problems. The documentary sale involving a letter of credit illustrates how the potentially large risks reviewed above can be distributed to third party intermediaries who have specialized relationships and expertise, and thus can evaluate each allocated risk more efficiently. In doing so, an international letter of credit can enable valuable transactions that otherwise may not take place.

THE DOCUMENTARY SALE TRANSACTION WITH A CONFIRMED LETTER OF CREDIT

The third party intermediaries enlisted in a letter of credit transaction are banks (one in the buyer's home country and usually a second one in the seller's home country) and at least one carrier. Thus, the parties involved are: (1) a buyer; (2) the bank at which the buyer does its banking (hereafter, "Buyer's Bank"); (3) a seller; (4) a bank with an office in the seller's trading area (hereafter, "Seller's Bank"); and (5) at least one carrier. These parties are able to take a large risk not subject to firm evaluation by any one of them, divide it into several small, calculable risks, and then allocate these smaller risks to the parties best able to evaluate them. Thus, the documentary sale with a letter of credit is an example that not all risk allocation is a zero sum game, but may in fact create a win-win situation.

The overall transaction comes together through a series of contracts—but not all of the parties to the transaction will be involved in all contracts. The contracts include (a) the sale of goods contract between the buyer and the seller; (b) a bill of lading, which is a contract with and a receipt issued by the carrier; and (c) the letter of credit, which represents a promise by Buyer's Bank (and, if "confirmed" (see below), also by Seller's Bank) to pay the seller upon proof that it has shipped the contract goods.

(a) The Sale of Goods Contract. The contract underlying the entire series of transactions is the contract for the sale of goods from the seller to the

buyer. The buyer and the seller are parties to this contract, but not the banks or the carrier. The seller is responsible for delivering the contracted quantity and quality of goods, and the buyer is responsible for taking the goods and paying the stated price. As described in Chapter 2, the law governing international sale of goods contracts in modern commerce is commonly, and increasingly so, the UN Convention on Contracts for the International Sale of Goods (CISG).

(b) The Bill of Lading. In documentary sales, buyers and sellers are usually distant from each other, and the goods must be moved. This requires the engagement of an international carrier, and— depending on the agreements in the sale of goods contract, and especially on the specific Commercial Term chosen, *see* Chapter 3—either the seller or the buyer will make a contract with the carrier to transport the goods. For our illustration, the seller will make that contract. The seller (or, in the language of a contract of carriage, the "shipper") makes a contract with the carrier that obligates the carrier to transport the goods to the buyer's location or some other distant place.

This second contract in our overall transaction is expressed in a "bill of lading," which is "issued" by the carrier. Under the terms of the bill of lading contract, the carrier, in return for payment of the freight charge, promises to deliver the goods to either (1) the "consignee" named in a nonnegotiable (*i.e.*, "straight") bill of lading, or (2) the person in possession ("holder") of an negotiable (*i.e.*, "order") bill of lading. As explained below, a documentary sale—especially one involving a letter of credit—generally requires a negotiable bill of lading, because this form means that the buyer is able to obtain delivery of the goods *only if* it has physical possession of the bill and the bill is properly indorsed over to it. Such a bill of lading controls access to and delivery of the goods, so that the bill of lading is also a "document of title." Chapter 3 above contains a detailed examination of the role of bills of lading in such a documentary transaction. *See* "The Role of Bills of Lading in International Sales Transactions."

(c) The Letter of Credit. Before it delivers the goods to the carrier, the seller ("shipper") wants assurance that the buyer will timely pay for them. A simple promise from a foreign buyer may not be sufficient. Even a promise from a bank in the buyer's country may not be sufficient, because the seller likely also knows very little about foreign banks. Instead, the seller wants a firm, legally binding promise from a bank known to it, preferably one in the seller's country and locality.

What the seller thus wants is the third contract in our transaction—a confirmed, irrevocable letter of credit. A letter of credit is a specialized contract involving a promise by a bank (Buyer's Bank) that it will pay to the seller the amount of the contract price subject to defined conditions. In the distinctive language of letter of credit law, the promise will be that Buyer's Bank will "honor a draft drawn on the bank by seller." Thus, if the seller secures such an obligation in the sales contract, the buyer must request that its bank "issue" such a letter of credit naming the seller as the "beneficiary." But again, the seller *also* will want a payment promise from a bank in its own country and region. Thus, if (again) agreed in the sales contract, the buyer must arrange for a "confirmed" letter of credit. This occurs through Buyer's Bank requesting that a bank in the seller's location obligate itself, through a separate "confirmation" letter sent to the seller, to "honor the draft" presented by the seller. Often, the seller will learn of both actions in the one confirmation letter from its local bank.

The banks' promises will be conditioned upon the seller presenting documentary evidence that it has shipped the goods via a carrier to arrive at the buyer's location, along with any other documents required by the sale of goods contract. What would furnish such evidence? The key document is the bill of lading issued by the carrier—the second contract in our transaction—which will describe the goods the carrier has received from the seller for shipment to the buyer.

Further, a negotiable (or "order") bill of lading will be required, one that thus also controls the right to obtain the goods from carrier. As described in more detail in Chapter 3 above, a negotiable bill of lading issued by the carrier and delivered by the seller to Seller's Bank serves three distinct functions: (1) It provides evidence that the described goods have been delivered to carrier; (2) it shows that the goods are destined for the location defined in the parties' sales contract; and (3) it gives the banks legal control over the goods. When, then, a bank pays the seller under the letter of credit, it will require that the seller indorse over to the bank the negotiable bill of lading, which is a document of title and thus gives the bank control over the carrier's delivery of the goods. Because the negotiable bill of lading controls access to the goods, the buyer cannot obtain possession of them from the carrier without physical possession of the bill. Thus, after the banks have paid the seller in return for that piece of paper, they can demand reimbursement from the buyer before they will release the negotiable bill to the buyer.

Consult the following diagram to illustrate the structure of a transaction involving a letter of credit:

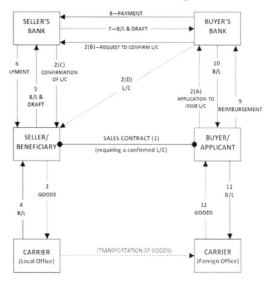

The process begins with the sale of goods contract. When the buyer and the seller are forming their contract, the seller will insist that it include both a "price term" and a "payment term." The price term is simply *how much* the buyer must pay; the payment term, in contrast, is *how* the buyer must pay. The challenge for the seller is that generally the buyer has a right to inspect the goods before payment. To avoid the risk of nonpayment after shipping the goods, the seller thus must bargain for and include in the sales contract a term that requires payment by an "irrevocable" letter of credit. Such an agreement normally will not be implied. The seller also should specify in detail what documents it must present to obtain payment. The reason for this is that even with a payment against documents transaction—such as the general presumptions for a CIF contract, see Commercial Terms in Chapter 3—the buyer will have a right to inspect the documents before payment, and this inspection also will come after the seller has shipped the goods through the carrier. When, then, the payment term is a letter of credit—which also requires a presentation of documents as a condition to payment—the seller must know in detail which documents it must present to obtain payment from the banks.

What documents will the banks require as a condition to payment under the letter of credit? In addition to the draft (see below), they usually include the following:

(1) A negotiable bill of lading showing the carrier's receipt of the described goods and reflecting an obligation to deliver them only to the holder of the document;

(2) a commercial invoice, which is a form of an itemized bill that sets out the terms of the sale, grade and quantity of goods, amount owed, etc.;

(3) a packing list, which is a separate confirmation from the seller's shipping department of the goods they packed for shipment, especially in sealed cartons or containers;

(4) a policy of insurance (if goods are to be transported by sea);

(5) a certificate of inspection, which is issued by a commercial inspecting firm and independently confirms that the seller has shipped the required number and type of goods (although the buyer must separately contract for such an inspection);

(6) an export license and/or health inspection certificate showing that the goods are cleared for export; and

(7) a certificate of origin, which documents the source of the goods sold and—depending on the trade agreements between the exporting and importing country—may be used by customs officials in the importing country to determine the amount of any required customs duties.

If it agrees to a letter of credit payment term, the buyer (the "account party," or, in the language of letter of credit law, the "applicant") will contract with Buyer's Bank ("issuer" or "issuing bank") to issue a letter of credit ("credit") in favor of the seller ("beneficiary"). The letter of credit is a direct promise by the issuing bank that it will pay the contract price to the seller/beneficiary, if the seller presents to it the documents specified in the letter of credit. Buyer's Bank will be aware of the buyer's creditworthiness, and will make appropriate arrangements to ensure reimbursement by the buyer (through either immediate payment or future repayment of a loan secured by appropriate collateral). These arrangements will be made before the letter of credit is issued, for with an irrevocable letter of credit Buyer's Bank is *independently* bound after issuance to pay the beneficiary according to the credit's terms.

As sketched above, for maximum protection the seller will demand that the sales contract require payment by "confirmed" letter of credit. In such a case, the buyer also must arrange for a payment promise by a local bank in the seller's area ("confirmer" or "confirming bank"). This is accomplished by Buyer's Bank forwarding its letter of credit to the seller through another bank in the seller's trading area (Seller's Bank) and requesting that Seller's Bank "add its confirmation." By merely indicating "We confirm this credit," Seller's Bank makes a direct and independent promise to the seller that it will pay the contract price to the seller, if (again) the seller presents the required documents. Most often, however, the confirmation comes in the form of a separate, formal letter from Seller's Bank to the seller. (Why do the banks provide these services? For an appropriate fee, of course. But these fees are fairly small, typically 1–2% of the amount of the letter of credit.)

If the sales contract does not require a confirmation of the credit, Buyer's Bank nonetheless can forward the letter of credit through a mere "advising bank" (also known as a "notifying bank") located near the seller. Such a bank will not be obligated to pay the seller, but merely will inform the seller of the issuance. It later also may take the presented documents from the seller and forward them to Buyer's Bank for collection purposes only. (Another role a bank may play is as a "nominated bank," one which the issuer authorizes (typically later) to accept the presented documents and pay the amount of stated in the credit, but which does not add its independent confirmation in advance.)

Once Buyer's Bank has issued the letter of credit and Seller's Bank has confirmed it, the seller will pack the goods, prepare a commercial invoice, and—again depending on the specific commercial term stated in the sales contract—secure insurance (another form of contract) covering the goods during transit. If the sales contract also requires an inspection certificate, the goods will be made available to the designated inspection firm (which the buyer will engage through another contract). The inspection firm then will issue a certificate stating that the goods conform to the description in the sales contract (or not). If the sales contract also so requires, the seller will prepare the necessary documents for the customs officials in its home country (*e.g.*, an export license) as well as a certificate of origin (if required by customs officials in the buyer's country).

The seller then will deliver the goods to the carrier, which issues the negotiable bill of lading as a combination contract, receipt, and document of title. As described above, in a letter of credit transaction this bill of lading most often must be negotiable, and will commonly require the carrier to deliver the goods only "to seller or order"—*i.e.*, only to the seller or a person the seller designates by an appropriate indorsement, provided in either case that the person also is in possession of the bill. See again "The Role of Bills of Lading in International Sales Transactions" in Chapter 3.

The seller now has the complete set of the required documents, and takes these documents to Seller's Bank, which (as a confirming bank) is obligated to pay the seller the contract price upon presentation of the specified documents. Because the letter of credit is merely a promise to pay, the seller also must use a legal vehicle to "draw on" the credit. To do this, the seller prepares a "draft" and then presents it to the bank along with the other required documents. The draft (sometimes known by an earlier term, "bill of exchange") resembles a check written by the seller and typically drawn on Buyer's Bank (the original issuer) for the amount of the goods shipped pursuant to the sales contract.

Just like a standard personal check, the seller (the "drawer") uses the draft to instruct Buyer's Bank (the "drawee") to pay a designated person (the "payee") from the "credit" created by the letter of credit. The payee, of course, is the seller itself.

A draft can be payable on demand ("at sight"), or at a defined later time (*e.g.*, "30 days after sight"). If a "demand draft" is used, the bank—in our case, Seller's Bank (the confirming bank)—will pay the amount immediately, usually by crediting the seller's bank account; if a time draft is used, the bank will "accept" it (*i.e.*, stamp its name on it) and thereby bindingly obligate itself to pay at the defined later time. In the latter case, the seller can still raise funds immediately by selling the draft to a third party on the strength of the bank's credit.

Seller's Bank never sees the goods, only the documents. Because of this, it inspects the documents rigorously to confirm that they comply exactly with the requirements of the letter of credit—for the documents are its only protection. Substantial performance by the seller is not enough.

If Seller's Bank determines that the presented documents conform to the requirements in the letter of credit, it will honor the presentation and pay the seller; if not, it will dishonor and refuse to pay. If it honors, Seller's Bank will require that the seller indorse both the draft and the negotiable bill of lading over to it and (of course) also transfer the other required documents. Seller's Bank, in turn, will indorse the draft and the bill of lading and forward both with their accompanying documents to

Buyer's Bank. As the issuer of the letter of credit, Buyer's Bank also is obligated to "honor" the draft and thus to reimburse Seller's Bank if the draft and the other documents from the seller conform to the requirements in the letter of credit.

Buyer's Bank then contacts the buyer, presents the documents to the buyer, and requests reimbursement. The buyer, like the banks, must pay against the documents and not the goods themselves, which is why it is necessary to have clear specifications for the required documents in the original sale of goods contract, and then to repeat those specifications precisely in the letter of credit. Upon payment by the buyer, Buyer's Bank will deliver the bill of lading, properly indorsed, to the buyer. Only then will the buyer have the power to obtain the goods from the carrier.

Note the limited risks to each party. If the seller ships conforming goods, it has independent promises of payment from both the buyer and the two banks. The banks' promises are enforceable despite assertions of non-conformity of the goods, so long as the documents conform to the requirements in the letter of credit. Thus, as a practical matter, the seller is exposed only if Seller's Bank fails, Buyer's Bank fails, and the buyer is either unable or unwilling to pay, a constellation of events so unlikely that the seller should have no noteworthy concern in shipping the goods. If Seller's Bank unjustifiably refuses to fulfill its promise to pay, the seller has a cause of action in a local court—which will use a familiar language and unfold in a familiar

legal   system—against   a   financially   secure
defendant.

Even though Seller's Bank is obligated to pay the
seller against the documents, its position also is
generally secure. It is entitled to reimbursement
from Buyer's Bank and from the buyer, and
practically is at risk only if both Buyer's Bank and
the buyer fail or refuse to perform their
obligations—risks which Seller's Bank should be
able to evaluate accurately. Moreover, Seller's Bank
has the security of the negotiable bill of lading,
which the seller has indorsed over to it and will
enable it to control the goods until it obtains
reimbursement.

For its part, Buyer's Bank is at risk only if the
buyer fails or refuses to perform; but these again are
risks which Buyer's Bank had an opportunity to
evaluate before issuing the letter of credit, and for
which it could adjust its price (the fee and the
interest rate on any loan). And again, after Seller's
Bank has indorsed the negotiable bill of lading over
to it, Buyer's Bank will have control over the goods
until it obtains reimbursement from the buyer.

Finally, upon its reimbursement of Buyer's Bank,
the buyer will receive from that bank a document
(the negotiable bill of lading) entitling it to delivery
of the goods from the carrier, an insurance
certificate protecting the buyer against casualty loss
in transit, and perhaps an inspection certificate
warranting that the goods in fact conform to the
sales contract. In other words, the buyer should
receive what it bargained for—delivery of

conforming goods or insurance proceeds sufficient to cover any loss.

THE GOVERNING LEGAL RULES

The law governing letters of credit developed before World War I principally in England, and thereafter in courts in the United States. But as the U.S. national economy matured in the 20th century, the need for uniform national rules led the drafters of the Uniform Commercial Code (UCC) to include a separate article (Article 5) on letter of credit law (as revised in 1995). As is true with the rest of the UCC, most of Article 5 is not mandatory law; as a result, nearly all of Article 5's provisions defer to the agreement of the parties as expressed in the terms of their contract.

For international letters of credit, the practically more significant rules are found in the Uniform Customs and Practices for Documentary Credits (UCP). The UCP (like the Incoterms, see "Commercial Terms" in Chapter 3) are a set of copyrighted contract terms published by the International Chamber of Commerce (ICC). The ICC published the original version of the UCP in 1933, and since then has updated it approximately every ten years. The most recent version is the 2007 Revision (No. 600).

THE UNIFORM CUSTOMS AND PRACTICES FOR DOCUMENTARY CREDITS (UCP)

The overwhelming majority of international letters of credit incorporate the UCP by express reference. The UCP constitutes a rather detailed set of rules that define the rights and obligations of the banks involved in letters of credit; but its legal status is as a statement of contract terms and banking trade usage, and not as generally applicable positive law. The unusual aspect of the UCP is that it takes effect by a unilateral declaration of a bank in the letter of credit, and not by formal agreement with the beneficiary. Nonetheless, the UCC expressly validates such a unilateral incorporation of the UCP in a letter of credit and also expressly provides that in such a case the UCP controls in the event of a conflict with the rules in the UCC. *See* UCC § 5–116(c).

Nonetheless, the rules set forth in the UCC and the UCP generally are quite similar in scope and substance, and indeed one key purpose of the 1995 revision of Article 5 was to align the UCC more closely with the UCP. But even if the UCP is incorporated in a particular letter of credit, the UCC continues to apply for gaps in the UCP. The most prominent example of this is that the UCP has no rules that address fraud. Based on this relationship between the UCP and the UCC, this chapter will describe the UCP rules for all non-fraud issues, and the UCC provisions for issues of fraud.

The UCP applies to any documentary credit (which it refers to merely as a "credit") "when the text of the credit expressly indicates that it is subject to these rules." Article 1. To begin, it describes four different roles of banks in letter of credit transactions: (1) issuing bank; (2) advising bank; (3) nominated bank; and (4) confirming bank (a subset of a nominated bank). An *issuing bank* means the bank that issues a letter of credit at the request of an applicant, and thus promises to honor a presentation if the presented documents conform to the terms of the letter of credit. An *advising bank* means a bank that advises the beneficiary (usually the seller) of the documentary credit at the request of the issuing bank. An advising bank makes no promise to pay against documents and is obligated only to take "reasonable care" to check the authenticity of the credit before advising. *Nominated bank* is an umbrella term under the UCP that covers any bank "with which the credit is available." This means a bank that is designated or authorized by the issuing bank to pay (or "negotiate," that is, purchase) the draft presented by the beneficiary. A *confirming bank* is a nominated bank that also confirms the letter of credit at the issuing bank's authorization or request, and thus (unlike other nominated banks) promises *in advance* to honor a conforming presentation.

THE FUNDAMENTAL PRINCIPLES OF LETTER OF CREDIT LAW

The letter of credit rules in the UCP (and also in UCC Article 5) are founded on two fundamental principles: (1) the "independence" principle, and (2) the "strict compliance" principle.

The Independence Principle. The most fundamental principle of letter of credit law is that the bank's obligation to pay upon the presentation of conforming *documents* is independent of the performance of the underlying transaction for the sale of the *goods*. In the words of UCP Article 4, a credit "by its nature is a separate transaction from the sale or other contract on which it may be based" and banks "are in no way concerned with or bound by such contract." This basic principle carries with it two important corollaries. First, the obligations of an issuing bank or a confirming bank are not subject to claims or defenses by the applicant (the buyer) that the beneficiary (the seller) has not performed its obligations under the sales contract. Second, in asserting its claim against a bank, the beneficiary likewise may not rely on rights outside of the letter of credit transaction.

The one exception to the independence principle relates to allegations of fraud or forgery. We will cover this important issue in detail below. *See* "The Fraud Defense."

The Strict Compliance Principle. The second fundamental principle of letter of credit law—which is closely related to the first—begins with the premise that in fulfilling their obligations the banks deal only with the *documents* required by the letter of credit. Thus, UCP Article 14(a) provides that the banks must examine a presentation to determine "on the basis of the documents alone" whether or not they appear "on their face" to constitute a "complying presentation."

Because the only protection for the banks in assessing a presentation is the documents themselves, the traditional standard has been "strict compliance" with the terms of the letter of credit. But modern versions of the UCP have introduced a slightly different linguistic formulation for the term "complying presentation." Article 14(d) provides that, as measured against "the context of the credit" and "international standard banking practice," data in a presented document "need not be identical to, but must not conflict with," the terms of the credit.

This language has generated substantial judicial and scholarly debate over the continued validity of the "strict" compliance standard. Nonetheless, modern opinions (as well as revised Article 5) have rejected a nascent line in some American cases that seemed to permit payment upon substantial performance by the beneficiary. Instead, the prevailing view among courts and scholars is that the strict compliance standard, properly calibrated, continues to apply under the UCP as well. Thus, one court held that an issuer was justified in dishonoring where the letter of credit mistakenly identified the beneficiary as Sung "Jin" Electronics, while the documents were correctly addressed to Sung "Jun" Electronics. *Hanil Bank v. PT. Bank Negara Indonesia*, 148 F.3d 127 (2nd Cir. 1998). More recently, an English court upheld a dishonor where a letter of credit identified the beneficiary as "Bulgrains Co. Ltd." but the presented documents referred to "Bulgrains & Co. Ltd." *See Bulgrains &*

Co. Ltd. vs. Shinhan Bank, [2013] EWHC 2498 (QB).

English courts have gained renown in applying the "strict compliance" standard, including in a famous case holding that the phrase "machine shelled groundnut kernels" did not comply with the required term "Coromandel groundnuts," even though it was "universally acknowledged" in the trade that both labels applied to the goods. *J.H. Rayner & Co. Ltd. v. Hambro's Bank, Ltd*, 1 K.B. 36 (1943). (This holding also reflects a further important principle: that banks are not responsible for, and are not expected to investigate, the customs or usages that may apply in a particular trade, other than in the banking trade. See below.)

Nonetheless, a clear typographical error seems to represent the edge of the strict compliance standard. The 2013 edition of the ICC's International Standard Banking Practice (ISBP) manual explains that "a misspelling or typing error that does not affect the meaning of a word or the sentence in which it occurs does not make a document discrepant." It cites as examples a description of goods as a "mashine" instead of "machine" or as a "fountan pen" instead of "fountain pen." *See* ICC Publ. 745E, A23 (2013). Thus, the prevailing norm, as one court sensibly explained, appears to be "a common sense, case-by-case approach [that] permit[s] minor deviations of a typographical nature because such a letter-for-letter correspondence between the letter of credit and the presentation documents is virtually impossible."

Voest-Alpine Trading USA Corp. v. Bank of China, 167 F. Supp. 2d 940 (S.D. Tex. 2000).

The primary document for describing the goods in a documentary sale transaction is the commercial invoice. The description in the commercial invoice must be specific and must "correspond with that appearing in the credit." UCP Article 18(c). Descriptions of the goods in all other documents "may be in general terms not conflicting with" the description in the credit. UCP Article 14(e).

The more difficult issues concerning the strict conformity of documents seem to arise in transportation terms. Express conditions in the credit that loading, presentment, or other acts must be performed by a certain time will be strictly enforced. A credit calling for "full set clean on board ocean bills of lading," for example, is not satisfied by a tender of "a trucker's bill of lading." Indeed, UCP Article 27 emphasizes the importance of a "clean" transport document with a rule that banks may only accept such a document if it bears "no clause or notation expressly declaring a defective condition of the goods or their packaging."

Unfortunately, discrepancies in tendered documents are an everyday occurrence. Indeed, some estimates are that as many as two-thirds of all presentations contain at least one discrepancy, and that one-half of presentations are rejected on this basis. That rate of error should not be surprising if one understands that the presentation may consist of many dozens of pages of documents.

THE BASIC OBLIGATIONS OF BANKS

When the beneficiary (seller) presents the required documents, an issuing or a confirming bank has two duties. The first is to examine the documents to determine whether they conform to the terms of the letter of credit. If the bank discovers discrepancies, its second obligation is to notify the beneficiary of the "dishonor."

Obligation to Examine the Documents for Discrepancies. As reviewed above, a bank's examination of presented documents is subject to a (properly calibrated) strict compliance standard. But a variety of related principles influence the application of this standard: (1) As indicated above, banks must determine the existence of a discrepancy on the basis of the presented documents alone. (2) As a corollary, banks may consider only those conditions that may be satisfied by documentary evidence. It is the responsibility of the issuing bank and its customer, the applicant (buyer), to ensure that, for each condition, the letter of credit stipulates a document to indicate compliance. Otherwise, "banks will deem such condition as not stated and will disregard it." UCP Article 14(h). (3) As noted in *Rayner & Co. Ltd.* case above, banks are not responsible for knowing, and are not expected to investigate, the customs or usages that may apply in a particular trade outside of the banking trade. (4) Banks also must disregard any document presented by a beneficiary that is *not* required by the letter of credit (which one might term "anomalous documents").

Obligation of Timely Notification of Discrepancies. A bank's second obligation is to notify the beneficiary in the event its examination reveals a discrepancy. The bank must give a notice of the dishonor, state the grounds, and return the documents to the beneficiary (or follow any previous instructions). Article 16(c). In addition, the bank must send any notice of dishonor "by telecommunication," and if this is not possible, "by other expeditious means." Article 16(d).

If it finds a discrepancy, the bank may give a notice of dishonor without consulting its customer, the applicant (buyer). However, in many situations, the discrepancies may be trivial, and the customer may want the payment made, and the goods delivered, despite the discrepancy. Thus, UCP Article 16(b) allows, but does not require, the bank to consult the applicant for a waiver of the discrepancies it has discovered. Evidence suggests that, if consulted, applicants in fact waive discrepancies discovered by the bank about 90% of the time. Thus, the system seems to work because the non-bank parties (buyer and seller) want the transaction to be completed despite the technical difficulties imposed by letter of credit law.

A bank not only must be thorough in its examination of a presentation, it also must be quick in its response. UCP Article 14(b) states that a bank has a "maximum of five banking days following the day of presentation to determine if a presentation is complying." (Under the UCC, the time limit is "a reasonable time . . . but not beyond the end of the seventh business day," but this should be an example of where the UCC defers to the UCP.) If the bank discovers no discrepancies, there is no particular difficulty in meeting this deadline, and "the maximum" may be shorter than five days. In a famous case from the past, an issuing bank examined 967 pages of documents twice in two and a half days. *Banco Español de Credito v. State Street Bank and Trust Co.*, 385 F.2d 230 (1st Cir. 1967).

If the bank discovers discrepancies, however, it may be subject to time pressures. The "five banking days" deadline includes not only the time to examine the documents, but also the time to consult the bank's customer about waiving the discrepancies *and* to give the required notice of dishonor. The latter two requirements, in particular, can create timing difficulties for the bank.

UCP Article 16(c) requires any bank that rejects a presentation of documents to state, "in a single notice" to the presenter, "each discrepancy in respect of which [it] refuses to honour." Under UCP Article 16(f), failure to state all the discrepancies, or to meet the time deadline, "precludes" the bank from claiming non-compliance due to any unstated discrepancy, without the necessity of proving waiver or estoppel. Thus, banks that reject documents have only one chance to identify all the discrepancies on which they can ever rely. The rationale for this rule is to inform the beneficiary of all the discrepancies at once, so that it can determine whether they are curable and whether such cure is cost-effective. But the rule also can lead the issuing bank to delay notification for additional re-examinations to ensure that all defects are discovered (as long as it does not breach the five-day deadline).

The banks' review of a presentation for discrepancies has direct consequences for the rights of the presenter, the obligations of the bank, and the right of the bank to seek reimbursement from another bank and the applicant:

(a) If the bank determines that a presentation complies with the letter of credit, it "must honour" and pay the beneficiary (or "accept" a time draft). Article 15(a), (b). In such a case, the bank is entitled to reimbursement. But if it refuses to pay in such a case, it will be liable to the presenter for "wrongful dishonor."

(b) If, in contrast, the documents do not comply, the bank "may refuse to honor." Article 16(a). In such a case, the presenter has no claim to payment under the letter of credit.

(c) Finally, if the documents do not comply, but the bank nonetheless honors (or waives its right to dishonor), it generally is not entitled to reimbursement ("wrongful honor").

The liability of the confirming bank is separate from and independent of, but parallels, the liability of the issuing bank. UCP Article 8 permits the beneficiary to present the documents to the confirming bank or to any other nominated bank. Once the presentation is made, the confirming bank has all of the examination, time, and notice obligations that apply to an issuing bank as described above. In turn, when a confirming bank accepts the documents from the beneficiary and presents them to the issuing bank, the latter has all of these examination, time, and notice obligations as against the confirming bank (which is now the "presenter").

The Special Role of the Transportation Document. Although, for the description of the goods, the commercial invoice is the document that must strictly conform to the letter of credit, the most important of the documents required by a letter of credit is the transportation document. Early versions of the UCP were premised principally on ocean bills of lading, evidencing an assumption that the goods would be carried by sea. New developments in the transport industry, however, have created new technological applications. Thus, the recent revisions of the UCP provide separate articles for negotiable ocean bills of lading; non-negotiable sea waybills; charter party bills of lading; multi-modal transport documents; air transport documents; road, rail or inland waterway transport documents; and courier receipts, post receipts, and certificates of posting.

Nonetheless, the most common form of required transport document in large international transactions remains the negotiable ocean bill of lading. Under UCP Article 20, an ocean bill of lading must name the port of loading, the port of discharge, and the carrier, and also be signed by the carrier or its agent. Banks have no duty, however, to check the signature or initials accompanying an "on board" notation, absent a special arrangement. The bill of lading may indicate an "intended vessel." In such cases, any "on board" notation must specify the vessel on which the goods have been loaded. The medieval custom of issuing "a set" of bills of lading, and hoping one of them would arrive and be honored, is now disapproved: UCP Article 20 requires as a norm only one original bill of lading.

In addition to nonnegotiable bills of lading (aka, "waybills," see above), two modern transportation practices are worthy of mention. A "charter party" bill of lading does not identify the carrier, and is now a permissible transport document for use with a letter of credit. UCP Article 22(b) relieves the banks from any duty to examine the terms of the charter party contract, under the assumption that only sophisticated parties with considerable knowledge of the trade will use them.

A second form of increasingly common transport document is a "multimodal" bill of lading. In multimodal transportation arrangements, the bill of lading—as its name implies—will cover the goods through "at least two different modes of transport." Article 19. An example would be where the goods are first loaded on a truck and then transferred to a railroad, before being loaded on a ship for ocean transport. Such a bill of lading is likely to be issued by a general services company known as a "freight forwarder" and not by a single carrier (because many carriers may be involved). Thus, it does not name a carrier and does not represent a receipt directly from the carrier, which is the norm for documents of title such as negotiable bills of lading. However, the UCP allows its use if the letter of credit authorizes a signature by a named agent of the carrier and the freight forwarder issues it in that capacity as a multimodal transport document.

ELECTRONIC ASPECTS OF LETTER OF CREDIT TRANSACTIONS

Electronic communications have taken over some aspects of letter of credit practice, but not others. They dominate the issuance process in bank-to-bank communications, and are sometimes used by applicants to initiate the issuance process. However, for a variety of reasons banks and other interested parties have not yet been able to create an entirely paperless transaction. First, the beneficiary still commonly wants a piece of paper—or at least a scanned electronic copy or pdf version of a formal letter—committing the banks to pay upon specified conditions. Second, even with an electronic letter of credit, most industries have not accepted electronic forms in the place of the significant documents typically required by a letter of credit. The principal example is an electronic negotiable bill of lading, which, for the reasons discussed in Chapter 3 (*see* "Electronic Bills of Lading"), has not yet found broad or stable acceptance. Thus, in the presentation phase for letters of credit, the parties commonly still use physical documents, while funds settlement (payment) likely will be electronic.

Over three quarters of letter of credit communications between banks—including the issuance, advice, and confirmation of letters of credit—is paperless; and nearly all informal communication is electronic. Nonetheless, bank-to-beneficiary communication is still paper-based. Letter of credit issuers of course now can communicate directly with beneficiaries via computer, however, and this is now the norm. UCP Article 11 also expressly contemplates "teletransmission," which will continue to facilitate the use of electronic practices. Moreover, the UCP has issued a separate set of rules, the Supplement to the Uniform Customs and Practice for Documentary Credits for Electronic Presentation ("eUCP"), which—if expressly incorporated in a letter of credit—permits a beneficiary to present equivalent "electronic records" for any required document.

The SWIFT System. Most bank-to-bank communications concerning letters of credit are routed through the dedicated lines of SWIFT (the Society for Worldwide Interbank Financial Telecommunication). SWIFT is a Belgian not-for-profit organization owned by banks as a cooperative venture for the transmission of financial transaction messages. It requires all such messages to be structured in a uniform format, and uses standardized elements for allocating message space and for message text. Each bank in the system has a unique SWIFT bank code (*e.g.*, Citibank in New York = CITIUS33), and each type of message has a unique number (*e.g.*, Issuance of Letter of Credit = MT700). Each message type also has a set of uniform fields for specific types of information (*e.g.*, 45A = Description of Goods and Services). In this way, banks may communicate their inter-bank messages on a computer-to-computer basis without human intervention.

A bank issuing a letter of credit communicates that message to the nearest SWIFT access point. The message is then routed on a dedicated data transmission line to a regional processor, where it is validated. From the regional processor, it is routed over a dedicated line to one of three main data centers, one each in the United States, the Netherlands, and Switzerland. From there it is routed through a regional processor to a SWIFT access point and to the receiving bank. There are also log in procedures, application-selection procedures, message numbering and error-checking capabilities, and control of access to the system hardware. SWIFT also retains records of each transaction. In all, the security devices are numerous and complex.

Under SWIFT rules, Belgian law governs all relations between SWIFT and its users. SWIFT is liable for negligence or fraud of its own employees and agents and for those parts of the communication system that it controls, such as regional processors, main switches and the dedicated lines that connect them. But SWIFT disclaims liability for those parts of the communication system that it does not control, such as the bank computers that issue and receive messages and the dedicated lines from bank to a regional processor. Even where SWIFT is liable, its liability is limited to "direct" damages (loss of interest); the contracts with SWIFT thus expressly disclaim liability for indirect, special, or consequential damages.

It is now possible for an applicant (buyer, in the documentary sale transaction) to draft a proposed electronic letter of credit. If properly formatted, the electronic proposed credit then can be transmitted to the issuing bank for electronic issuance through the SWIFT system. This procedure usually is used where the applicant seeks multiple credits and there is a master agreement between the issuing bank and the applicant. The issuing bank will first check to see whether the proposed credit is authorized and contains the required security codes. Then, it will determine whether it is within the previously authorized credit limit and is stated in the standardized elements and uniform format for electronic messages.

When is the issuer of an electronic letter of credit bound? The UCP has no formal rule on the subject, but UCC § 5–104 provides that a letter of credit "may be issued in any form," including an electronic format. UCC § 5–106(a) in turn makes clear that such an electronic credit "is issued and becomes enforceable" when the issuer "transmits it," not when it is delivered to the receiving bank; and for their part, SWIFT rules do not require a reply. This

UCC rule conforms to the understanding of bankers involved in the trade.

On the other end of the electronic communications, the beneficiary (the seller in the documentary sale) typically wants a "hard copy"—a written letter of credit in the traditional form. Thus, when the sending bank issues the letter of credit via a SWIFT message to the confirming bank, the latter will convert it into a formal letter sent to the beneficiary. (Again, today this often takes the form of a pdf. version of a formal letter sent by email.) However, the SWIFT message is designed for bank-to-bank use, and not necessarily for use by beneficiaries. This raises certain legal issues. First, the SWIFT message does not bear a signature in the traditional sense, even though it has been thoroughly authenticated through SWIFT's computer-based transmission mechanisms. Thus, the beneficiary is entitled to doubt whether the SWIFT electronic message alone creates a legal obligation of the sending bank to pay the beneficiary under the letter of credit.

The issue usually is framed as this: "Is the SWIFT inter-bank message *the* operative credit instrument as far as the beneficiary is concerned?" The issue is of importance to beneficiaries not only in the original issuance of the credit, but also in the myriad of amendments to the credit that may follow. Under SWIFT rules, SWIFT users treat the electronic message as a binding obligation, and treat the authentication as the functional equivalent of a signature. However, the beneficiary is not a SWIFT user, and under banking practice a beneficiary can rely on an electronic message only after it has been issued in a formal format, properly signed or otherwise authenticated. As noted, UCC § 5–104 permits electronic letters of credit; but that provision does not necessarily answer the question as to whether the unsigned record of a SWIFT message, generated by the recipient of that message, is the operative credit instrument and binds the issuing bank.

There also is some doubt about whether SWIFT-generated records or transcriptions are subject to the UCP. SWIFT internal rules provide that credits issued through its system are subject to the UCP, but the record or transcription into a hard copy may bear no reference to the UCP. UCP Article 1 states that the UCP provisions govern "where the text of the credit expressly indicates that it is subject to these rules."

Under the UCP, whether an electronic message is the operative credit instrument or not depends upon the terminology in the message itself. UCP Article 11(a) states a basic rule that an authenticated electronic message "will be deemed to be the operative credit," and that "any subsequent mail confirmation shall be disregarded." It also states, however, that if the electronic message states "full details to follow (or words of similar effect)," then the electronic message will not be the operative credit, and the issuing bank "must then issue the operative credit . . . without delay in terms not inconsistent" with the electronic message.

Chapter 3 discussed the attempts to create an electronic bill of lading. If successful, an electronic bill of lading could facilitate the electronic letter of credit transaction. However, to date, while an electronic bill of lading can replace a nonnegotiable (or straight) bill of lading, market participants have remained skeptical about its ability to replace a negotiable bill of lading. A number of institutions and business have tried, thus far without great success, to replicate the security of paper-based negotiable bills of lading. But some change may be on the horizon. As described in Chapter 3, the new provisions of UCC Articles 1 and 7 on "electronic documents of title" as well as the Rotterdam Rules of 2009 may provide a stable legal foundation for a broader acceptance of electronic bills of lading in the future.

Moreover, in 2013 collaboration between the ICC and SWIFT resulted in a new set of rules, the Uniform Rules for Bank Payment Obligations (URBPO), as an alternative for electronic letters of credit. These rules solely govern the relationship between a buyer's bank and a seller's bank and do not create any formal rights of the seller against either bank. Thus, except for stable, long-term relationships between and among the banks and specific buyer-seller pairs of traders, some doubt exists about whether the URBPO can displace the traditional international letter of credit transaction.

STANDBY LETTERS OF CREDIT

Foreign governments, or other foreign project developers with sufficient bargaining power, often require a financial assurance (by way of a financial guarantee) by multinational enterprises (MNEs) that they will supply goods, perform services, or construct a project competently and in accordance with the terms of the governing contract. Performance bonds can serve as an adequate assurance, but under prior U.S. federal law banks were not allowed to issue guarantees, performance bonds, or insurance policies. With a large market at stake, U.S. banks nonetheless developed a functional alternative—the "standby" letter of credit. This alternative form of a letter of credit is issued by the seller's (or other performer's) bank and runs in favor of the buyer—truly a backwards arrangement as compared to the commercial letters of credit described above.

A standby credit is payable against a writing that certifies that the seller has not performed its promises. Such a credit is not for the purpose of ensuring that the buyer performs its payment obligation to the seller for shipment of the goods. Rather, it serves as a form of guarantee or insurance that the seller will perform its obligations to the buyer (or to a foreign government, developer, etc.). Thus, although once not allowed to issue guarantees, performance bonds, or insurance policies at all, banks can achieve essentially the same end through standby letters of credit. The result is the creation of a new commercial device, which is now commercially accepted for its own value, and which has supplanted the performance bond in many fields of endeavor.

Consult the following diagram to illustrate the stages of the issuance and resort to a standby letter of credit:

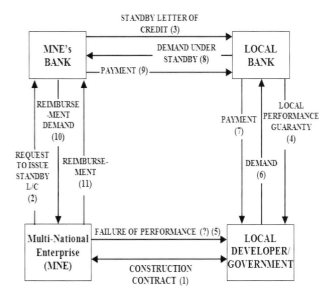

Below is also an example of a standby letter of credit issued by seller's bank in favor of the country of India. It is taken from *Dynamics Corp. of America v. Citizens & Southern Nat. Bank*, 356 F. Supp. 991 (N.D. Ga. 1973):

" . . . TO: THE PRESIDENT OF INDIA

INDIA

BY ORDER OF: ELECTRONICS SYSTEMS DIVISION OF DYNAMICS CORPORATION OF AMERICA

For account

of same

GENTLEMEN:

WE HEREBY ESTABLISH OUR IRREVOCABLE CREDIT IN YOUR FAVOR, FOR THE ACCOUNT INDICATED ABOVE, FOR A SUM OR SUMS NOT EXCEEDING IN ALL FOUR HUNDRED TEN THOUSAND FOUR HUNDRED SEVENTY TWO AND 60/100 US DOLLARS (US$410,472.60)— AVAILABLE BY YOUR DRAFT(S) AT sight,

DRAWN ON: us

Which must be accompanied by:

1. Your signed certification as follows: "The President of India being one of the parties to the Agreement dated March 14, 1971 signed and exchanged between the President of India and the Dynamics Corporation of America for the license to manufacture, purchase and supply of radio equipment as per Schedule I thereof for the total contract value of $1,368,242.00, does hereby certify in the exercise of reasonable discretion and in good faith that the Dynamics Corporation of America has failed to carry out *certain obligations of theirs under the said Order/Agreement. . ."*

Through this credit, the seller (applicant or account party) has contracted to have the seller's bank (issuing bank) issue an irrevocable letter of credit in favor of the foreign government (beneficiary) that payment will be made upon presentation of a simple documentary statement by the beneficiary. This is merely a unilateral declaration by the beneficiary, "in the exercise of reasonable discretion and in good faith," that the account party has failed to carry out its obligations under a contract.

This transaction is almost an exact reverse of the letter of credit in the documentary sale. In the standby credit, the account party (applicant) is the seller or contractor, the beneficiary is the purchaser, and the documents do not control the goods (and indeed have no independent value of their own). Some standbys require no formal documentary presentation at all, but merely a demand by the beneficiary that the issuer pay (a so-called "suicide credit"). Another, only slightly more limited version is one in which the issuer must pay whenever the beneficiary merely states that the contractor has failed to perform under the contract or, perhaps, has failed to return an advance payment.

Governing Law. As with commercial letters of credit, the principal sources of the legal rules for standby letters of credit are Article 5 of the UCC and the UCP. Both make clear that they may apply for a standby letter of credit. As to the UCC, a standby falls within § 5–102(a)(10)'s broad definition of a letter of credit to cover any "definite undertaking" by a bank "to honor a documentary presentation by payment." Since 1983, the UCP also has included standby letters of credit within its scope. The present version (UCP 600) thus states that, if a standby includes an express incorporation, the UCP rules apply "to the extent to which they may be applicable." Article 1. (Standby letters of credit also may have confirming banks; but the more common structure is for a standby to serve as support for a local performance guaranty by a foreign bank. A further set of ICC rules, the Uniform Rules for Demand Guarantees (URDG 758, 2010), addresses the subject of such independent guarantees, a civil law instrument that functions very much like a standby letter of credit.)

The two fundamental principles of commercial letters of credit also apply to standby credits. The first is that the banks' obligations under the letter of credit are independent of the buyer's and seller's obligations under the sale of goods or other underlying contract—the *independence principle*. Thus, the banks' payment obligation is not subject to defenses arising out of the underlying transaction, with the result that—with the exception of fraud as examined below—the disputes between the buyer and the seller in the underlying contract are irrelevant to the banks' payment decision.

The second fundamental principle of letter of credit law is that the banks deal only with documents required by and presented under the letter of credit. The result again is that the presented documents must strictly comply with the requirements of the letter of credit—the *strict compliance principle*. Some legal commentators question whether these traditional rules should be applied to standby credits. The reasoning is that standby credits serve a different function: They do not provide a *primary* vehicle to assure payment to a seller/exporter, but rather a *secondary* assurance of performance for a foreign government or developer if a seller/contractor fails to fulfill its contractual obligations. However, as noted, both the UCP and UCC Article 5 make it clear that they may apply to standby letters of credit, and thus the fundamental independence and strict compliance principles should apply to this form of bank credit as well.

INTERNATIONAL RULES FOR STANDBY LETTERS OF CREDIT

Even though both the UCP and UCC Article 5 expressly include standby letters of credit within their coverage, it is clear that they were designed principally to cover the documentary letter of credit transaction and not the standby transaction. Thus, they impose many unnecessary document-related conditions on the use of standbys. The UCP, in particular, contains many provisions on the proper presentation of transportation documents, all of which are irrelevant to the usual standby letter of credit transaction. The UCP also does not address several issues, such as fraud and choice of law, which are significant to standby transactions.

In response to these difficulties, the UN Commission on International Trade Law (UNCITRAL)—the institution responsible for the CISG—developed the United Nations Convention on Independent Guarantees and Stand-by Letters of Credit (1995). This Convention entered into force on January 1, 2000, but as of April 2016, only eight countries have ratified it (and not the United States nor any other major trading country). For the same reason, the ICC developed the Rules on International Standby Practices (ISP 98), which became effective on January 1, 1999. The ISP 98 was designed to replace the UCP and be its equivalent in international practice regarding standby letters of credit.

The U.N. Convention. The U.N. Convention on standbys applies to an "international undertaking." Article 1(1). Under Article 4(1), a letter of credit is "international" if the place of business of any two of the following typical actors are in different countries: the issuer, the beneficiary, the applicant, an "instructing party" (an entity that applies for the letter of credit on behalf of the applicant), or a confirmer.

The international undertaking also must be an "independent commitment" given by a bank or other person (the "guarantor/issuer") to the beneficiary. Article 2. Under Article 3, an undertaking is independent if the bank's obligation to the beneficiary is not dependent upon "the existence or validity of the underlying transaction, or upon any other undertaking." Likewise, the undertaking must not be "subject to any term or condition not appearing in the undertaking." Finally, the undertaking may not be subject to any "future, uncertain act or event" except for the presentation of documents. In this way, the Convention adopts a standard that any conditions on payment must have a "documentary" character.

The Convention also provides choice of law rules, and allows the parties to choose the applicable law. If the parties do not agree on a choice of law, the Convention provides a default rule that the law of the issuer's place of business shall govern the transaction. Articles 21, 22. The Convention nonetheless gives full freedom to the parties to exclude its application (Article 4(1)), with the result that otherwise-applicable domestic law will apply.

Now that the Convention has entered into force, letters of credit can be issued subject to its provisions. Indeed, even in countries that have not ratified the Convention, standby letters of credit may be issued subject to it if so permitted by the choice of law rules of the issuer's state. Because most such rules emphasize party autonomy, the law of many different countries may permit an issuer to choose the Convention as the law governing a standby letter of credit.

Article 14 of the Convention states the basic principle that an issuer must "act in good faith and exercise reasonable care" and must adhere to "generally accepted standards of international practice" for stand-by letters of credit. The core provision of the Convention, however, is found in Article 16 on "examination of [the] demand and accompanying documents." Under that provision, the issuer must examine any demand for payment in accordance with the Article 14 standard, and determine "whether documents are in facial conformity with the terms and conditions of the undertaking, and are consistent with one another." The bank also has a "reasonable time, but not more than seven business days" following the demand, to examine the documents and, if it decides not to honor, to give the beneficiary notice by "expeditious means . . . indicat[ing] the reason for the decision not to pay."

The ISP 98. The ICC's Rules on International Standby Practices (1998) apply to any international or (notwithstanding its title) domestic standby credit—however named or described—that expressly incorporates it. When so incorporated, the ISP 98 provides that the standby credit is "an irrevocable, independent, documentary and binding undertaking."

Because in many respects standby and commercial credit practices are the same, the ISP has a number of rules that are similar to those in the UCP. Like the UCP, the ISP 98 permits the parties to incorporate all of its rules by simple reference in the standby credit. The ISP 98 nonetheless differs from the UCP in style and approach. The ISP 98 contains 89 rules, in contrast to the UCP's 39, and covers many issues on which the UCP is silent.

The ISP also sets out detailed rules for documentary compliance of a presentation. The general principle is that a demand for payment must comply on its face with the terms and conditions of the standby credit "in the context of standard standby practice." Rule 4.01. In many respects, however, the ISP 98 rules on this subject are similar to those in the UCP. Rule 4.02 thus provides that documents that are presented but are not required by the standby "shall be disregarded"; Rule. 4.06 states that the date on a document may be "earlier but not later that the date of its presentation"; Rule 4.07 has detailed rules on when and by whom a required document must be signed; Rule 4.11 provides that non-documentary conditions "must be disregarded"; and Rule 4.15 declares that a presented document must be an original, but that a presented document is deemed to be an original "unless on its face it appears to be reproduced from an original."

The ISP 98 nonetheless has certain rules in this regard that have special reference to standbys. Thus, Rule 4.03 states that presented documents need be examined for inconsistencies with each other "only to the extent provided in the standby"; Rule 4.05 requires that any required document "must be issued by the beneficiary," unless the standby itself or the nature of the document indicates that it is to be issued by a third party; and Rule 4.08 declares that even if a standby does not specify any required document as a condition to payment, "it will still be deemed to require a documentary demand for payment."

On the issue of the time frame for the issuer to respond to a demand for payment, the ISP 98 follows the traditional rule of a "reasonable time" not to exceed seven banking days (which is contrary to the five day rule under the UCP). Rule 5.01. But to balance the uncertainty of the reasonable time standard, the same rule establishes a three-day safe harbor for examination of documents, within which notice of dishonor is deemed to be timely. The statement of discrepancies in a notice of dishonor need not be detailed. Rule 5.02.

Like the UCP, the ISP 98 does not contain rules that address the subject of forgery or fraud in a presentation. Indeed, Rule 1.01(b) states expressly that the ISP 98 does not address "defenses to honor based on fraud, abuse or similar matters." For such issues, therefore, the parties must look to otherwise applicable law such as the UCC (or, where applicable, the U.N. Convention on Standby Credits). The next section addresses this important subject.

THE FRAUD DEFENSE

One important tension that arises from a strict application of the independence principle in letter of credit law is the effect of fraud. The independence principle promotes the utility of the letter of credit transaction by offering certainty of payment to the beneficiary who complies with a credit's requirements. But where a required document is forged or fraudulent, or the beneficiary has engaged in material fraud beyond a "mere" breach of the underlying sales contract, a counter principle comes into play. As one court long ago observed, "There is as much public interest in discouraging fraud as in encouraging the use of letters of credit." *Dynamics Corp. of America v. Citizens & Southern Nat. Bank*, 356 F. Supp. 991 (N.D. Ga. 1973). The famous case in this regard is *Sztejn v. J. Henry Schroder Banking Corp.*, 31 N.Y.S.2d 631 (N.Y. Sup. 1941), in which the court observed that the principle of "the independence of the bank's obligation under the letter of credit" should not be extended to protect an unscrupulous beneficiary where its fraudulent actions become apparent before the bank decides to honor a presentation.

Thus, the law is subject to two competing principles, and the courts have attempted to accommodate both when allegations arise that a payment will facilitate a material fraud by the beneficiary or a transaction otherwise is tainted by forged or fraudulent documents. The conflict between the two principles becomes especially acute when an applicant makes a vigorous claim of fraud but the supporting evidence is equivocal. Nonetheless, the UCC and, in varying degrees, other legal systems recognize the fraud exception to the independence principle. The policy underlying this exception is that the courts will not allow their process to be used by a dishonest person to carry out a fraud. However, an enduring debate exists about how broad this fraud exception should be.

Claims of Fraud Under the UCC. As noted above, neither the UCP nor the ISP 98 has provisions that address the subject of fraud. As a result, otherwise applicable law will step in to fill the gap. Indeed, UCC § 5–116(c) expressly provides that, even where a credit incorporates rules of custom or practice (such as the UCP or ISP), the UCC will continue to apply in absence of a conflict. With the UCP and ISP 98 silent, no such conflict exists on the issue of fraud. *See, e.g., Mid-America Tire, Inc. v. PTZ Trading Ltd.*, 768 N.E.2d 619 (Ohio 2002).

The courts generally have been skeptical regarding enjoining payment due to fraud in the documentary letter of credit transaction. This is less true, however, for the standby letter of credit transaction. A principal reason for the difference is that some of the limiting concepts in the documentary letter of credit transaction—such as the extensive documentary requirements and the strict compliance standard—become largely meaningless when the required document contains a mere assertion by the beneficiary that the other party failed to perform properly under the contract. When the limitations that give structure to a transaction become meaningless, the transaction can become a breeding ground for fraud.

UCC § 5–109 imposes, however, a series of important limitations on the fraud exception. The first is an absolute requirement that an issuer honor a presentation by certain intermediary banks that already have paid in good faith. Thus, § 5–109(a)(1) provides that the issuer "shall honor" a conforming presentation made by either (i) "a nominated person who has given value in good faith without notice of forgery or material fraud," or (ii) "a confirmer who has honored its confirmation in good faith" (as well as certain other good faith parties in quite rare situations). Thus, a confirming bank that has paid against the documents in good faith is entitled to reimbursement even if strong evidence of fraud or forgery later surfaces. The same applies for other nominated banks (*i.e.*, those authorized, but not obligated, to honor a presentation) if they have paid in good faith and without notice. Under the UCC, therefore, if such a good faith intermediary bank has already paid the beneficiary, and the documents on their face comply with the terms of the credit, the issuing bank *must* provide reimbursement, even if the documents are forged or fraudulent or there is material fraud in the transaction.

A second limitation on the fraud exception is that, even if the documents are presented by anyone else (*e.g.*, the beneficiary or any other intermediary bank), the issuing bank *may* still pay, even though it has been notified that the documents are forged or fraudulent, or that there is fraud in the transaction. The only requirement is that the issuer act "in good faith," and Article 5 defines this term with the very limited notion of "honesty in fact." § 5–102(a)(7) (sometimes called the "pure heart, empty head" test). Thus, an issuing bank or confirming bank may honor a presentation even in the face of allegations of fraud as long as it is not itself involved in deceitful activity.

The issuing bank also may *refuse* to pay in such a situation, but for a variety of reasons that is not very likely. First, banks have a limited ability to evaluate the available evidence of fraud and have little desire to become involved in the buyer-seller dispute in any event. Second, banks are paid to handle documents, not to become judge and jury. Third, banks likely will be reluctant to develop a reputation as an unreliable source of funds in letter of credit transactions. Fourth, a decision to dishonor almost certainly will cause a lawsuit by the beneficiary for wrongful dishonor, with all of the attendant litigation costs and attorneys' fees for the bank. Finally, if the issuing bank honors a conforming presentation in good faith, even with no investigation whatsoever, Article 5 makes clear that it has an absolute right of reimbursement from the applicant. § 5–108(i). Thus, all of the incentives point in the direction of the issuer honoring and allowing the applicant and the beneficiary to fight it out among themselves.

Injunction Sought by the Applicant. The applicant (buyer) may, however, seek an injunction on its own. UCC § 5–109(b) grants an applicant the right to a court order against payment if it can prove forgery or fraud in a required document under the letter of credit or fraud by the beneficiary in the underlying transaction. But UCC Article 5 leaves only a very narrow avenue for this option. In specific, UCC § 5–109(b) limits the right to an injunction based on the fraud exception in several important ways:

First, in parallel with a point discussed above a court may not issue an injunction against payment to an intermediary bank that has already honored a conforming presentation in good faith.

Second, the fraud must be "material," and this is a severe standard. Of course, whether a fraud is "material" will depend on the facts of each specific case. Nonetheless, the courts generally have imposed a very high burden, and have required proof of fraud that has "so vitiated the entire transaction that the legitimate purposes of the independence of the issuer's obligation would no longer be served." *See, e.g., ACE American Ins. Co. v. Bank of the Ozarks*, 2014 WL 495356684, at *12 (S.D.N.Y. 2014); *Ground Air Transfer, Inc. v. Westates Airlines*, Inc., 899 F.2d 1269 (1st Cir. 1990). *See also* § 5–109, Comment 1 (endorsing this standard).

Third, the applicant must present sufficient evidence of fraud or forgery, not merely allegations of it. This may be a difficult given the tight time frame for a decision by the bank (five banking days under the UCP) on honoring a presentation.

Fourth, the applicant must satisfy all of the traditional equitable requirements for injunctive and similar relief. Thus, the applicant must demonstrate that it would suffer irreparable harm without an injunction; that a later money judgment would not be an adequate remedy (that there is "no adequate remedy at law"); and in most jurisdictions also that the balance of harm does not weigh too heavily against the beneficiary and that an injunction would not be contrary to the public interest.

Fifth, a court must require as a condition of an injunction that the beneficiary, the issuer, and any affected confirming or nominated banks are "adequately protected." This typically means that the applicant must post a bond against any losses by affected third parties. The Comments to § 5–109 expand this concept to include even protection against incidental damages, such as legal fees.

Finally, UCC § 5–109 adds a significant limitation on the "locus" of the fraud. A forgery or a fraud in a document required by the letter of credit may permit an injunction if perpetrated by anyone. But as to conduct in the underlying transaction, § 5–109(b) permits an injunction only if payment would facilitate a material fraud "by the beneficiary"—not by some third party, such as a carrier.

The importance of this distinction is illustrated by the approach of other common law courts. English and some Canadian courts also have recognized the fraud exception, based upon fundamental contract principles and the persuasive precedent of the American cases. These courts require the applicant to establish that the beneficiary itself was involved in the fraudulent activity; a fraud or forgery by any other party, including in the letter of credit transaction itself, will not suffice.

This different approach of non-U.S. common law courts is illustrated by comparing three scenarios in which a letter of credit requires an on board bill of lading dated May 15: (1) if the applicant can prove that the beneficiary fraudulently delivered worthless trash to the carrier (instead of the required goods) to meet the May 15 deadline, a court may issue an injunction against honor; (2) if the applicant can prove that the beneficiary fraudulently altered a May 16 bill of lading to state May 15, a court may issue an injunction against honor; but (3) if the carrier or another third party fraudulently puts a May 15 date on a bill of lading actually issued on May 16, a court may *not* issue an injunction against honor. Indeed, the English Court of Appeals in *Montrod Ltd. v. Grundkötter Fleischvertriebs GmbH*, [2002] 1 W.L.R. 1975, refused to allow any flexibility in the requirement of beneficiary involvement, even if a document presented under the letter of credit is so fraudulent as to be a "nullity."

Under § 5–109, in contrast, a court may issue an injunction in all three cases. Of special importance, this includes the third scenario in which a document required by the letter of credit is forged or materially fraudulent, even though the beneficiary was not involved. In such a case, the identity of the perpetrator is irrelevant.

The traditional difference between fraud doctrines and breach of contract concepts was that the former considers the state of mind of a party, while the latter focuses only on whether a particular performance conformed to the contractually agreed standard. Fraud concepts have expanded enormously since the middle of the last century, however, and conduct that would not have been actionable then now may well amount to fraud. The modern fraud doctrines often do not require any evil intent; rather, the law now requires merely that a party state a fact with indifference about its truthfulness or make an innocent statement of fact under circumstances that leave the impression of complete knowledge, when that is not true. In spite of all of this, in letter of credit law the courts have continued to place a high burden on applicants to demonstrate "material fraud" by the beneficiary.

Because of this, courts commonly decline to enjoin payment because of insufficient evidence of fraud. Applicants thus have sought other means for protection. One option is a "notice injunction." Under this vehicle, an applicant with only limited evidence of fraud nonetheless may be able to convince a court to require that an issuer give notice to the applicant (usually a matter of days) before honoring a presentation by the beneficiary. This would permit the applicant to accelerate its efforts to obtain sufficient evidence to justify a preliminary or permanent injunction against payment by the issuer under the letter of credit.

As suggested above, injunctions against honor are rare in traditional commercial letters of credit, but are more common in standby letters of credit. The principal reason for this is the extremely limited documentary presentations typically required with standbys. Often, the beneficiary need merely make a documentary demand that states an entitlement to payment. Substantial political and economic upheavals thus often trigger aggressive demands under standby letters of credit. One prominent example is the political changes brought about by the revolution in Iran in the 1970s. After an initial period of strict adherence to the independence principle, U.S. courts became increasingly skeptical of demands made by Iranian governmental institutions and began issuing injunctions against honor under standby letters of credit that supported pre-revolution projects. *See, e.g., Harris Corp. v. Nat'l Iranian Radio and Television*, 691 F.2d 1344 (2nd Cir. 1982). One court found similarly convincing evidence of fraud in the chaos surrounding the recent events in Iraq and thus entered an injunction against honoring a demand under a standby letter of credit. *See, e.g., Archer Daniels Midland Co. v. JP Morgan Chase Bank, N.A.*, 2011 WL 855936 (S.D.N.Y. 2011).

Claims of Fraud Under the UNCITRAL Convention. As noted above, UNCITRAL also has attempted to bring about international uniformity on fraud allegations under the 1995 Convention on Independent Guarantees and Stand-by Letters of Credit. The Convention includes two important provisions (Articles 19 and 20) that address this subject: Article 19 covers the right of a bank to refuse payment, and Article 20 covers the authority of a court to grant a provisional measure against payment upon the request of an applicant.

Article 19 of the Convention permits a bank to refuse payment if the applicant can show that (1) a document is not genuine, (2) no payment is due, or (3) "the demand has no conceivable basis." The same provision also describes five expansions on the last option. These include that (a) a covered risk "has undoubtedly not materialized"; (b) a court or arbitral tribunal already has declared the underlying obligation is "invalid"; (c) the underlying obligation "has undoubtedly been fulfilled to the satisfaction of the beneficiary"; (d) fulfillment of that obligation "has clearly been prevented by willful misconduct of the beneficiary"; and (e) a confirming or similar bank seeking reimbursement has made payment "in bad faith."

Article 20 provides that, if the issuer is nonetheless intent on honoring the presentation, the applicant itself may seek provisional court measures to prevent that action. These may include blocking payment or freezing the proceeds of an undertaking. But this right exists *only* for the grounds recognized in Article 19.

Moreover, the Convention imposes other important limitations on the right to such "provisional relief" by a court. First, such relief must be based on "immediately available strong evidence." Second, the evidence must show a "high probability" that one of the grounds recognized in Article 19 is present. Third, in deciding whether to block payment of the proceeds, the court must take into account whether failing to do so "likely" will cause the applicant "serious harm." Finally, as a condition to issuing such an order, the court "may require the [applicant] to furnish such form of security as the court deems appropriate." As under the UCC, therefore, the court may require that the applicant post a bond against any losses by affected third parties

OTHER LETTER OF CREDIT TERMS; BACK TO BACK AND REVOLVING CREDITS

A complete understanding of international letters of credit also requires familiarity with a range of specialized terminology. First, although the UCP presumes that letters of credit are irrevocable (*see* Article 7(b)), the parties instead may expressly agree that a letter of credit is revocable. The latter gives the beneficiary a right to payment, but only until it is cancelled by the issuer or applicant— something beneficiaries rarely are willing to accept.

Letters of credit may be payable by sight draft (on demand) or time draft (*e.g.*, one month after presentation of documents). In a time draft transaction, the issuing bank does not pay on presentation, but must "accept" the draft that accompanies the documents. This makes the bank liable to pay at the prescribed later time. The beneficiary then can negotiate (sell) the accepted draft to another financial institution to raise cash immediately. A "general" letter of credit is freely transferable by the beneficiary, while a "special" one limits permissible transferees, usually to one or more banks. A letter of credit "expires" when the time period stated therein for the presentation of drafts and other documents has passed.

A broker of goods may rely on a "back-to-back" letter of credit arrangement to finance an entire transaction without using any of its own capital (or even having any). By definition, a broker buys goods in one transaction and sells them in another. If it is able to structure the two deals such that it is, first, a beneficiary of a letter of credit in the downstream sales transaction (in which the broker is the seller), it can use this credit as collateral for a bank to issue a letter of credit to support the upstream transaction (in which the broker is the buyer). Both the terms and the timing, however, can be tricky. The broker must ensure that the bank credit in the downstream sale is set up *before* it is obligated to arrange for a bank credit to support the upstream purchase. In addition, it must ensure that the documents required by the two letters of credit are *identical*, such that it can use the exact documents from the upstream transaction to satisfy the requirements in the downstream letter of credit.

Back-to-back credits also can become unworkable if one of the credits is amended, and no similar amendment is made to the other. Thus, most banks prefer not to become involved in a back-to-back letter of credit transaction. Instead, they recommend that sellers and brokers obtain financing through a "transferable letter of credit" or an "assignment of proceeds" from a letter of credit.

A transferable letter of credit is one that expressly states that it can be transferred by the original beneficiary to a third party, which then becomes a new and substitute beneficiary. UCP

Article 38; *see also* UCC § 5–112. Thus, a broker that is the beneficiary of a transferable letter of credit can use its rights under that credit to finance the purchase of the goods from suppliers by transferring all or part of its rights under the downstream credit to the upstream suppliers. Partial transfers are allowed, so the broker can use this device to finance purchases from several suppliers. However, although substitute commercial invoices and drafts may be used, all other necessary documents ultimately will be presented—through the issuing bank—to the original account party (applicant), which will reveal the identity of the substitute beneficiary. That may compromise commercially sensitive information, and so brokers tend to avoid such arrangements.

The beneficiary of a letter of credit instead may irrevocably assign a portion of the credit's proceeds to a third party. That is, a broker that is the beneficiary of a letter of credit that permits assignment of proceeds can use its rights under that credit to finance the purchase of goods from a supplier by assigning a part of the broker's rights under the downstream credit to the upstream supplier. The assignment of proceeds does not change the parties to the letter of credit. Nonetheless, the original account party (applicant under the letter of credit) is obligated to pay only if it receives—through the issuer—documents that conform to the credit, so the assignee will not be paid unless it ships goods using conforming documents. The assignee is not a party to the letter of credit and may not know the precise terms of the credit, so it must trust the broker (the beneficiary) to both accurately convey the content of and then later fulfill those terms. The assignment is not governed by the UCP, but by the applicable law of contract. UCP Article 39. *See, e.g.,* UCC § 5–114.

Rapid expansion of turn-key construction contracts (*e.g.,* for building a complete steel mill or cement plant such that a buyer need only to "turn a key" to begin plant operation) has expanded the use of "revolving" letters of credit. This form of a credit serves as a vehicle to enable contractors to receive progress payments promptly as sequential construction phases are completed, and in turn to support further construction phases.

Revolving letters of credit are usually clean (no documents required) sight letters that work in the same way and are subject to the same legal rules as fixed amount letters of credit. The principal difference relates to the amount of the credit and how much the beneficiary may draw at any given time. They commonly are used to cover the payment obligation of an importer—such as a developing country's government—for import services (*e.g.,* building skills) or raw materials. Such a letter of credit is then funded in stages. Each time the construction company (the beneficiary) performs a defined set of services and then draws on the letter of credit for payment, the importer (the applicant under the letter of credit) must arrange with the issuer to restore the amount of the credit to an agreed level in favor of the beneficiary.

Revolving letters sometimes require presentation of specific documents such as certificates of construction phase completion (often prepared by a supervising architect). But a variety of administrative challenges of obtaining such interim certifications prompts many contractors to seek less formal arrangements, ones that may require the applicant to trust the contractor not to draw upon the letter before such action is appropriate. In such a case, the payment ceiling (amount of credit) under the revolving letter may be a substantially smaller amount than the total value of the construction contract.

CHAPTER 5
TECHNOLOGY TRANSFERS

Issues surrounding the transfer of knowledge across national borders have provoked intense discussions during the last decade. The discussions promise to continue unabated. At the core is the desire of third world countries (often advanced developing countries like China, Brazil, and India) to obtain protected information quickly and affordably irrespective of the proprietary rights and profit motives of current holders (usually persons from the most developed countries).

Developing countries want production processes which maximize inexpensive labor but which result in products that are competitive in the international marketplace. Capital intensive production processes (e.g., robot production of automobiles) may be of less interest. MNEs may be willing to share (by way of license or sale) a good deal of proprietary information, but are reluctant to part with their "core technology."

Among the industrialized countries, efforts often occur to acquire (even by way of stealing) "leading edge" technology. One example involved attempted theft of IBM computer technology by Japanese companies ultimately caught by the F.B.I. In the United States, the Office of Export Administration uses the export license procedure to control strategic technological "diversions." But falsification of licensing documents by prominent Norwegian and

Japanese companies allowed the Soviets to obtain the technology for making vastly quieter submarine propellers. In the ensuing scandal, "anti-Toshiba" legislation was adopted in the U.S. Congress. See Section 2443 of the 1988 Omnibus Trade and Competitiveness Act. Leading Japanese executives resigned their positions, which is considered the highest form of apology in Japanese business circles.

The predominant vehicle for controlling technology transfers across national borders is the "license" or "franchise" contract. Some $180 billion in licensing royalties flow annually across borders. The holder of information in one country first acquires the legally protected right to own the information in another country. With few exceptions, IP rights are national in origin, products of territorial domestic regimes. This makes the acquisition of IP rights around the globe remarkably expensive.

Once acquired, the holder then licenses the right, usually for a fee, to a person in that other country. The very sharing of information raises a risk that proprietary control of the technology may be lost or, at a minimum, that a competitor will be created. Absent authorized transfers, piracy of intellectual property is increasingly commonplace. Indeed, in some countries such theft has risen to the height of development strategy.

The developing nations (as a "Group of 77"), the industrialized nations and the nonmarket economy nations tried to agree in UNCTAD upon an international "Code of Conduct" for the transfer of technology. Wide disparities in attitudes toward such a Code were reflected by the developing nations' insistence that it be an "internationally legally binding Code," and the industrialized nations' position that it consist of "guidelines for the international transfer of technology".

Some economics of the debate are illustrated by the fact that persons in the United States pay about one-tenth in royalties for use of imported technology than they receive in royalty payments from technology sent abroad. Many considered development of an international technology transfer Code the most important feature of the North–South dialogue. But it was not to be. Instead, to some degree, the TRIPs Agreement of the World Trade Organization functions as such a code.

THE TRIPs AGREEMENT

The World Trade Organization agreements effective January 1995 include an agreement on trade-related intellectual property rights (TRIPs). This agreement is binding upon the over 150 nations that are members of the World Trade Organization. In the United States, the TRIPs agreement was ratified and implemented by Congress in December of 1994 under the Uruguay Round Agreements Act. There is a general requirement of national and most-favored-nation treatment among the parties.

The TRIPs Code covers the gamut of intellectual property. On copyrights, there is protection for computer programs and databases, rental authorization controls for owners of computer software and sound recordings, a 50-year motion picture and sound recording copyright term, and a general obligation to comply with the Berne Convention (except for its provisions on moral rights).

On patents, the Paris Convention (1967 version) prevails, 20-year product and process patents are available "in all fields of technology", including pharmaceuticals and agricultural chemicals. However, patents can be denied when necessary to protect public morals or order, to protect human, animal or plant life or health, and to avoid serious environmental prejudice. The TRIPs provisions did not stop the Indian Supreme Court in 2013 from denying Novartis a patent on its cancer drug, Gleevac. The court took the view that Novartis was engaged in "evergreening", i.e., making small, inconsequential changes to existing patents and that Indian law could require proof of "improved therapeutic efficacy" before a patent grant.

Article 31 of the TRIPs permits compulsory licensing of patents in national emergencies or other circumstances of extreme urgency, subject to a duty to reasonably compensate the patent owner. Thailand has issued compulsory licenses on a range of cancer, heart disease and AIDS drugs. There is considerable controversy over pharmaceutical patents based on traditional medicines of indigenous peoples, which some see as bio-piracy. Proposals have been made to amend TRIPs to require disclosure of the origins of bio-patents, obtain informed consent from the indigenous communities involved, and share the benefits of such patents.

For trademarks, internationally prominent marks receive enhanced protection, the linking of local marks with foreign trademarks is prohibited, service marks become registrable, and compulsory licensing is banned. Geographical indicators of origin (Feta cheese, Bordeaux wines, Tennessee whiskey) are to be protected, though Wisconsin Feta and California Champagne continue. In addition, trade secret protection is assisted by TRIPs rules enabling owners to prevent unauthorized use or disclosure. Integrated circuits are covered by rules intended to improve upon the Washington Treaty. Lastly, industrial designs are also part of the TRIPs regime.

Infringement and anti-counterfeiting remedies are included in the TRIPs, for both domestic and international trade protection. There are specific provisions governing injunctions, damages, customs seizures, and discovery of evidence.

Pharmaceuticals

Late in 2001, the Doha Round of WTO negotiations were launched. These negotiations have reconsidered the TRIPs agreement, particularly as it applies to developing nations. In addition, a Declaration on the TRIPs Agreement and Public Health was issued at the Qatar Ministerial Conference. This Declaration includes the following statement:

> We agree that the TRIPs Agreement does not prevent Members from taking measures to protect public health. Accordingly, while reiterating our commitment to the TRIPs Agreement, we affirm that the Agreement can

and should be interpreted and implemented in a manner supportive of WTO Members' right to protect public health and, in particular, to promote access to medicines for all.

By mid-2003, a "Medicines Agreement" was finally reached on how to implement this Declaration. Compulsory licensing and/or importation of generic copies of patented medicines needed to address developing nation public health problems are authorized. Such activities may not pursue industrial or commercial policy objectives, and different packaging and labeling must be used in an effort at minimizing the risk of diversion of the generics to developed country markets. Under pressure from the United States, a number of more advanced developing nations (such as Mexico, Singapore and Qatar) agreed not to employ compulsory licensing except in situations of national emergency or extreme urgency. Canada, China, the EU, India, South Korea and other WTO members, on the other hand, have licensed production of drugs nations incapable of pharmaceutical production.

TRIPs Disputes

TRIPs disputes decided by WTO Panels or the Appellate Body have required India to reform its "mailbox rule" for pharmaceutical and agricultural chemical patent applications (patentable since 2005), Canada to give 20 year terms to pre-TRIPs patents and limit its generic pharmaceutical regulatory review and stockpiling patent rights' exceptions, the European Union to remove information technology tariffs and amend discriminatory regulations regarding geographical indicators, the United States to pay for small "business use" of copyrighted music and to remove a prohibition against registration of Cuban confiscated trademarks without the original owner's consent (HAVANA CLUB rum), and China's copyright coverage and entertainment product restraints.

PATENT PROTECTION

For the most part, patents are granted to inventors according to national law. Thus, patents represent *territorial* grants of exclusive rights. The inventor receives Canadian patents, U.S. patents, Mexican patents, and so on. The European Union, however, has recently created a Unitary EU Patent that provides an alternative to 28 member state patents obtained individually or en masse via the longstanding European Patent Convention (a non-EU agreement).

Since over one hundred countries have laws regulating patents, there are relatively few jurisdictions without some form of patent protection. Approximately 2 million patents are issued around the world each year. However, legally protected intellectual property in one country may not be protected similarly in another country. For example, some third world nations refuse to grant patents on pharmaceuticals. These countries often assert that their public health needs require such a policy. Thailand was traditionally one such country and unlicensed or compulsory licensed "generics" have been a growth industry there, and also in Brazil and India.

Nominal patent protection in some developing nations may lack effective forms of relief-giving the appearance but not the reality of legal rights. Since international patent protection is expensive to obtain, some holders take a chance and limit their applications to those markets where they foresee demand or competition for their product. Nevertheless, U.S. nationals continue to receive tens of thousands of patents in other countries. But the reverse is also increasingly true. Residents of foreign countries now receive over 50 percent of the patents issued under U.S. law. In many countries, persons who deal with the issuance and protection of patents are called patent agents. In the United States, patent practice is a specialized branch of the legal profession. Obtaining international patent protection often involves retaining the services of specialists in each country.

What constitutes a "patent" and how it is protected in any country depends upon domestic law. In the United States, a patent issued by the U.S. Patent Office grants the right for 20 years to exclude everyone from making, using or selling the patented invention without the permission of the patentee. The United States traditionally granted patents to the "first to invent," not (as in many other countries) the "first to file."

In 2011, the United States switched to first to file rules. Patent infringement, including the supply of "components" for patented inventions, can result in injunctive and damages relief in the U.S. courts. "Exclusion orders" against foreign-made patent infringing goods are also available. Such orders are frequently issued by the International Trade Commission under Section 337 of the Tariff Act of 1930, and are enforced by the U.S. Customs Service.

A U.S. patent thus provides a short-term legal, but not necessarily economic, monopoly. For example, the exclusive legal rights conveyed by the patents held by Xerox on its photocopying machines have not given it a monopoly in the marketplace. There are many other producers of non-infringing photocopy machines with whom Xerox competes.

There are basically two types of patent systems in the world community, registration and examination. Some countries (e.g., France) grant a patent upon "registration" accompanied by appropriate documents and fees, without making an inquiry about the patentability of the invention. The validity of such a patent grant is most difficult to gauge until a time comes to defend the patent against alleged infringement in an appropriate tribunal.

In other countries, the patent grant is made following a careful "examination" of the prior art and statutory criteria on patentability or a "deferred examination" is made following public notice given to permit an "opposition." The odds are increased that the validity of such a patent will be sustained in the face of an alleged infringement. The United States and Germany have examination systems.

To obtain U.S. patents, applicants must demonstrate to the satisfaction of the U.S. Patent Office that their inventions are novel, useful and nonobvious. Nevertheless, a significant number of U.S. patents have been subsequently held invalid in the courts and the Patent Office has frequently been criticized for a lax approach to issuance of patents. Much of this growth is centered in high-tech industries, including computer software and business methods patents. The United States also been criticized for sometimes allowing patents on "traditional knowledge" (e.g., Mexican Enola Beans) found primarily in the developing world.

The terms of a patent grant vary from country to country. For example, local law may provide for "confirmation," "importation," "introduction" or "revalidation" patents (which serve to extend limited protection to patents already existing in another country). "Inventor's certificates" and rewards are granted in some socialist countries where private ownership of the means of production is discouraged. The state owns the invention. This was the case in China, for example, but inventors now may obtain patents and exclusive private rights under the 1984 Patent Law.

Some countries, such as Britain, require that a patent be "worked" (commercially applied) within a designated period of time. This requirement is so important that the British mandate a "compulsory license" to local persons if a patent is deemed unworked. Many developing nations have similar provisions in their patent laws . . . the owner must use it or lose it.

INTERNATIONAL RECOGNITION OF PATENTS

The principal treaties regarding patents are the 1970 Patent Cooperation Treaty and the 1883 Convention of the Union of Paris, frequently revised and amended. To some extent, the Paris Convention also deals with trademarks, service marks, trade names, industrial designs, and unfair competition. Other treaties dealing with patents are the European Patent Convention (designed to permit a single office at Munich and The Hague to issue patents of 35 countries party to the treaty), and the proposed European Union Patent Convention (intended to create a single patent valid throughout the EU).

Paris Convention

The Paris Convention, to which over 170 countries including the United States are parties, remains the basic international agreement dealing with treatment of foreigners under national patent laws. It is administered by the International Bureau of the World Intellectual Property Organization (WIPO) at Geneva. The "right of national treatment" prohibits discrimination against foreign holders of local patents and trademarks. Thus, for example, a foreigner granted a Canadian patent must receive the same legal rights and remedies accorded Canadian nationals.

Furthermore, important "rights of priority" are granted to patent holders provided they file in foreign jurisdictions within twelve months of their home country patent applications. But such rights may not overcome prior filings by others in "first to file" jurisdictions.

Patent applications in foreign jurisdictions are not dependent upon success in the home country. Patentability criteria vary from country to country. Nevertheless, the Paris Convention obviates the need to file simultaneously in every country where intellectual property protection is sought. If an inventor elects not to obtain patent protection in other countries, anyone may make, use or sell the invention in that territory. The Paris Convention does not attempt to reduce the need for individual patent applications in all jurisdictions where patent protection is sought. Nor does it alter the various domestic criteria on patentability.

Patent Cooperation Treaty

The Patent Cooperation Treaty (PCT), to which about 140 countries including the United States are parties, is designed to achieve greater uniformity and less cost in the international patent filing process, and in the examination of prior art. Instead of filing patent applications individually in each nation, filings under the PCT are done in selected countries. The national patent offices of Japan, Sweden, Russia and the United States have been designated International Searching Authorities (ISA), as has the European Patent Office at Munich and The Hague.

The international application, together with the international search report, is communicated by an ISA to each national patent office where protection is sought. Nothing in this Treaty limits the freedom of each nation to require expensive translations, establish substantive conditions of patentability and determine infringement remedies.

However, the Patent Cooperation Treaty also provides that the applicant may arrange for an international preliminary examination in order to formulate a non-binding opinion on whether the claimed invention is novel, involves an inventive step (non-obvious) and is industrially applicable. In a country without sophisticated search facilities, the report of the international preliminary examination may largely determine whether a patent will be granted. For this reason alone, the Patent Cooperation Treaty may generate considerable uniformity in world patent law. In 1986 the United States ratified the PCT provisions on preliminary examination reports, thereby supporting such uniformity.

KNOWHOW

Knowhow is commercially valuable knowledge. It may or may not be a trade secret, and may or may not be patentable. Though often technical or scientific, e.g. engineering services, knowhow can also be more general in character. Marketing and management skills as well as simply business advice can constitute knowhow. If someone is willing to pay for the information, it can be sold or licensed internationally.

Legal protection for knowhow varies from country to country and is, at best, limited. Unlike patents, copyrights and trademarks, you cannot by registration obtain exclusive legal rights to knowhow. Knowledge, like the air we breathe, is a public good. Once released in the community, knowhow can generally be used by anyone and is almost impossible to retrieve. In the absence of exclusive legal rights, preserving the confidentiality of knowhow becomes an important business strategy. If everyone knows it, who will pay for it? If your competitors have access to the knowledge, your market position is at risk. It is for these reasons that only a few people on earth ever know the Coca Cola formula, which is perhaps the world's best kept knowhow.

Protecting knowhow is mostly a function of contract, tort and trade secrets law. Employers will surround their critical knowhow with employees bound by contract to confidentiality. But some valuable knowledge leaks from or moves with these employees, e.g. when a disgruntled retired or ex-employee sells or goes public with the knowhow. The remedies at law or in equity for breach of contract are unlikely to render the employer whole.

Neither is torts relief likely to be sufficient since most employees are essentially judgment proof, though they may be of more use if a competitor induced the breach of contract. Likewise, even though genuine trade secrets are protected by criminal statutes in a few jurisdictions, persuading the prosecutor to take up your business problem is not easy and criminal penalties will not recoup the trade secrets (though they may make the revelation of others less likely in the future).

The Economic Espionage Act of 1996 creates *criminal* penalties for misappropriation of trade secrets for the benefit of foreign governments or anyone. For these purposes, a "trade secret" is defined as "financial, business, scientific, technical, economic or engineering information" that the owner has taken reasonable measures to keep secret and whose "independent economic value derives from being closely held." In addition to criminal fines, forfeitures and jail terms, the Act authorizes seizure of all proceeds from the theft of trade secrets as well as property used or intended for use in the misappropriation (e.g., buildings and capital equipment).

Despite all of these legal hazards, even when certain knowhow is patentable, a desire to prolong the commercial exploitation of that knowledge may result in no patent registrations. The international chemicals industry, for example, is said to prefer trade secrets to public disclosure and patent rights with time limitations. Licensing or selling such knowhow around the globe is risky, but lucrative.

TRADEMARK PROTECTION

Virtually all countries offer some legal protection to trademarks, even when they do not have trademark registration systems. Trademark rights derived from the use of marks on goods in commerce have long been recognized at common law and remain so today in countries as diverse as the United States and the United Arab Emirates. The latter nation, for example, had no trademark registration law in 1986, but this did not prevent McDonald's from obtaining an injunction against a local business using its famous name and golden arches without authorization. However, obtaining international trademark protection requires separate registration under the law of each nation.

Over three million trademarks are registered around the globe each year. In the United States, trademarks are protected at common law and by state and federal registrations. Federal registration is permitted by the U.S. Trademark Office for all marks capable of distinguishing the goods on which they appear from other goods. U.S. law notably allows trademarks on distinct smells, colors, sounds and tastes. Unless the mark falls within a category of forbidden registrations (e.g. those that offend socialist morality in the People's Republic of China), a mark becomes valid for a term of years following registration.

In some countries (like the United States prior to 1989), marks must be used on goods before registration. In others, like France, use is not required and speculative registration of marks can occur. It is said that ESSO was obliged to purchase French trademark rights from such a speculator when it switched to EXXON in its search for the perfect global trademark. Since 1989, U.S. law has allowed applications when there is a bona fide intent to use a trademark within 12 months and, if there is good cause for the delay in actual usage, up to 24 additional months. Such filings in effect reserve the mark for the applicant. The emphasis on bona fide intent and good cause represent an attempt to control any speculative use of U.S. trademark law.

The scope of trademark protection may differ substantially from country to country. Under U.S. federal trademark law, injunctions, damages and seizures of goods by customs officials may follow infringement. Other jurisdictions may provide similar remedies on their law books, but offer little practical enforcement.

Thus, trademark registration is no guarantee against trademark piracy. A pair of blue jeans labeled "Levi Strauss made in San Francisco" may have been counterfeited in Israel or Paraguay without the knowledge or consent of Levi Strauss and in spite of its trademark registrations in those countries. Trademark counterfeiting is not just a third world problem, as any visitor to a U.S. "flea market" can tell. Congress created criminal offenses and private treble damages remedies for the first time in the Trademark Counterfeiting Act of 1984.

In many countries trademarks (appearing on goods) may be distinguished from "service marks" used by providers of services (e.g., The Law Store), "trade names" (business names), "collective marks" (marks used by a group or organization), and "certification marks" (marks which certify a certain quality, origin, or other fact). Although national trademark schemes differ, it can be said generally that a valid trademark (e.g., a mark not "canceled," "renounced," "abandoned," "waived" or "generic") will be protected against infringing use. A trademark can be valid in one country (ASPIRIN brand tablets in Canada), but invalid because generic in another (BAYER brand aspirin in the United States).

Unlike patents and copyrights, trademarks may be renewed continuously. A valid mark may be licensed, perhaps to a "registered user" or it may be assigned, in some cases only with the sale of the goodwill of a business. A growing example of international licensing of trademarks can be found in franchise agreements taken abroad. And national trademark law sometimes accompanies international licensing. The principal U.S. trademark law, the Lanham Act of 1946, has been construed to apply extraterritorially (much like the Sherman Antitrust Act) to foreign licensees engaging in deceptive practices.

Foreigners who seek a registration may be required to prove a prior and valid "home registration," and a new registration in another country may not have an existence "independent" of the continuing validity of the home country registration. Foreigners are often assisted in their registration efforts by international and regional trademark treaties.

INTERNATIONAL RECOGNITION
OF TRADEMARKS

The premium placed on priority of use of a trademark is reflected in several international trademark treaties. These include the Paris

Convention, the 1957 Arrangement of Nice Concerning the International Classification of Goods and Services, and the 1973 Trademark Registration Treaty done at Vienna. The treaties of widest international application are the Paris Convention and the Arrangement of Nice, as revised to 1967, to which the United States is signatory. The International Bureau of WIPO plays a central role in the administration of arrangements contemplated by these agreements.

The Paris Convention reflects an effort to internationalize some trademark rules. In addition to extending the principle of national treatment in Article 2 and providing for a right of priority of six months for trademarks (see patent discussion ante), the Convention mitigates the frequent national requirement that foreigners seeking trademark registration prove a pre-xisting, valid and continuing home registration. This makes it easier to obtain foreign trademark registrations, avoids the possibility that a lapse in registration at home will cause all foreign registrations to become invalid, and allows registration abroad of entirely different (and perhaps culturally adapted) marks.

Article 6bis of the Paris Convention gives owners of "well known" trademarks the right to block or cancel the unauthorized registration of their marks. One issue that frequently arises under this provision is whether the mark needs to be well known locally or just internationally to obtain protection.

The Nice Agreement addresses the question of registration by "class" or "classification" of goods. In order to simplify internal administrative procedures relating to marks, many countries classify and thereby identify goods (and sometimes services) which have the same or similar attributes. An applicant seeking registration of a mark often is required to specify the class or classes to which the product mark belongs. However, not all countries have the same classification system and some lack any such system. Article 1 of the Nice Agreement adopts, for the purposes of the registration of marks, a single classification system for goods and services. This has brought order out of chaos in the field.

The 1973 Vienna Trademark Registration Treaty (to which the United States is a signatory) contemplates an international filing and examination scheme like that in force for patents under the Patent Cooperation Treaty. This treaty has not yet been fully implemented, but holds out the promise of reduced costs and greater uniformity when obtaining international trademark protection.

Numerous European and Mediterranean countries are parties to the Madrid Agreement for International Registration of Marks (1891, as amended). Since 2002, the United States has joined in the Madrid Protocol of 1989. This Protocol permits international filings to obtain about 60 national trademark rights and is administered by WIPO. A Common Market trademark has been developed by the European Union, an alternative to national trademark registrations and the "principle of territoriality" underlying IP laws.

COPYRIGHT PROTECTION

Nearly one hundred nations recognize some form of copyright protection for "authors' works." The scope of this coverage and available remedies varies from country to country, with some uniformity established in the roughly 80 nations participating in the Berne and Universal Copyright Conventions (below). In the United States, for example, the Copyright Act of 1976 protects all original expressions fixed in a tangible medium (now known or later developed), including literary works, musical works, dramatic works, choreographic works, graphic works, audiovisual works, sound recordings, computer programs and selected databases.

It is not necessary to publish a work to obtain a U.S. copyright. It is sufficient that the work is original and fixed in a tangible medium of expression. Prior to 1989, to retain a U.S. copyright, the author had to give formal notice of a reservation of rights when publishing the work. Publication of the work without such notice no longer dedicates it to free public usage.

U.S. copyright protection now extends from creation of the work to 70 years after the death of the author. The author also controls "derivative works," such as movies made from books. Only the author (or her assignees or employer in appropriate cases) may make copies, display, perform, and first sell the work. Registration with the U.S. Copyright Office is not required to obtain copyright rights, but is important to federal copyright infringement remedies. Infringers are subject to criminal penalties, injunctive relief and civil damages. Infringing works are impounded pending trial and ultimately destroyed. But educators, critics and news reporters are allowed "fair use" of the work, a traditional common law doctrine now codified in the 1976 Copyright Act.

The marketing of copyrights is sometimes accomplished through agency "clearinghouses." This is especially true of musical compositions because the many authors and potential users are dispersed. In the United States, the American Society of Composers, Authors and Publishers (ASCAP) and Broadcast Music, Inc. (BMI) are the principal clearinghouses for such rights. Thousands of these rights are sold under "blanket licenses" for fees established by the clearinghouses and later distributed to their members. Similar organizations exist in most European states. Their activities have repeatedly been scrutinized under U.S. and EU antitrust law.

A Joint International Copyright Information Service run since 1981 by WIPO and UNESCO is designed to promote licensing of copyrights in the third world. This Service does not act as an agency clearinghouse for authors' rights, a deficiency sometimes said to promote copyright piracy.

Copyright protection in other countries may be more or less comprehensive or capable of adaptation to modern technologies. Copyrights on computer programs, for example, are less certain in many jurisdictions. In some developing countries, "fair use" is a theme which is expansively construed to undermine copyright protection. But these differences seem less significant when contrasted with the worldwide problem of copyright piracy, ranging from satellite signal poaching to unlicensed music and books.

In the United States, the Copyright Felony Act of 1992 criminalized all copyright infringements. The No Electronic Theft Act of 1997 (NET) removed the need to prove financial gain as element of copyright infringement law, thus ensuring coverage of copying done with intent to harm copyright owners or copying simply for personal use. The Digital Millennium Copyright Act of 1998 (DMCA) brought the United States into compliance with WIPO treaties and created two new copyright offenses; one for circumventing technological measures used by copyright owners to protect their works ("hacking") and a second for tampering with copyright management information (encryption). The DMCA also made it clear that "webmasters" digitally broadcasting music on the internet must pay performance royalties.

INTERNATIONAL RECOGNITION OF COPYRIGHTS

Absent an appropriate convention, copyright registrations must be tediously acquired in each country recognizing such rights. However, copyright holders receive national treatment, translation rights and other benefits under the Universal Copyright Convention (UCC) of 1952 (U.S. adheres). Most importantly, the UCC *excuses* foreigners from registration requirements provided notice of a claim of copyright is adequately given (e.g., Folsom, Gordon, Van Alstine and Ramsey, 2016). Some countries like the United States took advantage of an option *not* to excuse registration requirements. The exercise of this option had the effect at that time of reinforcing the U.S. "manufacturing clause" requiring local printing of U.S. copyrighted books and prohibiting importation of foreign copies. This protectionist clause finally expired under U.S. copyright law in 1986.

The UCC establishes a minimum term for copyright protection: 25 years after publication, prior registration or death of the author. It also authorizes compulsory license schemes for translation rights in all states and compulsory reprint rights and instructional usage in developing countries.

National treatment and a release from registration formalities (subject to copyright notice requirements) can be obtained in Pan-American countries under the Mexico City Convention of 1902 and the Buenos Aires Convention of 1911, the United States adhering to both. Various benefits can be had in many other countries through the Berne Convention of 1886 (as revised). Like the UCC, the Berne Convention suspends registration requirements for copyright holders from participating states. Unlike the UCC, it allows for local copyright protection independent of protection granted in the country of origin and does not require copyright notice.

The Berne Convention establishes a minimum copyright term of the life of the author plus 50 years, a more generous minimum copyright than that of the UCC. It also recognizes the exclusive translation rights of authors. The Berne Convention does not contemplate compulsory licensing of translation rights. Most U.S. copyright holders previously acquired Berne Convention benefits by simultaneously publishing their works in Canada, a member country.

In 1989, the United States ratified the Berne Convention. U.S. ratification of the Berne Convention created copyright relations with an additional 25 nations. Ratification has eliminated U.S. registration requirements (reserved under the UCC) for foreign copyright holders and required protection of the "moral rights" of authors, i.e. the rights of integrity and paternity. The right of paternity insures acknowledgment of authorship. The right of integrity conveys the ability to object to distortion, alteration or other derogation of the work. It is generally thought that unfair competition law at the federal and state levels will provide the legal basis in U.S. law for these moral rights. A limited class of visual artists explicitly receive these rights under the Visual Artists Rights Act of 1990.

FRANCHISING IN THE UNITED STATES

Franchising is an important sector in the U.S. economy. Thousands of franchisors have created and administer franchise systems throughout the nation. U.S. franchisees number in the hundreds of thousands. These franchisees are typically independent business persons, and their local franchise outlets employ millions of people. It has been estimated that approximately one-third of all retail sales in the United States take place through franchised outlets. Just as U.S. franchisors have found franchising particularly effective for market penetration abroad, Canadian, European and Japanese companies are increasingly penetrating the U.S. market through franchising.

Franchising is a business technique that permits rapid and flexible penetration of markets, growth and capital development. In the United States, there are traditional distinctions between product franchises and business format franchises. Product franchises involve manufacturers who actually produce the goods that are distributed through franchise agreements. For example, ice cream stores, soft drink bottling companies and gasoline retailers are often the subject of product franchises. Business format franchises are more common. These do not involve the manufacture by the franchisor of the product being sold by the franchisee. More typically, the franchisor licenses intellectual property rights in conjunction with a particular "formula for success" of the business. Fast food establishments, hotels, and a variety of service franchises are examples of business format franchising.

U.S. regulation of franchise relationships occurs at both the federal and state levels of government. Such regulation can be as specific as the Federal Trade Commission Franchising Rule and state franchise disclosure duties or as amorphous as the ever present dangers of state and federal antitrust law.

INTERNATIONAL FRANCHISING

International franchising raises a host of legal issues under intellectual property, antitrust, tax, licensing and other laws. The significance of these issues is magnified by the rapid growth of international franchising. Many U.S. franchisors start in Canada, with Japan and Britain following. Some U.S. investors have found franchising the least risky and most popular way to enter Central and Eastern Europe. U.S. franchising in China is expanding rapidly. Franchising is not just a U.S. export. Many foreign franchisors have entered the U.S. market.

Most franchisors have standard contracts which are used in their home markets and receive counsel on the myriad of laws relevant to their business operations. Such contracts need to be revised and adapted to international franchising without significantly altering the franchisor's successful business formula. Franchise fees and royalties must be specified, the provision of services, training, and control by the franchisor detailed, the term and area of the franchise negotiated ("master franchises" conveying rights in an entire country or region are common in international franchise agreements), accounting procedures agreed upon, business standards and advertising selected, insurance obtained, taxes and other liabilities allocated, and default and dispute settlement procedures decided.

At the heart of all franchise agreements lies a trademark licensing clause conveying local trademark rights of the franchisor to the franchisee in return for royalty payments.

Were franchising unaffected by regulation, the attorney's role would be limited to negotiation and drafting of the agreement. But international franchising is increasingly regulated by home and host jurisdictions, including regional groups like the EU. In third world countries, especially Latin America, technology transfer laws, aimed principally at international patent and knowhow licensing, also regulate franchise agreements. These laws benefit franchisees and further development policies, e.g., conservation of hard currencies by control of royalty levels.

In 1986, the European Court of Justice issued its first major opinion on the legality of franchise agreements under competition law. The *Pronuptia* decision indicates that European law can depart significantly from leading American antitrust law on market division arrangements for distributors. The Europeans subsequently implemented a comprehensive regulation on franchise agreements, which in turn was replaced by the EU "vertical restraints" Regulation No. 330/10.

There is often a perception of being invaded culturally that follows franchising. Local laws sometimes respond to the cultural impact of foreign franchises, as when McDonald's wishes to introduce its large golden arch into the traditional architecture of Europe. But this did not stop McDonald's from opening in Moscow with great success. In India and Mexico, nationalist feelings hostile to the appearance of foreign trademarks on franchised products have produced laws intended to remove such usage. For example, the Mexican Law of Inventions and Tradenames (1976, repealed 1987) anticipated requiring use of culturally Mexican marks in addition to marks of foreign origin.

Other nations require local materials (olive oil in the Mediterranean) to be substituted. This could, for example, alter the formula for success (and value) of fast food franchises. Still others (e.g., Alberta, Canada) mandate extensive disclosures by franchisors in a registered prospectus before agreements may be completed. Disclosure violations can trigger a range of franchisee remedies: rescission, injunction, and damages. Such laws are also found in many of the American states.

Franchise advertising must conform to local law. For example, regulations in the People's Republic of China prohibit ads which "have reactionary . . . content." Antitrust and tax law are important in international franchising. Double taxation treaties, for example, will affect the level of taxation of royalties.

Antitrust law will temper purchasing requirements of the franchisor, lest unlawful "tying arrangements" be undertaken. Tying arrangements involve coercion of franchisees to take supplies from the franchisor or designated sources in return for the franchise. Such arrangements must, by definition, involve two products: the tying and tied products. They are subject to a complex, not entirely consistent, body of case law under the U.S. Sherman Antitrust

Act, Articles 101 and 102 of the Treaty on the Functioning of the European Union (TFEU) and other laws.

For example, U.S. antitrust case law on franchise tying arrangements is quite diverse. One decision treats the trademark license as a separate tying product and the requirement of the purchase by fast food franchisees of non-essential cooking equipment and paper products unlawful. Another case permits franchisors to require franchisees to purchase "core products" (e.g., chicken) subject to detailed specifications, or from a designated list of approved sources. Sometimes, the "core product" (e.g., ice cream) and the trademark license (e.g., Baskin-Robbins) are treated as a single product incapable of being tied in violation of the law. Still another leading case involving McDonald's suggests that anything comprising the franchisor's "formula for success" may possibly be tied in the franchise contract. This may be especially lawful if there was full pre-contract disclosure by the franchisor.

INTERNATIONAL PATENT AND KNOWHOW LICENSING

This section concerns the most common form of lawful international technology transfer—patent and knowhow licensing. Before any patent licensing can take place, patents must be acquired in all countries in which the owner hopes there will be persons interested in purchasing the technology. Even in countries where the owner has no such hope, patent rights may still be obtained so as to foreclose future unlicensed competitors. Licensing is a middle ground alternative to exporting from the owner's home country and direct investment in host markets. It can often produce, with relatively little cost, immediate positive cash flows.

International patent and knowhow licensing is the most critical form of technology transfer to third world development. From the owner's standpoint, it presents an alternative to and sometimes a first step towards foreign investment. Such licensing involves a transfer of patent rights or knowhow (commercially valuable knowledge, often falling short of a patentable invention) in return for payments, usually termed royalties. Unlike foreign investment, licensing does not have to involve a capital investment in a host jurisdiction. However, licensing of patents and knowhow is not without legal risks.

From the licensee's standpoint, and the perspective of its government, there is the risk that the licensed technology may be old or obsolete, not "state of the art." Goods produced under old technology will be hard to export and convey a certain "second class" status. On the other hand, older more labor intensive technologies may actually be sought (as sometimes done by the PRC) in the early stages of development. Excessive royalties may threaten the economic viability of the licensee and drain hard currencies from the country. The licensee typically is not in a sufficiently powerful position to bargain away restrictive features of standard international licenses.

For all these reasons, and more, third world countries frequently regulate patent and knowhow licensing agreements. Such law is found in the Brazilian Normative Act No. 17 (1976) and the Mexican Technology Transfer Law (1982, repealed 1991), among others. Royalty levels will be limited, certain clauses prohibited (e.g., export restraints, resale price maintenance, mandatory grantbacks to the licensor of improvements), and the desirability of the technology evaluated.

Regulation of patent and knowhow licensing agreements is hardly limited to the third world. The Common Market, for example, after several test cases before the European Court of Justice, issued a "block exemption" controlling patent licensing agreements. Many of the licensing agreement clauses controlled by this 1984 Regulation were the same as those covered by third world technology transfer legislation. Its successors, Regulations 240 of 1996, 772 of 2004 and 316 of 2014, broadly cover technology transfer agreements (including, since 2004, software copyright licensing).

EU regulation prohibits production restraints, forbids the fixing of retail prices for the licensed product by the licensor, limits the licensor's power to select to whom the licensee may sell, controls the "grant back" of product improvements and determines the licensee's right to challenge the validity of intellectual property. It also affects exclusive licensing arrangements, the allocation of geographic territories among licensees, trademark usage, tying arrangements, fields of use, the duration of the license, quality controls, and discrimination between licensees by the licensor. Regulation of patent, knowhow and software copyright licensing in the United States is less direct and predominantly the concern of patent and antitrust law (e.g., tying practices).

The licensor also faces legal risks. The flow of royalty payments may be stopped, suspended or reduced by currency exchange regulations. The taxation of the royalties, if not governed by double taxation treaties, may be confiscatory. The licensee may produce "gray market" goods which eventually compete for sales in markets exclusively intended for the licensor. In the end, patents expire and become part of the world domain. At that point, the licensee has effectively purchased the technology and becomes an independent competitor (though not necessarily an effective competitor if the licensor has made new technological advances).

Licensing is a kind of partnership. If the licensee succeeds, the licensor's royalties (often based on sales volumes) will increase and a continuing partnership through succeeding generations of technology may evolve. If not, the dispute settlement provisions of the agreement may be called upon as either party withdraws from the partnership. Licensing of patents and knowhow often is combined with, indeed essential to, foreign investments. A foreign subsidiary or joint venture will need technical assistance and knowhow to commence operations. When this occurs, the licensing terms are usually a part of the basic joint venture or investment agreement.

Licensing may also be combined with a trade agreement, as where the licensor ships necessary supplies to the licensee, joint venture partner, or subsidiary. Such supply agreements have sometimes been used to overcome royalty limitations through a form of "transfer pricing," the practice of marking up or down the price of goods so as to allocate revenues to preferred parties and jurisdictions (e.g., tax havens).

REGULATION OF TECHNOLOGY TRANSFERS

When transfer of technology rules do not exist in the recipient country, the technology transfer (TT) agreement is the conclusion of the bargaining of the two parties. The agreement will not be public; it will not be registered. But in some nations, especially developing nations and nonmarket economy nations such as China, the government may be involved in the determination and regulation of the technology transfer agreement.

Typically, without approval from a technology transfer commission, the TT agreement is void and unenforceable. In such jurisdictions, the parties end up negotiating terms for their agreement that are acceptable to the TT Commission.

Developing World Technology Transfer Regulations

During the 1970s a number of developing nations enacted transfer of technology laws. In Latin America, Decision No. 24 of the ANCOM group pioneered the use of regulatory TT Commissions. The ANCOM approach spread like wildfire throughout Latin America. The laws were adopted both as part of the general attempt to control foreign investment and technology transfers, but also to preserve scarce hard currency at a time of severe balance of payment problems. The developing nations viewed technology transfer agreements as an area where there were serious abuses, and believed that their laws would adequately address these issues. The principal abuses were thought to include the following:

1. Transfer of obsolete technology;

2. Excessive price paid for the technology;

3. Limitations on use of new developments by the transferee by grant back provisions;

4. Little research performed by the transferee;

5. Too much intervention by the transferor in transferee activities;

6. Limitations on where the transferee may market the product;

7. Requirements for components be purchased from the transferor which are available locally or could be obtained from other foreign sources more cheaply;

8. Inadequate training of transferee's personnel to do jobs performed by personnel of the transferor;

9. Transfer of technology which has adequate domestic substitutes and is therefore not needed;

10. Too long a duration of the agreement; and

11. Application of foreign law and use of foreign tribunals for dispute resolution.

These do not establish an exclusive list. Some nations had different reasons for wishing to more closely govern technology transfers. But these reasons provide an outline of what areas transfer of technology laws in the 1970s attempted to govern.

The result of these restrictive laws was the transfer of less technology, and of technology less valuable to the source. It was often older technology over which the company was willing to relinquish some control. The bureaucracies established to register and approve or disapprove the agreements were often staffed with persons who knew little about technology, less about international business, but who possessed all of the inefficiency and incompetence of many government agencies.

These laws did not bring in more technology, but less. The consequence was that they did not serve the purpose of helping the balance of payments. Furthermore, the nations which adopted strict rules regulating the transfer of technology often did not have laws which protected intellectual property.

In the 1980s and 1990s, some of these restrictive laws were dismantled, whether by formal repeal or replacement by more transfer encouraging and intellectual property protecting laws, or by a relaxed interpretation of the laws and a general automatic approval of what the transferor and transferee agreed upon. Mexico, for example, eliminated its Technology Transfer Commission in 1991.

Ironically, some technology agreements which were used in the 1960s before the enactment of the strict laws, and which became unusable after such enactments, are now once again being used in the developing world, but regulated (as noted above) in the European Union. However, a substantial number of "technology transfer" control laws remain in force in Latin America, notably Brazil, and elsewhere in the developing world.

CHAPTER 6

FOREIGN INVESTMENT TRANSACTIONS

Defined broadly, foreign investment includes any movement of assets or business operations from an investor's home country to a foreign nation (often called the "host" country) in hopes of making a profit. The investment could be passive, and might include as simple a transaction as purchasing a share of stock in a foreign corporation or making a small loan to a foreign business. Usually, however, in considering the legal aspects of international business transactions, "foreign investment" refers to buying or establishing an active business operation abroad—a factory, sales and distribution center, infrastructure project, natural resources extraction and processing operation, or similar undertaking. Such an undertaking raises different concerns from the sales or licensing transactions discussed in earlier chapters because the investor exports capital assets, not just products or services, to the foreign country, and thus risks greater loss if things go wrong.

REASONS FOR ESTABLISHING A FOREIGN INVESTMENT

Foreign investments are initiated for many reasons. Sometimes an investment is the natural succession to a successful period of increasing export sales to a foreign nation, when the exporter decides the foreign market is sufficiently large to justify foreign production. Foreign production will reduce transportation costs of finished products sold in the foreign nation and may allow the use of local resources available at lower costs, especially labor. Foreign investment may follow immediately after a successful period of export sales, or follow a period of foreign production through licensing the technology for foreign production to a firm in the foreign nation. An example is the aircraft manufacturing industry. In order to assure participation in sales in the increasing Asian market, especially China, U.S. and European aircraft manufacturing companies have moved the manufacture of some parts to Asia, both by licensing and by direct foreign investment.

Investors may also establish foreign operations to produce goods for export to other countries (often including their own home country). Lower costs of production, especially as a result of low labor costs and less regulation, may encourage overseas production, particularly in developing countries, even if the foreign domestic market is not large; the model is to export the lower-cost goods to developed markets. Another common motivator of foreign investment is acquisition of natural resources such as oil or minerals to sell on the world market.

Companies interested in developing foreign operations could do so though contractual arrangements with firms in the foreign country, including through transfers of technology (see Chapter 5). But companies may dislike transferring technology to a company owned by foreign nationals, due to fear of losing control over the technology or inability to control production quality. Protection of technology is of special concern when the technology consists of knowhow, which often lacks the legal protection provided patents, trademarks and copyrights. Such concerns are particularly well founded with respect to nations that do not afford strong protection to intellectual property rights. Even if a license of technology to an unrelated company in another nation has resulted in a profitable relationship, the technology owner may prefer to establish a wholly or majority owned subsidiary to take over the production of the goods or services. The owner may not wish to share the profits with the licensee when it could do the production itself and keep better control over production quality.

Foreign investment that follows export sales or transfers of technology tends to be *voluntary* in the sense that the investor makes the decision for business reasons, not because the framework of laws and policies of the foreign government require local production. In some cases, however, especially in developing nations with balance-of-payments problems, the government may make it difficult or impossible for other nations' businesses to export to the country. Tariffs, quotas and other nontariff trade barriers may be used to reduce imports and the consequent demand for scarce foreign currency to pay for the imports, and also to protect domestic industries. The answer may be to establish a direct foreign investment. This would be to some degree an *involuntary* investment, in that it is not one of several alternatives available, but is the only allowable form of doing business in that country.

WHERE TO ESTABLISH THE FOREIGN INVESTMENT

Lawyers are not usually asked this question, but they may be asked to undertake a risk analysis of investing in several possible foreign locations. The legal climate may be the deciding factor in location. For example, a company may be interested in starting an investment in the European Union (EU). One of the newer EU members may have attractive incentives such as lower labor costs. But what is the legal climate in such nations? Are there vestiges of the old socialism that will be hard to deal with? Are incentives likely to short–lived? Might the nation return to socialism, or borrow so extensively that it cannot pay its debts and risk collapse? If the investment is proposed for a lightly regulated market economy, will the nation retain that form? Can you predict the future for Venezuela better than for Hungary? Is there an unwritten law, or "operational code," that governs investment and differs from the written law? If so, does it differ very much, and is it more or less restrictive?

WHAT LAWS GOVERN FOREIGN INVESTMENT?

Foreign business operations are governed primarily by the law of the place in which they occur. The host country may or may not have an express foreign investment law governing foreign-owned operations, but in any event it will have many generally applicable business regulations such as corporate or company law, labor law, environmental regulations, bankruptcy laws and perhaps investment incentive programs. Investors (and their lawyers) must be aware that in many cases these laws may differ sharply from the rules in the United States or other developed nations, and may vary widely from country to country. An assumed way of doing business in the United States may simply not be an option in another country because of these legal differences.

In addition, the investor's home nation may govern its companies' activities abroad in such areas as antitrust, securities regulation, prohibitions of payments to foreign officials, export restrictions, and boycott or anti-boycott rules. Issues of this so-called extraterritorial regulation are discussed further in Chapter 8.

International law also provides some rules, though not a comprehensive code. Customary international law (arising from the traditional practices of nations) may provide some protection for the foreign investor, but its rules remain contested (see Chapter 7). Regional organizations, especially the EU, may have extensive rules that must be considered. As discussed below, multilateral treaties such as the North American Free Trade Agreement (NAFTA) and the treaties establishing the World Trade Organization (WTO), as well as Bilateral Investment Treaties (BITs), Free Trade Agreements (FTAs) and other agreements between nations, have provisions governing investment. As a result, lawyers advising foreign investment must become conversant with multiple sources of law.

STRUCTURING THE FOREIGN INVESTMENT

Branches Versus Subsidiaries. Foreign investment is often done through a subsidiary (a company owned, in whole or part, by the investing company). Sometimes this is a legal requirement, as in countries that require local operations to be conducted by companies incorporated in that country or partially owned by nationals of that country. Often it is a strategic decision. Investors may be allowed to structure their foreign operations as a branch of their larger business, without any legal separation. However, for tax and liability purposes, they will generally prefer to operate through a separate subsidiary, or sometimes through multiple tiers of subsidiaries. Where this structure is adopted, counsel must assure that legal formalities are followed; otherwise the parent and subsidiary might be deemed "alter egos" and treated as a single company, thus losing the benefits of corporate separateness.

Joint Ventures. Foreign investment may be structured as a joint venture, meaning that ownership is shared between two or more foreign investors, or between foreign investors and local investors. Sometimes the latter arrangement is required by local law. A joint venture is not typically a distinct corporate form; rather, it usually involves creating a subsidiary to own the investment, with ownership of the subsidiary divided among the joint venturers.

Ownership and Control. Ownership and control issues are often complex, especially in cross–border situations, as, for example, when a corporation incorporated in one nation has its center of management in a second nation and its owners (shareholders) are citizens of a third nation. While identifying the nation of the corporation's place of incorporation (charter) is usually easy, it may not be easy to determine who owns or controls the entity or where that control occurs. When an investor owns all the equity in the foreign investment, there is usually little question regarding who has ownership and control. But where there are multiple owners, who has control may be less certain. Foreign ownership of a majority of the voting equity of the subsidiary usually means it is under the control of the investor.

If an investor from abroad has exactly half the equity, who has control may be quite uncertain. No one has control solely by virtue of ownership of 50 percent, but one of the 50 percent owners may be able to exert control. It may depend on the ability to control proxies, if such method of voting is permitted. Where the ownership is less than 50 percent—often true of a joint venture where the foreign owner is limited by law to 49 percent equity—control is quite likely to be the result not of the equity split, but of some form of management agreement. Few multinational corporations are willing to hold 49 percent equity without very substantial participation in management, if not assurance of absolute control.

Restrictions on control and ownership are most likely to be part of a developing nation's foreign investment legal and policy framework. As developing and transitional nations join international trade organizations and regional economic groups such as the WTO, EU or NAFTA, they are required to reduce or abolish restrictions on foreign investment. But often they are permitted to retain reservations that allow mandated reductions or abolitions to occur over long periods of time, or are even allowed to permanently retain limited restrictions, especially in key sectors of the economy.

BEYOND OWNERSHIP AND CONTROL

Foreign investment usually involves the ownership and control of some form of service or manufacturing industry that is located in another country. That country may be close to the United States geographically and similar in many ways, such as Canada, or far away and different in many ways, such as Indonesia. The foreign investor may confront many new methods of living and working. Different legal systems may be involved, as may different languages, currencies, cultures, forms of doing business, concepts of legal practice, forms of labor participation and workers' rights, levels and forms of officer compensation, risks of expropriation, intrusiveness of government participation, attitudes towards democracy and socialism, standards of business dress and decorum, methods of finance and rules governing discrimination in the workplace. These differences, not merely the concepts of ownership and control, must be understood and dealt with for the foreign investment to succeed. A successful international business lawyer knows how to give advice on more than the different legal systems; non–legal advice may extend to any of the above areas, and more.

RESTRICTIONS ON FOREIGN INVESTMENT

Some nations impose numerous legal obstacles to foreign investment. These may occur at formation of the investment, during operation, or during withdrawal. Restrictions may include mandatory joint ventures, export mandates, import substitution, use of a subsidiary rather than a branch, limits on the number of foreign employees or directors, and many others. Some nations make it easy to establish an investment but not easy to operate. Currency controls, mandated benefits and protections for employees, workers' participation in management, and limits on profit transfers and payment for technology may undermine the profitability of the investment. Finally, there may be restrictions on withdrawal, from inability to repatriate capital to difficult insolvency laws. Many of the "laws" may actually be unwritten policies that are difficult to know about in advance.

RESTRICTION ON FOREIGN INVESTMENT IN DEVELOPING NATIONS

Until the early 1970s, there were few restrictions on foreign ownership in market economy developing nations. During the 1960s, many large multinational corporations expanded abroad by opening new operations or acquiring locally owned enterprises. These moves generated concern and often hostility, leading to the adoption of laws in many developing nations regulating foreign investment. Those laws tended to have fairly common approaches to foreign investment. First, acquisition of host-nation enterprises was either limited or prohibited. Second, new investment was required to have certain percentages of local equity participation. Some areas of investment, such as export-oriented extractive industries, communications, transportation, banking, insurance and electricity, often were reserved for state-owned enterprises or enterprises owned by nationals to the exclusion of all foreign participation. Other areas of business could have only specific levels of participation by foreign investors, often less than 50 percent. A government agency had to approve acquisitions or new investment. The agency usually was allowed discretion in granting exceptions, and frequently the governing statutes provided a list of open-ended criteria for approving or disapproving the proposed investment. Common criteria, whether in those lists or in the unwritten policy of the approving agency, included (1) assisting in generating economic development, (2) agreeing on the number of workers to be employed, (3) considering the effect on existing national businesses,

(4) considering the effect on balance of payments, (5) mandating the use of domestic materials and parts, (6) requiring financing be obtained from abroad, (7) contributing to the host nation's acquisition of advanced technology, (8) locating operations in designated development zones, and (9) establishing local research and development facilities.

Investment laws were often supplemented by regulations, guidelines and decisions of foreign investment registration and review agencies. Frequently the decisions of review agencies were not made available to the public. Attorneys occasionally gained access to these decisions through personal contacts in the government, and counsel with such access were better able to predict how agencies would respond to applications for exceptions to restrictive investment laws. Potential investors in developing nations thus confronted not only the restrictive investment laws on the books but also written and unwritten guidelines and policies that generally moderated many of the restrictions.

In addition to mandates for local ownership, developing nations often had similar requirements for local management. Where foreign equity was limited to 49 percent, that same percentage would apply to the number of foreigners allowed on the board. But a minority in numbers did not necessarily mean a minority in influence, and the local board members usually were motivated by the same profit goals as the foreign parent appointees. Nationalism might arise among the board members, however, if the parent wanted the foreign affiliate to shift production to another nation or take any action that appeared to benefit the company's activities in another nation at the expense of operations in the host nation.

Some developing countries began to wonder why they had not increased their rates of development under these rules. No one gave much thought to the fact that private shareholders from developing nations had the same aspirations to earn profit as developed nation shareholders, and directors from developing nations acted in much the same way as their counterparts in developed nations. Shifting ownership from foreign to domestic was no guarantee of economic development in the nation as a whole. To encourage more investment, many nations with restrictive laws began to allow total foreign ownership under written or unwritten "exception" provisions. The foreign investor was allowed to retain total ownership if it transferred its most modern technology to the host nation, or located the proposed investment in an area of high unemployment or a zone designated for economic development, exported a high percentage of its output, or located research and development facilities in the host nation.

IBM is a good example of a company with a pragmatic approach to investment but with a firm no joint venture policy. In Mexico, IBM expanded production considerably even after the enactment of the strict Mexican foreign investment law in 1973, by agreeing to produce the most recent models and by exporting a high percentage of production. In contrast, when told by the Indian government in the

1980s that it had to alter its Indian investment structure to an equity joint venture with majority Indian ownership, IBM withdrew its investment. It later returned when the restrictive Indian rules were altered.

After the debt crisis in the early 1980s, the opening to investment by many former nonmarket economies in the 1990s, and the election of less populist governments in many developing nations, the rules of the game began to change dramatically. Developing nations and former nonmarket economies began a push toward privatization, selling off many state-owned industries. Restrictive investment laws were interpreted in favor of foreign investors' wishes and subsequently replaced by laws encouraging investment. New bilateral and multilateral agreements prohibited many of the old restrictive practices and mandated greater openness to foreign investment.

Modern foreign investment laws usually allow total foreign ownership of investment in most areas while restricting some sectors for continued state ownership. Joint ventures are still encouraged, but when formed they tend to be voluntary (e.g., tax motivated) rather than required. Sometimes continuing restrictions on foreign ownership of land induces a joint venture, as might risk analysis suggesting limited equity participation.

The ability under local law to form a foreign investment is now less the issue than the method chosen. For the host nation, the initiation of a new investment ("greenfields" investing) may be preferred over the acquisition of an existing company, and a joint venture is sometimes preferred over total foreign ownership, although the foreign investor often is the one making the final choice. Many nations (including developed nations, as discussed below) have some method of reviewing acquisitions for reasons such as national security or national economic interests.

In the new century, a few nations returned to restrictive policies, including Venezuela and Bolivia, resulting in a lessening of foreign investment. Others never fully accepted the move to a more open investment environment, or embraced it only in limited areas. And even in countries whose governments fully embraced the new approach, that embrace may be far less than unanimous, with opposition groups calling for a return to greater restrictions. It is essential to understand that there is a dynamic process to investment attitudes among nations. The laws of a host nation in place at one time ought not to be viewed as representative of the legal framework likely to exist a decade or two in the future. Investors must be aware that the dynamic process of economic and political development and change is the engine that pulls the train of rules regulating trade and investment.

POLICY VERSUS LAW: DEALING WITH THE OPERATIONAL CODE OF THE WAY THINGS WORK

Many developing economies have specific laws governing foreign investment. These laws are what the public (and too often the foreign investor) believes comprise the *exclusive* framework for investment. But nations often have another level of law that is unwritten. It is the "way things work," an "operational code." It consists of unpublished regulations and rulings that are applied in some cases but not even mentioned in others. The Brazilians call them "drawer regulations." Investors in China are sometimes confronted with laws they have never heard of, and which they are told may not even be read by foreigners. This operational code allows the government to give different treatment to different investors. Fortunately, many local attorneys know what they are and how to use them. They are a reason for choosing local counsel wisely.

RESTRICTIONS ON FOREIGN INVESTMENT IN DEVELOPED NATIONS

Laws affecting foreign investment are not limited to developing nations. Investors attempting to establish equity investments in Japan confront numerous obstacles, although no written restrictive foreign investment law exists. Many foreign investors began to establish a base in the EU, fearing a "Fortress Europe" (the consequence of the achievement of a "Europe without internal frontiers") that would restrict foreign investment. Canada adopted a fairly restrictive foreign investment law in 1973, but following much criticism from abroad and debate within, the law was replaced with the far less restrictive Investment Canada Act in 1985, which is further limited (for North American investors) by NAFTA's Chapter 11 (discussed below). France,

Korea and other developed nations additionally review some foreign investment on national interest grounds. One should not assume that control of foreign investment is limited to developing nations, or assume that there are no controls on foreign investment in the United States.

The United States has long promoted an image of an investment-encouraging nation where only a few areas are subject to ownership and control limitations, such as national defense, nuclear energy and domestic air transportation. This is largely but not entirely true, and on occasion fears of foreign "buy up" of key U.S. industries have provoked proposals for greater restrictions in Congress.

A Committee on Foreign Investment in the United States (CFIUS) was first created in 1975 to monitor foreign investment. Initially CFIUS had power only to monitor and review foreign investment of behalf of the President. In 1988 Congress enacted the Exon–Florio Amendment to the 1950 Defense Production Act (DPA), partly in response to the proposed acquisition of Fairchild Semiconductor Corporation, a defense contractor, by the Japanese company Fujitsu, Ltd. CFIUS reviewed this proposed acquisition (before the enactment of Exon–Florio) and determined that U.S. national security interests were at risk, but it had no authority to stop the acquisition. Fujitsu nevertheless terminated its proposed acquisition in the face of government pressure. Exon-Florio gave the President authority to block such acquisitions on the advice of CFIUS, within certain statutory guidelines. Congress further amended Exon-Florio in 1992, after dissatisfaction with the way the President and CFIUS handled the proposed takeover of part of LTV Corporation by Thomson–CSF, a conglomerate with majority ownership by the French government. The expected purchase by Thomson of LTV's missile division was terminated by Thomson when it believed it could not expect to gain approval under Exon–Florio from the Department of Defense. Congress intervened because members were upset with the failure of the administration to act more strictly.

In 2007, the Foreign Investment and National Security Act (FINSA) reformed and codified the responsibilities of the CFIUS. As in the case of both the original CIFUS and the 1992 amendments, proposed investment in the United States drove the changes. This time it was the 2006 proposed sale to Dubai Ports World International of a British company that held leases to operate six major U.S. ports. There was additional concern over the 2005 proposal by China National Offshore Oil Corporation to purchase shares of the U.S. oil company Unocal.

FINSA covers "any merger, acquisition, or takeover . . . by or with any foreign person which could result in foreign control of any [entity] engaged in interstate commerce in the United States." FINSA continues presidential authority through CFIUS to investigate effects on national security from covered transactions. It sets forth eleven statutory factors to be considered. If national security is threatened, the President may prohibit the action. Review must occur if the purchasing foreign entity is controlled by or acting on behalf of a foreign government. The law additionally prohibits the sale of some U.S. companies to certain foreign investors, principally those entities involved with foreign governments. FINSA has caused a significant increase in the number of proposed transactions subject to review. The Department of Homeland Security is now an important player within CFIUS. It may be tempted to use CFIUS to gain control over actions of the parties, regardless of the presence or absence of any serious national security link, especially in the area of cyber security.

Although the President, through CFIUS, has reviewed a large number of transactions, only a handful have been blocked or seriously delayed, causing critics to charge that the law is not being used to block investment as allegedly intended. One case where a presidential order blocked the acquisition involved the proposed acquisition by China's National Aero–Technology Import and Export Corp. (CATIC) of MAMCO Mfg., a Seattle aircraft parts manufacturer. The investigation disclosed that CATIC had previously violated U.S. export control laws in purchases of General Electric aircraft engines. There were also concerns about CATIC attempting to gain technology to build jet fighters able to refuel during flight and carrying on covert operations in the United States for the Chinese government. The Executive Order calling for divestment referred only to the threat to national security, providing no detailed supporting reasons.

More recently, a presidential order blocked a Chinese-owned corporation, Ralls Corp., from acquiring a wind energy development near a U.S. military installation. In a surprising development, Ralls successfully challenged the order in U.S. court on the ground that the review process had not been fair under the U.S. Constitution's due process clause because Ralls had not been given adequate opportunity to review and rebut the evidence on which the order was based. It is not clear, however, how much protection this ruling will ultimately provide foreign investors because it relates only to CFIUS's procedures.

The U.S. foreign investment laws have been used by U.S. target corporations whose management is hostile to a proposed takeover. The target company may use the post–notification review period to try to delay the takeover, even to the extent of providing misleading information to CFIUS. The intention would be to cause CFIUS to undertake an investigation. Such delay may be enough to discourage the foreign would–be acquirer even though there are no legitimate national security grounds to expect an ultimate presidential blockage. There are no clear sanctions for using FINSA to block a hostile takeover, but providing false or misleading information to CFIUS would seem to violate federal criminal statutes. If the U.S. government intends to be receptive to foreign investment, including investment by way of acquisition, the misuse of FINSA is counterproductive to that policy of openness.

Exon–Florio and FINSA did not solve all congressional concerns. Remaining open issues include: clearer definitions; consideration of economic impacts as well as national security; consideration of the concentration in the industry, including as a factor whether the target company has received U.S. government funds; and transferring the chair of CFIUS from the Department of Treasury to the Department of Commerce.

PRIVATIZATION

The lessening of state ownership of the means of production and distribution has been carried out principally by the process of privatization. This conversion was a critical aspect of the transition of nonmarket economies to market economies. Privatization also is a continuing feature of developing and developed market economies. State ownership of the means of production and distribution of goods and services is increasingly viewed as philosophically inappropriate. More practically, most state enterprises have been unable to operate at a profit, causing a drain on state resources. Privatization is viewed as a way to reduce subsidies for state-owned enterprises, a way to raise revenue to improve national infrastructure, and a future source of tax revenue if private ownership allows the enterprise to operate at a profit and compete in world markets.

Additionally, privatization is thought to be a better way to provide goods and services demanded by a nation's population. This view extends to the largest developed nations. Britain, Italy, France and Germany have all privatized large state-owned industries. U.S. privatization has included highways, ports, wastewater facilities, gas utilities, and local government services such as parking garages, prisons and recreational facilities.

Privatization has raised new issues for foreign investors. It is a process based on a mix of law and policy. The policy may be very pro–privatization, but it may be backed by weak laws that do not answer many important questions. Many countries have adopted privatization laws that are periodically amended to govern such major issues as determining what to sell, the role of workers in approving the sale, valuation of the business, the level of foreign participation allowed in a sale, rights of nationals and/or employees to ownership preferences, method of financing, and the creation of an adequate legal infrastructure (corporation laws, securities laws, bankruptcy laws, etc.) to support the process. In many cases these questions are not resolved in the written privatization laws and must be dealt with in negotiations with the government.

One of the most difficult issues in privatization is how to value the business. State-owned enterprises may possess little of value for the new owner except the right to function as the business. Obsolete equipment must be replaced. New markets must be found. Modern technology must be introduced. Workforces often must be reduced and the remaining workers trained in more efficient methods of production and the use of new technology. It may be difficult to establish a market value, so valuation may need to be negotiated without many of the usual reference points in a business acquisition.

The process of privatization is only partly completed. It is a necessary concomitant to becoming a market economy, and has continued into the new century. While recent figures indicate some decrease in the level of privatization activity (in part the result of the successful privatizations of the former non-market economies), privatization remains an important part of the investment and development process.

BILATERAL INVESTMENT TREATIES

International law has been slow to establish standards regarding how nations ought to treat foreign investment. Bilateral investment treaties (BITs) have provided some help. These treaties typically limit restrictions that can be placed on foreign investment and provide protections for investors against expropriation and other interference with the investment once it is established.

To protect U.S. investors abroad, the United States embarked on its BIT program in the early 1980s. The BIT program followed earlier Friendship, Commerce, and Navigation (FCN) treaties, which often had some protections for investment among other provisions. Unlike the FCNs, BITs focus more exclusively on investment-related issues. But investment screening mechanisms and key sectors often remain exempt from BIT protection, typically listed in a BIT Annex.

While elimination of foreign investment screening and imposition of performance requirements has been an object of the BIT program, these provisions of the model BIT have been weakened in the treaties currently in force.

BITs have become common features of most developed nations in their relations with host nations for foreign investment. For example, China has investment protection agreements with such nations as Australia, Austria, Belgium/Luxembourg, Denmark, France, Germany, Japan, the Netherlands, and the United Kingdom.

The United States has approximately 40 BITs currently in force, mostly with relatively small developing countries, including most Eastern European countries and a scattering in Africa and Latin America, as well as some larger countries such as Egypt, Turkey and Argentina. Most major U.S. investment destinations, including India, Brazil, and China, are not covered by U.S. BITs; a BIT with Russia has been signed but not ratified. However, many countries not covered by BITs are instead covered by similar provisions in bilateral or multilateral free trade agreements (FTAs), discussed below.

U.S. BITs typically feature the following protections: (1) national treatment (meaning that foreign investors are to be treated the same as local investors); (2) most favored nation treatment (meaning that U.S. investors are treated as favorably as investors from other foreign nations); (3) protection against expropriation and other taking of or interference with the investment (discussed in Chapter 7); (4) transferability of funds into and out of the country; (5) limits on performance requirements; (6) a right to choose senior management regardless of nationality; and (7) dispute settlement through arbitration.

BITs do not prohibit nations from enacting investment laws, but they require that such laws should not interfere with any rights in the treaty. The treaties often require the host country to give "fair and equitable treatment" to the investment, a phrase that is subject to some uncertainty in application. An important provision of most BITs requires the host country to submit to international arbitration in the event a foreign investor feels the country has not honored its obligations under the BIT. BIT arbitrations, and other investor-state arbitration provisions, are discussed further in Chapter 7.

The BIT process is dynamic. Each successive agreement with a new country may include some new provisions. The United States has a model agreement, but it has been modified as host nations have sought new foreign investment and have been willing to sign BITs to establish the most attractive conditions for that investment. The BITs in existence today will not be identical to BITs executed in years ahead.

FOREIGN INVESTMENT UNDER NAFTA AND OTHER FREE TRADE AGREEMENTS

Free Trade Agreements (FTAs) principally involve matters such as reduction or elimination of tariffs and other trade barriers. Many U.S. free trade agreements also contain investment protections similar to those in BITs. The United States is currently party to two regional free trade agreements, NAFTA (with Canada and Mexico) and the Dominican Republic-Central America Free Trade Agreement (DR-CAFTA), with the Dominican Republic, Costa Rica, El Salvador, Guatemala, Honduras, and Nicaragua. It has bilateral free trade agreements (FTAs) with an additional 12 countries. In 2015, the United States signed the Trans Pacific Partnership (TPP) with 11 Pacific nations including Japan, and is in negotiations with the EU for a Transatlantic Trade and Investment Partnership (TTIP). The TPP and TTIP, if finally adopted, will contain similar protections for investment as existing FTA agreements.

NAFTA's Chapter 11 covers foreign investment from one NAFTA party made in another NAFTA party. Section A includes provisions affecting investment, while Section B addresses the settlement of disputes between a party and an investor of another party. The investment provisions in Chapter 11 to some extent reflect provisions in the earlier Canada–United States FTA, but there are some provisions unique to NAFTA. For example, provisions for local management and control were important provisions in the 1973 Mexican Investment Law.

NAFTA, as well as the contemporaneous 1993 Mexican Investment Law, prohibit mandating the nationality of senior management. But NAFTA allows requirements that the majority of the board of a foreign investment entity be of a particular nationality, or be resident in the country, provided that such a requirement does not materially impair the investor's control over the investment. These provisions attempt to balance eliminating the distortions associated with mandating local management with ensuring that host nation input is provided.

Like BITs, NAFTA's investment rules are based on the concepts of national treatment and most–favored–nation status. Thus, each nation must grant investors of the other NAFTA nations treatment no less favorable than it grants to domestic investors and no less favorable than it grants to investors from any non-NAFTA country. NAFTA specifically lists seven areas of prohibited performance requirements, but a nation may impose measures to protect life or health, safety, or the environment. Incentives to invest may not be conditioned on most performance requirements, but may be conditioned on location, provision of services, training or employing workers, constructing or expanding facilities, or undertaking research.

NAFTA allows investors to freely transfer profits, dividends, interest, capital, royalties, management and technical advice fees and other fees, as well as proceeds from the sale of the investment and various payments (such as loan repayments). Limitations on transfers may be made involving certain bankruptcy actions, securities dealings, criminal acts, issues involving property, reporting of transfers, and to ensure satisfaction of judgments.

Each NAFTA nation listed exceptions to the investment rules, thus deviating from the basic principle of national treatment. Some exceptions were mandated by the nation's constitution, others by federal law. Where a nation has made exceptions that disallow foreign participation, it may either reserve the area for national ownership or exclusively for private domestic ownership. But it may also allow some foreign participation. Thus, some of the restrictive nature of earlier investment laws is preserved, but in a considerably more limited form.

Like the BITs, NAFTA also protects investors against expropriation and requires the investment to be given fair and equitable treatment (a standard that is not well defined and has caused some controversy). Also like the BITs, NAFTA requires host nations to submit to arbitration where an investor claims its rights have been violated. Investor-state dispute resolution under NAFTA is discussed in more detail in Chapter 7.

Investment protections in DR-CAFTA and many U.S. FTAs generally follow the model of NAFTA.

FOREIGN INVESTMENT UNDER THE WORLD TRADE ORGANIZATION

Like FTAs, the World Trade Organization is principally concerned with tariffs and other trade barriers. However, one of the WTO agreements, the Agreement on Trade–Related Investment Measures (TRIMs), provides some protection for investment. As must be expected in any large organization with divergent views, its negotiated provisions are not as comprehensive as those in FTAs such as NAFTA. The WTO's TRIMs provisions are considerably briefer than those in NAFTA, and they have a weaker dispute settlement process. TRIMs disputes are subject to the provisions of the WTO General Agreement relating to dispute resolution rather than having a separate arbitration process for investment disputes like NAFTA. The WTO dispute resolution mechanism only addresses disputes between member nations; it does not provide any remedies for private parties. While NAFTA's investment dispute provisions have been extensively used to date, the TRIMs provisions have received relatively little attention.

The TRIMs Agreement first sets forth a national treatment principal. TRIMs which are considered inconsistent with WTO obligations are listed in an annex, and include such performance requirements as minimum domestic content, limiting imports or linked them to exports, and restrictions on access to foreign exchange. Developing countries are allowed to "deviate temporarily" from the national treatment concept, thus diminishing in value the effectiveness of the WTO investment provisions and obviously discouraging investment in nations which have a history of imposing investment restrictions.

The essence of the TRIMs Agreement is to establish the same principle of national treatment for investments as has been in effect for trade. Its investment protections are incorporated in the overall structure of the WTO, alongside trade measures, rather than being treated as a distinct area. Because the measures are much less extensive, and less subject to effective dispute resolution, than those included in BITs and FTAs, the regulation of foreign investment has developed and is likely to continue to develop in the context of the latter rather than within the WTO.

THE OECD AND THE MULTILATERAL AGREEMENT ON INVESTMENT

Attempting to build on the BITs and FTAs, the Organisation for Economic Cooperation and Development (OECD) for a while pursued a Multilateral Agreement on Investment (MAI). The nature of the OECD, dominated by developed nations, although less so than in its earlier years, meant that the MAI tended to focus on concerns of the multinational corporations of developed nations rather than the aspirations of the developing nations that host investment, thus making agreement difficult. But there were insurmountable disagreements in the negotiations even among developed nations. For example, most of the OECD members wished to include limits on the extraterritorial application of laws, such as attempts to impose a nation's boycott laws in other nations, or to govern the acts of foreign subsidiaries, while the United States generally opposed such limitations. A draft agreement, produced in 1997, encountered widespread opposition on various grounds. As a result, the process has, for the present, been effectively abandoned.

FINANCING THE FOREIGN INVESTMENT

Some foreign investment is done using the parent corporation's retained earnings or using its traditional borrowing sources for operations in the United States. The foreign investment opens other possible sources, including lending institutions in the foreign host nation and international banks specializing in such projects. Additional possible sources exist, such as international development banks and agencies, including the World Bank's International Finance Corporation (IFC) and the U.S. Overseas Private Investment Corporation (OPIC). Some international lending authorities invest primarily in infrastructure, which may not benefit many production companies but may be of interest to a U.S. construction business.

PROJECT FINANCING

"Project financing" is a specialized form of financing typically used for large industrial projects. Large enterprises may finance projects on the basis of their own credit, using their accrued cash reserves, borrowing from a bank or other financial institution, or raising capital through equity (stock) and debt (bond) offerings. But for particularly large industrial projects, even quite substantial enterprises may not have the ability or desire to assume the corresponding debt burdens (often, many billions of dollars). Also, agreements with existing lenders may disallow additional borrowing if it would exceed defined levels or ratios (such as assets to debts)

In project financing, the project itself represents the source for repayment of the project debt. The enterprise that initiates the project (the "sponsor") creates the legal structures for the project, secures the financing, and otherwise arranges the myriad related contracts—but lenders and other creditors must look only to the revenues and assets of the *project* for payment. The sponsor will establish a separate legal entity (a "special purpose vehicle" or SPV) as a wholly or partially owned subsidiary to construct, own, and operate the project. The SPV, not the sponsor, will then serve as the borrower for project loans.

This arrangement contains two significant elements: First, the project debt is "off balance sheet" for and "nonrecourse" to the sponsor. That is, the project sponsor does not include the project debt on its own accounts and has no direct legal obligation to repay the debt if the project fails. Second, and closely related, the viability of the project financing—the ability to attract lenders and other investors—depends on the project's merits and not on the sponsor's credit. The sponsor will need to convince the project finance lenders that the project will generate sufficient revenue to repay the loans, with interest, and satisfy any priority claims of other investors. Thus, secure and sufficient revenue from the project represents the foundation of project financing. The project also will need to provide collateral to protect the lenders upon default, and the sponsor will need to assure the lenders that they will have secure, first-priority access to that collateral under applicable legal rules.

All project financings involve the same essential elements. The project sponsor or other project participants will arrange for the issuance of nonrecourse debt (short- or long-term notes or bonds). The nonrecourse aspect of such loans is worthy of emphasis. The project sponsor (and any affiliates) will require that they have no liability to the lender if the project defaults in payment or breaches any other provisions of the loan contracts. The lenders must agree to have recourse only to the project assets to enforce their rights.

This structure reinforces the central role of the project's viability. To convince the lenders, the project sponsor will undertake and present a feasibility study for the project that analyzes the project's business plan and addresses all its significant commercial, economic, political, and legal risks. The study will contain an analysis of the market for the product the project will generate, the sources and strength of competition in the field, expected future market conditions, and all the related risks for each of these issues. The lenders likely will commission experts to analyze these matters on an independent basis as well.

In addition, project lenders will demand collateral rights—which decrease the risk and thus the interest rate on loans—in a variety of forms. The principal one will be an assignment of the project revenues in the event of default. That is, the lenders will demand that, should the project fall short in its payments, they will have a direct right to the project's future revenues and may assert claims against buyers of the project's output. The lenders will also typically want the right to seize the project's assets in the event of default. The sponsor will need to convince the lenders that the collateral assignments are economically valuable and legally enforceable against third parties. As explained in more detail below, however, various legal issues may create significant uncertainty on this subject.

If all goes well, the sponsor may be able to structure a project financing to address all noteworthy risks and convince the lenders to rely solely upon their rights against the project and its future revenues as security for their loans. However, lenders often will demand further protection in the form of "credit enhancements," which provide financial support for the project. Credit enhancements typically come from two sources. The most common is some form of guarantee from the sponsor. The sponsor will, of course, resist this as contrary to the nonrecourse nature of project financing; thus, even if forced to give one, it will seek to carefully circumscribe the nature, extent, and triggering events for any guarantee.

The second form of credit enhancement comes from creditworthy third parties. These may include, among others, letters of credit from banks, capital contributions from investors, and third-party guarantees or insurance. The structure and details of these arrangements will differ greatly depending on the nature of the project, the goals of the project sponsor, the legal and political stability in the project's region, and, most important, the project's economic viability. Where political or market instability is high or economic development support is needed, a credit enhancement may take the form of a guarantee from a governmental or multilateral financial institution such as the World Bank (through the IFC or the Multilateral Investment Guarantee Agency (MIGA)), the Inter-American Development Bank (IDB), the European Bank for Reconstruction and Development (EBRD), or the Asian Development Bank (ADB). The host country (or a political subdivision such as a state or province) also may provide credit enhancements.

Project financing is a complicated endeavor. The project sponsor and its lawyers will need to negotiate and conclude a dizzying array of interrelated contracts. Contracts will be needed with, among others, the lenders; third-party investors; issuers of letters of credit, guarantors, or similar third-party credit enhancements; project developers; construction contractors; and project operators. As well, the sponsor and its lawyers will need to conclude security agreements or assignments of rights governing the lenders' access to collateral, especially future project revenues and project assets. This likely will involve negotiations with third-party buyers of the project's output, the goal of which will be to secure binding purchase commitments into the future (discussed further below).

Allocation of the myriad risks involved in the construction and financing of the project is an essential aspect of these negotiations. The specifics of this allocation vary significantly depending on the nature of the transaction and especially on the bargaining position of the participants and the overall viability of the project. As a general goal, the sponsor will seek an arrangement that allocates each of the risks to the party best able to control it. For example, the sponsor will seek to have the construction contractor assume risks relating to subsurface conditions at the project site, construction delays arising from known risks, and material and labor shortages.

The project also will have unique risks at each of its three principal stages: design engineering and construction; start-up; and operation. As the project unfolds, new risks will arise and others will diminish. Principally for this reason, project financing typically involves at least two types of lenders (or lender groups). The first extends the construction loan, which has a relatively short term. The second makes the long-term or "take-out" loan, for the operation of the project throughout its life. Both groups, however, will be interested in the construction phase, and each will seek assurances that the project will be completed on time and for the price included in the project's financial projections. Before concluding the loan contracts, therefore, the lenders will require that the sponsor or the construction contractor present design drawings, land surveys, construction schedules, and resumes on the experience of the contractor and expected subcontractors. Again, the lenders likely will hire their own experts to examine each of these matters.

As reflected by the two separate phases of lending, the start-up of a project commonly is the most sensitive phase for project financing. For one thing, performance tests for project output may trigger third-party or sponsor performance guarantees. It is also the point at which short-term construction lenders are "taken out" by the long-term lenders. The latter will want assurances that all construction risks have been addressed and all conditions for the long-term viability of the project (and thus for the disbursement of the long-term loans) have been satisfied. At this point the long-term lenders (as well as any third-party investors) will require that the sponsor or construction contractor provide contractually mandated proof that the project is able to generate the type and level of production necessary to pay the project's operating costs and service the project's debts.

A variety of risks also exists during the project's operation. The project must demonstrate its ability to meet the benchmarks set in the market viability studies that convinced the lenders to provide financing in the first place. But as in all commercial ventures, unlikely events may occur, known risks may become worse, and unanticipated risks may arise. Prominent operating risks include the supply of input raw materials; demand for project output; currency fluctuations; strikes or other employee unrest; governmental expropriation; regulatory or legal changes; management errors; political instability; and insolvency by suppliers or customers. Unless carefully considered in the project design and carefully allocated in the related contracts, any of these risks may cause substantial friction among the project participants. Even with a clearly allocated risk, negative developments may cause severe harm and even compromise a participant's solvency. These considerations point to the importance of carefully negotiated "*force majeure*" clauses—ones that allocate among the participants the various remote risks that may affect the project in the future.

From a legal perspective, the most important risks of project financing relate to the availability of security for project loans under applicable legal rules. As noted, the project lenders must rely on project revenues for repayment. The lenders, therefore, will want assurances that buyers are both available and willing to pay for project output. Ideally, the lenders will want financially secure buyers legally bound to purchase the output under long-term contracts. A variety of contractual arrangements are possible in this regard. They range from "take-if-offered" contracts (buyers must pay only if the output is delivered) to "take-or-pay" contracts (buyers must either take or pay for project output, but excess payments may be credited against future deliveries) to "hell-or-high-water" contracts (buyers must pay even if the project is not able to make any deliveries at all).

The lenders will also want assurance that they have a first-priority claim to the project's rights against the obligated buyers. This raises a variety of difficult legal questions. First, the concept of a registered and enforceable security interest, including in future payment obligations (so-called "floating" liens or charges), is well established under U.S. law. *See* UCC §§ 9–102(a)(2), 9–203, 9–204, 9–308. But civil law countries generally do not recognize floating liens that extend to future assets. The lenders may seek agreement that U.S. law will govern the enforcement of security rights, but the buyers' home country or countries may not enforce such an agreement. If this option is not available, the lenders will need to rely on another conceptual device that is recognized by local law, such as an "assignment" or a "pledge" of the project's contract rights against the buyers.

There are also issues of priority. Even if applicable local law recognizes and enforces the lenders' rights to the buyers' future payment obligations, does it establish formal registries of creditor interests and will it enforce priority rights between competing creditors? And even if all of these rights exist, the lenders will need to assess the costs and extent of delays that attend enforcement through litigation in local courts. To address such concerns, the lenders may insist on an international arbitration agreement with the third-party buyers of project output, to facilitate a more efficient and impartial resolution of any future disputes (see Chapter 10).

Separately, the lenders likely will seek to secure rights in the project's fixed assets. A common assumption is that such "immoveable" assets are the most secure forms of collateral. But a variety of challenges arise for this form of illiquid collateral which are not present for claims against monetary obligations. The first is the most obvious: Does local law permit the creation of a mortgage or similar right in real property? Second, if so, the lenders will need to identify and carefully follow the local formalities. Third, some local jurisdictions require that a lender place a formal value on the mortgage, and this will both set the ceiling for recovery and determine the amount of required fees or taxes. The two considerations obviously are in tension. Moreover, local law may require that the value be denominated in the local currency, and this implicates currency fluctuation risks (an especially serious matter if the currency is a "soft" one, as discussed below).

Fourth, the lenders will need to determine what their foreclosure rights are and how they are properly exercised. Substantial and idiosyncratic differences exist on this subject across jurisdictions. Prominent among these will be the costs and length of foreclosure proceedings. Delays of five or ten years are not uncommon. In light of this, the lenders will need to determine whether they may operate the project during the foreclosure process or afterwards. Required governmental permits and foreign ownership controls (especially in the field of natural resources) may impose severe restrictions in this regard. Finally, some local laws give priority to the claims of governmental bodies or other "preferred" creditors. The extent of such preferences obviously can have a significant effect on the value of the lender's mortgage rights in the fixed assets. The complexity of all of these matters will mean that the lenders must engage competent local counsel for careful advice and planning.

The logical solution for these problems is an international treaty. The International Institute for the Unification of Private Law (UNIDROIT) has proposed a treaty on the assignment of debtors' claims against third parties from the sale of goods or services ("receivables," also known as "factoring"). *See* UNIDROIT Convention on International Factoring (1988). As of 2016, however, only a handful of countries had ratified this treaty. A similar treaty from the U.N. Commission on International Trade Law (UNCITRAL), the U.N. Convention on the Assignment of Receivables in International Trade (2001), has not entered into force as of 2016. A more successful treaty from UNIDROIT, the Convention on International Interests in Mobile Equipment (2001), has over 60 ratifications as of 2016. This is a framework convention that will allow focused protocols for special categories of mobile equipment in the future, such as the already-concluded protocols on Matters Specific to Aircraft Equipment (2001), Matters Specific to Railway Rolling Stock (2007), and Matters Specific to Space Assets (2012).

THE EFFECT OF A DIFFERENT CURRENCY ON THE FOREIGN INVESTMENT

When a business invests in a foreign nation with a different currency, many issues arise. They may generally be grouped into two categories. The first is valuation. Currencies change value relative to each other—sometimes gradually, sometimes abruptly. If the investment's revenues and expenses are in a foreign country, they may be denominated in the foreign currency; if the currency gains or loses value relative to the investor's home country currency, the investor may find that in terms of the home country currency the expenses are much greater, or the revenues much less, than expected.

Currencies are typically either fixed rate currencies or floating rate currencies. A floating rate currency changes its value continuously based on market conditions—that is, how much people are willing to pay in one currency to obtain a unit of the other currency. The currencies of most major developed nations, including the U.S. dollar, the U.K. pound, the Euro and the Japanese yen, are floating rate currencies (as are the currencies of a number of developing nations). A fixed rate currency has its value tied to another currency by government decree. For example, the government might declare that one unit of its currency is worth one U.S. dollar. Some nations have intermediate approaches such as a "managed float" in which the government frequently changes the fixed rate to approximate market rates, or intervenes in the currency market to try to maintain a desired rate.

One might suppose that a fixed rate currency is more attractive to foreign investors, but that is not necessarily so. For one thing, fixed rates are hard to maintain because they will get out of alignment with the market rate (that is, what the rate would be if it were allowed to be determined by the market). Thus the government will come under pressure to change the fixed rate, which it may do dramatically and without warning. It is important to remember that fixed rates are fixed only until the government changes them, which it can do at any time. In addition, to maintain a fixed rate, the government may engage in various types of currency controls to manage problems created by a fixed rate that is out of alignment with the market rate. As discussed below, currency controls are a serious threat to the viability of foreign investment.

A related aspect of currency valuation is the idea of "hard" and "soft" currencies. A hard currency is one that tends to hold (or increase) its value relative to other currencies, while a soft currency is one that tends to lose value over time. The currencies of most major developed countries, most of the time, have been hard currencies. Though they change in value relative to one another over time, they (usually) do not experience dramatic sustained declines. But that has not always been true; difficult economic situations and misguided government policies have caused abrupt collapses in even supposedly "hard" currencies. Many developing nations have soft currencies, generally meaning a fairly gradual but sustained loss in value over time—due to high inflation, economic conditions and government policy—with the risk of more rapid loss. Foreign investors obviously prefer hard currencies and see substantial risk in soft currencies: keeping money in a soft currency may result in substantial loss of value relative to the home currency.

The second major area of currency risk for foreign investors is currency exchange controls and related regulations of currency exchange and repatriation. Government regulations may prevent the foreign currency from being readily converted into dollars or another foreign currency.   They may limit the amount of conversion or the purposes for which currency can be converted. Even if conversion is allowed, there may be restrictions on how much money is taken out of the country.

Exchange controls may arise from political motivations—for example, to keep foreign investors from taking "excess" profits out of the country rather than reinvesting them. Commonly, they arise from fixed exchange rates that do not align with market rates and thus result in shortages of hard foreign currency in developing nations. In such a circumstance the government will not want the foreign investor to exchange local currency for scare foreign currency it plans to take out to the country.

These issues create significant planning problems for foreign investors. How should revenues and expenses to be incurred in foreign currency be valued? How much local currency should be retained for business needs? The investor must learn about hedging—buying contracts that assure later conversion at a determined rate. All this attention to a different currency costs money, and that usually means passing such costs on to the ultimate consumer.

TRANSFER PRICING

Another significant issue in operating a foreign investment is transfer pricing. Transfer pricing refers to the exchange of goods, services and technologies between related entities such as a parent and a subsidiary. For example, suppose a U.S. parent company supplies parts and technology to its manufacturing subsidiary in China. How is the value of the parts and technology to be determined for purposes of calculating profits and losses of the parent and the subsidiary? In an "arm's length transaction" (one between unrelated entities), the price would be negotiated. But if the parent owns and controls the subsidiary, it can set any price it wants. A high price for the parts and technology will increase profits of the parent and reduce profits of the subsidiary; a low price will make the subsidiary appear more profitable and the parent less profitable.

There are several reasons a company might wish to manipulate the price of transfers between itself and its subsidiaries. If a U.S. investment in another nation faces laws that restrict repatriating profits to the U.S. parent but allow payments for technology, perhaps the parent will simply raise the price it charges the foreign subsidiary for technology. It can thus operate without showing any profits abroad that, if they existed, would be frozen in the non-transferrable foreign currency. In addition, transfer pricing can be used to shift profits to jurisdictions with lower taxes. For example, if the U.S. parent's subsidiary is located in a country with lower taxes than the United States, the parent might want to show more profits in the subsidiary (and less in the parent) by charging a low price for transferred goods, services and technology. Finally, transfer pricing may be used to divert profits away from joint venture partners. For example, a U.S. parent with a majority owned subsidiary might charge a high price for technology transfers to its subsidiary; the joint venture partners would lose dividends because the subsidiary's profits (in which they would share) would be transformed into technology payments to the parent (in which they would not share).

Because transfer pricing can lead to various abuses, including manipulation of tax laws and unfair treatment of minority shareholders, it is closely regulated (at least in theory) in most jurisdictions. In general, the regulating authority will require the related companies to price their transfers as if they were arm's-length transactions (that is, market-based transactions between unrelated parties). This is an easy rule to state, and it may be an easy rule to apply if the items transferred are generic goods for which a price can readily be found on the open market. However, when the transferred items are unique—such as proprietary technology or services of particular individuals—the "arm's length" price may be difficult to identify. In addition, it may not be obvious that companies are using inappropriate pricing unless they are closely scrutinized by knowledgeable regulators, which may especially difficult for developing nations.

THE SETTLEMENT OF INVESTMENT DISPUTES

Foreign investments may result in disputes among private parties. Although similar in nature to disputes arising from domestic investments, these disputes may be difficult to resolve because they cross international boundaries and thus create special problems in litigation. One partial solution is the use of international commercial arbitration rather than litigation, although as discussed below this creates a separate set of issues and cannot completely avoid a role for courts. Private dispute resolution through international litigation and arbitration is described in Chapter 10.

Investment disputes also involve claims by the foreign investor that the host nation improperly interfered with the investment to the degree that it constitutes a taking of property or otherwise violates the rights of the investor. Resolution of disputes between investors and host nations can be especially difficult, both because the standards of conduct are poorly defined and vigorously disputed in international law, and because litigation against foreign sovereign defendants is procedurally difficult. As noted, numerous treaties, particularly BITs and FTAs, have attempted to mitigate these problems by providing standards of conduct (albeit somewhat imprecise ones) and requiring arbitration of investor-state disputes. Resolution of disputes with foreign governments, particularly in the context of expropriation of foreign investments, is discussed in Chapter 7.

CHAPTER 7
PROPERTY TAKINGS AND REMEDIES

Investments in foreign nations create risks that the host governments may "take" property and refuse to provide "proper" compensation. What is a "taking" and what is "proper" compensation have long been debated. The right to take is difficult to challenge; most nations have some form of eminent domain allowing government taking of private property for public purposes. Thus, the issue usually becomes proper compensation. Investors are likely to view compensation as improper unless it is (1) paid promptly, (2) adequate in amount, and (3) paid in an effective form. And as a practical matter, investors will want to know what remedies, if any, they may have if proper compensation is not paid.

DEFINING THE TAKING

The terms most frequently used when referring to the taking of foreign property are often neither clear in meaning nor consistently applied. The least intrusive act is usually called an *intervention*. That assumes the taking is intended to be temporary, and that the investment will be returned when the problems that motivated the taking are corrected. If the property is not returned in a reasonable period of time, the taking becomes at least a *nationalization*. The words *nationalization* and *expropriation* are often used interchangeably. They are usually intended to mean a taking followed by some form of compensation. But if no payment or inadequate payment follows the taking, the act may be labeled a *confiscation*. The more usual case of a taking involves a nationalization or expropriation followed by an offer of some payment, with disagreement arising about whether the payment standard should be "just," "appropriate," "prompt, adequate and effective," or some other phrase. These payment terms have never been very clearly defined.

Government interference with a foreign investment may alternatively involve a series of steps that amount to a disguised, constructive, de facto, or "creeping" expropriation. A taking may occur almost imperceptibly and often over a substantial period of time. It nevertheless maybe labeled a taking. Reasonable taxes on an investment might be raised to become confiscatory; mandatory labor legislation might attempt to transfer the financial resources of an investment to nationals of the host country; remittances and repatriations might be blocked or delayed while host-country inflation effectively consumes them; necessary government approvals might prove unobtainable; and other regulations might become burdensome to the point of rendering the investment valueless. The line between reasonable regulation and taking is notoriously difficult to establish.

Expropriations may take all property of all investors, or be *selective, discriminatory,* or *retaliatory.* They may be selective by taking only one industry, or discriminatory by taking the property of a particular foreign investor or the property of all investors from a particular foreign nation, or retaliatory by taking property in response to acts of the foreign investor or its government.

TAKINGS OF THE PAST CENTURY AND TODAY

Expropriation in the last century effectively began when Russia (after the 1917 revolution) and Eastern European nations (after World War II) eliminated private ownership of the means of production and distribution. Mexico expropriated oil in 1938. Indonesia nationalized most Dutch-owned property in the 1950s. Egypt expropriated the Suez Canal Company in 1956. Expropriations were frequent in the 1960s, beginning with Cuba's extensive takings of all foreign-owned properties.

In the late 1970s the revolutionary government in Iran seized U.S. investment property. But generally in the 1970s the pace of nationalization slowed. Many developing nations turned to a new *"ization"* (*e.g.*, "Mexicanization" or "Peruvianization"): mandating the conversion of wholly foreign-owned subsidiaries to joint ventures with majority local ownership. That approach in turn began to diminish in the early 1980s, particularly after the debt shock in 1982 led many developing nations to encourage more foreign investment in the hope that exports would increase and generate hard currency earnings to help pay foreign debts. The next stage was *privatization*, the reduction of state ownership by the sale of state-owned enterprises invariably operating with government subsidies. The most significant privatizations of the final decade of the century took place in the former nonmarket economy nations of Eastern Europe.

The new century has seen some new nationalizations, especially in Venezuela, Bolivia and Argentina. The meaning of expropriation has been tested in actions brought under the North American Free Trade Agreement (NAFTA) and other trade and investment treaties, as the concept is seemingly being expanded to include regulatory practices that impede a foreign investment.

Nationalization of property has not been limited to acts by socialist or developing nations. The United Kingdom nationalized coal, steel, airline service and production, and other industries after World War II. France nationalized nearly all banks in 1982. (Many of the U.K. and French nationalized properties were later returned to the private sector, through privatization.) But in the United Kingdom and France, the takings were mostly of property owned by nationals rather than by foreign investors. The United States has some government ownership of business. For example, much of the nation's passenger railway service was transferred to government ownership. But that involved an industry in severe financial distress. National ownership was viewed as a means of saving a dying, vital service sector, rather than displacing ownership successfully operated by the private sector. Nationalizations as an alternative to bankruptcy are a special and separate classification of property takings.

Events that lead a country to nationalize a foreign-owned commercial enterprise are difficult to predict. A taking of property may follow a change in government, whether resulting from revolution (Cuba, Indonesia, Iran, the USSR) or election (Chile, Venezuela, Bolivia). But takings are also pursued by stable governments (Mexico, Great Britain). Nationalism and a sense of exploitation by foreigners may inspire a takeover. Or the taking may occur because other methods of ownership are viewed as economically unsound, or politically or socially inappropriate. Most nationalizations are politically motivated; few have occurred where a thorough economic study was first undertaken showing that certain sectors of industry ought to be state-owned, or at least owned by nationals rather than foreigners.

A particular investment's susceptibility to nationalization increases if it engages in what are seen as essential national industries, such as extractive export-oriented natural resources, banking, insurance, international transportation (airlines, shipping), communications, national defense or agriculture. An entity is also more vulnerable if it uses people or processes that can be easily duplicated locally; if it uses supplies that can be obtained easily from sources other than the affected investors; or if it does not have an essential value dependent upon the investor's goodwill or good name in the marketing of goods or services produced by the investment, and it has enough overall value to outweigh any bad press or other offsetting loss following a takeover.

TAKINGS AND INTERNATIONAL LAW

Even if a nationalization is legal under local domestic law, it may be challenged under international law. Customary international law is a set of unwritten rules said to derive from nations' traditional interactions with each other, giving rise to a sense of legal obligation. What constitutes the customary international law of expropriation, however, is not easy to discern, particularly since developing nations in the late 1960s began to demand participation in formulating rules of international law applying to taking of property. Nations differ about what constitutes a public purpose and, most importantly, what is required compensation. They also differ regarding the legitimacy of discriminatory nationalizations (in which the property of only one nation is taken), especially when that nation is the former colonial ruler. Furthermore, some nations have developed deductions applied to a multinational's valuation of its property, such as the Chile's deduction for what it considered excess profits by foreign copper companies. Finally, taking nations often reject the idea that any law other than their own domestic law should apply to their sovereign act of taking property, whether the property belongs to their own nationals or to foreigners.

The right of a nation to full and permanent sovereignty over its natural resources and economic activities and the right to take privately owned property are long accepted international legal norms. That is true whether the property belongs to the country's own nationals or to foreigners. Most nations and commentators agree that the taking must be for a public purpose or in the public interest. The difficulty of assessing the public interest, however, as well as doubt that such measurement may be undertaken outside the taking nation, have rendered the public purpose element of expropriations largely theoretical. Even though many expropriations appear to have been motivated by little more than revolutionary fervor with no sound economic justification, courts and other governments are not anxious to challenge the validity of the taking nation's claim of public purpose.

As a result, the expropriation debate focuses not on whether there was justification for the taking but on whether there was sufficient compensation. The U.S. government has repeatedly stated its view that nationalization requires "prompt, adequate and effective" payment in compensation. But this formulation has only limited support from other governments, jurists, arbitrators and international law scholars. The more commonly used terms are "just" or "appropriate" compensation. While the U.S. adherence to a "prompt, adequate and effective" standard may create obstacles in the settlement of an expropriation case, that standard is applied in determining whether certain benefits of U.S. laws may be extended to countries which carry out expropriations. It is not clear, however, whether more than semantics is at stake: when the "just" or "appropriate" compensation standard is applied, the measurement commonly seems to include elements of the "prompt, adequate and effective" standard.

The conflict regarding the proper standard of compensation and the debate whether international law or domestic law applies to a taking have their modern roots for the United States in the 1938 Mexican expropriation of foreign-owned petroleum investments. The United States recognized Mexico's sovereign right to take foreign property, but only upon payment of prompt, adequate and effective compensation according to international law. Mexico rejected both the alleged "prompt, adequate and effective" standard and the fundamental premise that international law rather than domestic law was the proper source of the applicable law. Mexico said it would pay because the Mexican constitution required payment, and it would pay according to Mexican standards of compensation. A diplomatic settlement was ultimately reached regarding payment, but it did not resolve the standard under which the payment ought to be made. The next large-scale nationalization of U.S. property was by Cuba after the Castro revolution in 1960. Like Mexico, Cuba rejected the prompt, adequate and effective standard. But unlike Mexico, Cuba's continued isolation from the United States for more than fifty years has prevented any settlement.

Soon after the Cuban expropriations, the U.N. General Assembly passed the Resolution on Permanent Sovereignty Over Natural Resources (1962), affirming the right of nations to exercise permanent sovereignty over their resources and mandating the payment of "appropriate" compensation "in accordance with the rules in force in the State taking such measures in the exercise of its sovereignty and in accordance with international law." Although U.N. General Assembly Resolutions do not create international law, this Resolution appeared to express the customary international law of the day. A dozen years later, after the United Nations had expanded with the addition of many newly independent nations, the General Assembly addressed the issue again in the Declaration on the Establishment of a New International Economic Order (1974), passed with reservations by Japan, West Germany, France, the United Kingdom and the United States. The developed countries' objected to the absence of any reference to the application of international law in the settlement of nationalization compensation issues. Later that same year, the General Assembly passed the Charter of Economic Rights and Duties of States, with most of the major developed nations opposed to the article that stated that compensation for nationalization was exclusively a domestic law matter.

The developing nations' view expressed in the U.N. resolutions was consistent with how they justified expropriations in practice. Chile expropriated the Kennecott Copper Company's holdings, offering to pay according to Chilean law, but only after deducting excess profits that Kennecott allegedly had withdrawn from its Chilean operation. Similar refusals to compensate were expressed by other developing nations. Unfortunately, the U.N.'s principal judicial organ, the International Court of Justice (ICJ), was unable to provide guidance due to a lack of jurisdiction. Its narrow ruling in the Barcelona Traction decision (*Belgium v. Spain*) (1970) did not reach the issue of expropriation, holding instead that only the country where the expropriated company is incorporated may object and rejecting a claim brought by the country where most of the investors resided. The ICJ's predecessor, the Permanent Court of International Justice, held in 1927 in the Chorzów Factory case (*Germany v. Poland*) that there was a duty of "payment of fair compensation," and the *Norwegian Shipowners' Claims* arbitration in 1922 adopted a "just" standard. The U.S. Supreme Court, in *Banco Nacional de Cuba v. Sabbatino*, 376 U.S. 398 (1964), observed that "[t]here are few if any issues in international law today on which opinion seems to be so divided as the limitations on a state's power to expropriate the property of aliens."

Several arbitration awards and national court rulings have helped establish further foundations of an international rule of compensation. The *TOPCO–Libya* arbitral award of 1977 declared that customary international law required "appropriate compensation." *Banco Nacional de Cuba v. Chase Manhattan Bank*, 658 F.2d 875 (2nd Cir. 1981), suggested that the consensus of nations was "appropriate compensation." The 1982 *Aminoil–Kuwait* arbitral award also approved "appropriate" as the accepted international standard. But the U.S. executive branch continued to argue for "prompt, adequate and effective" compensation. The American

Law Institute rejected that standard in the Restatement (Third) of Foreign Relations Law of the United States (1987), adopting instead a standard of "just" compensation. That standard is believed to avoid the possible inclusion of deductions under an "appropriate" standard, but has received little support.

Following resolution of the Iran-U.S. hostage crisis in 1980, the two countries agreed to establish the Iran-United States Claims Tribunal, meeting at The Hague, to resolve claims, including expropriation claims. The tribunal did not formally adopt a "prompt, adequate and effective" compensation standard, but claims approved by the Tribunal for the most part have been paid "promptly" from the funds established for such payment, and they have been paid in dollars, thus meeting any "effectiveness" standard. With respect to the "adequacy" element the tribunal has used various measurements of valuation that seem to satisfy any reasonable "adequacy" standard. By 2012, nearly all the 4,700 private claims filed against Iran had been resolved and more than $2.5 billion in awards were made. The decisions add significantly to the development of expropriation law. Although this experience may support the "prompt, adequate and effective" standard espoused by the U.S. government, the Iranian claims process is *sui generis* because of the vast funds that Iran owned on deposit in the United States at the time of the nationalizations: the United States seized these assets, and later agreed to turn them over to the Tribunal to pay claims. If any conclusions are to be made regarding the current international law of compensation, it seems clear that it is not *called* prompt, adequate and effective, but something very close to those terms may be included in the definition of appropriate or just compensation.

If the issue of compensation is reached, the value of the expropriated property must be established. That value may be established by direct negotiations with the taking government. Alternatively, valuation might be decided by an arbitral panel, as in the case of the Iranian nationalizations. If the taking state refuses to pay compensation, the issue of valuation may come before a court outside the taking state. That could be an international forum, or, more likely, a court either in the nation of the expropriated investor or in a third nation where the taking nation has assets. However, because of various barriers to adjudication, satisfaction of the claim may have to wait until the U.S. government has negotiated a lump sum settlement with the taking nation. The wait may be long; the 1960 Cuban nationalizations remain unresolved. Once payment is made to a nation which has negotiated the claims on behalf of its nationals, international law plays no role in how that sum is divided among claimants.

TREATIES AFFECTING THE NATIONALIZATION PROCESS

Treaty commitments between the host nation and the investors' home nation may narrow expropriation uncertainties. As discussed in Chapter 6, Bilateral Investment Treaties (BITs) and their predecessors, Friendship, Commerce and Navigation (FCN)

Treaties, frequently have provisions protecting foreign investment, typically including limits on expropriation and requiring compensation. One important provision the United States seeks to include in its BITs is the "prompt, adequate and effective" concept (if not always the language) for compensation following expropriation. Many nations which have agreed to this concept in BITs disputed its appropriateness during the nationalistic North–South dialogue of the 1960s and 1970s. But as they began to promote rather than restrict investment, they had to accept the idea that expropriated investment should be compensated reasonably soon after the taking ("prompt"), based on a fair valuation ("adequate"), and in a realistic form ("effective"). The Argentina–United States BIT, for example, refers to the "fair market value . . . immediately before the expropriatory action." But the United States has not concluded BITs with many important developing nations where there is much foreign investment by U.S. nationals (e.g., China, India, Brazil). And where BIT treaties exist there is always the risk that a successor government may reject them, even if that would violate international law. They are important treaties, nevertheless, and investors gain added protection if their property is taken by a nation which has signed such a bilateral treaty with the United States.

In addition, also as discussed in Chapter 6, the North American Free Trade Agreement (NAFTA) has protections for foreign investment in NAFTA's Chapter 11, including provisions governing the taking of property of foreign investors from a NAFTA party, and a number of post-NAFTA free trade agreements (FTAs) also have some similar investor protections. NAFTA acknowledges the right to take property, but only where there is a public purpose, a non–discriminatory taking, due process of law and minimum standards of treatment, plus the payment of compensation. The compensation provisions do not recite the prompt, adequate and effective standard urged by the United States, but quite clearly meet that standard by more specific language.

NAFTA Chapter 11 cases are developing a jurisprudence on taking of foreign property that has drawn criticism from challenged NAFTA governments and observers, especially environmental law groups. Government regulations, often directed to environmental issues, have been ruled to constitute expropriation in the manner they have been implemented. While NAFTA covers the compensation side of expropriation in considerable detail, it does not adequately define what constitutes an expropriation. In addition, NAFTA and many FTAs require that investors be given "fair and equitable treatment," a standard that remains unclear and debated in application.

The World Trade Organization (WTO) Agreement on Trade–Related Investment Measures (TRIMs) does not include provisions governing the taking of investment property. As noted in Chapter 6, attempts to develop a worldwide Multilateral Agreement on Investment (MAI) that would have included expropriation provisions have been unsuccessful and for now appear to have been abandoned.

REMEDIES FOR TAKINGS

For foreign investors, regardless of the level of protection the law purports to offer, as a practical matter much depends upon whether any viable remedies exist for a violation. Pursuing remedies against foreign sovereign governments poses multiple challenges, and depending on the circumstances an investor may conclude that no practical remedy is available.

Suit in the Expropriating Nation. The investor might choose to sue in the courts of the nation carrying out the expropriation, and indeed under customary international law and some treaties, this process (called "exhausting local remedies") may be required prior to seeking international remedies. Where the host nation has strong constitutional or other protections for property and a strong independent judiciary, this may be a viable course; for example, in the United States the Fifth and Fourteenth Amendments to the U.S. Constitution require compensation for takings, and these requirements are commonly enforced by U.S. courts. But other nations, particular developing nations, may not have the constitutional protection of property or judicial independence to provide a practical remedy.

Suit in International Courts. Few if any international courts are open to private investors to seek remedies for expropriation. The ICJ, for example, only hears cases between nations (as do the Dispute Resolution Panels of the WTO). It is theoretically possible that the investor's home government might bring a case on the investor's behalf (called "espousal") but this has rarely occurred. In addition, the ICJ's jurisdiction depends on the consent of both countries that are parties to the litigation, which often may be difficult to obtain.

Diplomatic Solutions. More commonly, expropriation disputes will be resolved through government-to-government negotiations, especially in the case of large-scale expropriations. Sometimes these disputes are settled by lump-sum payments or other adjustments. Another approach is for the governments to agree to establish claims tribunals to resolve claims on a case-by-case basis. In modern times the best-known of these tribunals is the U.S.-Iran claims tribunal, discussed above, established to resolve claims arising from the 1979 Iranian revolution. Various U.S. domestic laws limit foreign aid and provide other punishments for nations that have expropriated property of U.S. nationals without compensation.

Arbitration Clauses. If there is a contract between the investor and the host nation, the parties may agree to submit future claims arising from the contract to international arbitration. Contract-based arbitration is discussed further in Chapter 10; in general, arbitration clauses are typically enforced, even against sovereign nations, and resulting arbitral awards can be enforced in domestic courts (subject to some limitations in the case of foreign sovereigns). An investor and an expropriating nation may also agree to arbitration after a dispute has arisen, although this is not common.

Approximately 150 nations are parties to the 1966 Convention on the Settlement of Investment Disputes between States and Nationals of Other States. The Convention provided for the creation of the International Centre for the Settlement of Investment Disputes (ICSID) as part of the World Bank. The Convention and the Centre provide for the arbitration of investor-state investment disputes, offering an institutional framework for the proceedings. Jurisdiction under the Convention extends to "any legal dispute arising directly out of an investment, between a Contracting State or . . . any subdivision . . . and a national of another Contracting State." But the parties must consent in writing to the submission of the dispute to the Centre, either by contract or after the dispute has arisen. Once given, consent may not be withdrawn.

Because the ICSID procedures are open only to nations that are parties to the ICSID Convention, ICSID also created the Additional Facility, which may conduct conciliation and arbitration proceedings for special disputes not otherwise within ICSID's jurisdiction. It was created to deal with disputes between parties with long–term special economic relationships involving substantial resource commitments. The Additional Facility may be used only with the approval of the ICSID Secretary General.

Treaty-Based Arbitration. Many BITs and other trade and investment treaties contain provisions allowing arbitration of investment disputes between the private investor and the host nation (called investor-state arbitration).

For example, NAFTA provides a mechanism to settle investment disputes by arbitration where a party to NAFTA has allegedly breached an obligation under Section A of Chapter 11's provisions relating to investment or under provisions in NAFTA's Chapter 15 governing monopolies and state enterprises, and damage or loss has occurred from the breach. Investors of a NAFTA party may submit the claim directly, the first such provision in a trade agreement. The process first requires consultation and negotiation. If unsuccessful, it proceeds to mandatory arbitration. The arbitration is governed either by the Arbitration Rules of the U.N. Commission on International Trade Law (UNCITRAL) or the ICSID Additional Facility. The arbitrators are selected by the parties to the dispute and the arbitration is enforceable. The process is to some degree a mini–ICSID procedure, with participation limited to disputants and arbitrators of the three NAFTA parties.

Dispute settlement activity under NAFTA's Chapter 11 has been extensive. Several Chapter 11 investment disputes have raised doubt about the intended scope of the Chapter 11 protections. Private investors have challenged the application of regulations adopted in NAFTA countries that have allegedly prevented foreign investment from functioning. There is debate regarding whether the challenged regulatory provisions constitute regulation or expropriation. When the challenged regulations have been environmental protection laws, the concern over the use of Chapter 11 has been most vocal. Another contentious case involved a Canadian funeral home chain subjected to a huge punitive damages decision in a Mississippi state court with severe limitations on the ability to appeal the decision. The investor challenged the fairness of the state legal system itself, rather than traditional expropriatory measures.

BITs often similarly contain provisions allowing private investors to initiate mandatory arbitration for investment disputes (often through ICSID if the nations are party to the ICSID Convention). Substantial investment arbitration activity has taken place pursuant to BITs, sometimes leading to enforcement in domestic courts. For example, the arbitration of a dispute between British investors and Argentina, under the U.K.-Argentina BIT, ended up being litigated in part in U.S. courts. *See BG Group, PLC v. Republic of Argentina*, 134 S.Ct. 1198 (2014) (concerning whether the British investor was required under the BIT to exhaust local remedies in Argentina before proceeding to arbitration).

Suit in Home-Country Courts. It may be possible for an investor to sue the expropriating government in the investor's home courts (for example, a U.S. investor might sue in U.S. court). But substantial barriers exist.

Most importantly, customary international law generally provides that nations have immunity from suit in the courts of other nations, subject to various exceptions. In the United States, this rule is implemented by the Foreign Sovereign Immunities Act (FSIA), a federal law generally providing immunity with a list of statutory exceptions. An investor wishing to sue a sovereign government (or an agency or instrumentality of a sovereign government) in U.S. court must find an exception to the FSIA's general rule of immunity.

One possibility is the FSIA's exception for takings in violation of international law. The investor would, as a threshold matter, have to establish that the taking violated international law. For example, litigation under this provision has debated whether expropriation of a foreign investor's locally incorporated subsidiary implicates international law, because international law generally does not govern taking of property of a nation's own corporations. *See Helmerich & Payne International Drilling Co. v. Bolivarian Republic of Venezuela*, 784 F.3d 804 (2d Cir. 2015) (acknowledging this limitation but finding an exception to immunity because the taking discriminated against U.S.-owned subsidiaries).

In addition, the statutory exception requires that the taken property, or property exchanged for the taken property, be present in the United States in connection with a commercial activity, or that the taken property be owned or operated by an agency or instrumentality of the foreign sovereign that conducts commercial activity in the United States. These conditions may be difficult to meet, particularly with respect to non-moveable investment property.

The FSIA also has an exception where the foreign sovereign has waived its immunity, which may be done in an investment contract. For example, in *Capital Venture International v. Republic of Argentina*, 552 F.3d 289 (2d Cir. 2009), the court enforced Argentina's contractual waiver of immunity. In addition, the FSIA has an exception for claims based on commercial activity of the foreign nation that occurs in or has a direct effect in the United States. In general this exception is not helpful to expropriation claims, which are usually considered sovereign acts rather than commercial acts. However, in unusual circumstances an interference with an investment might be considered a commercial act. *See Foremost-McKesson, Inc. v. Islamic Republic of Iran*, 905 F.2d 438 (D.C. Cir. 1990).

A further potential barrier to investor remedies in U.S. court is the common law Act of State doctrine. In *Banco Nacional de Cuba v. Sabbatino*, 376 U.S. 398 (1964), the U.S. Supreme Court held that the Act of State doctrine prevented U.S. courts from hearing cases of foreign expropriation, even where there were allegations of violations of international law. The Court applied the longstanding rule that courts in one country will not sit in judgment on the acts of a foreign government done within its own territory. Accordingly, the Court refused to consider whether Cuba's nationalization of its sugar industry after the Castro revolution violated international law.

Like the FSIA, the Act of State doctrine has various exceptions that may or may not be useful to foreign investors. After *Sabbatino*, Congress passed a statute (called the Second Hickenlooper Amendment after its sponsor, Senator Hickenlooper), allowing U.S. courts to hear expropriation claims despite the Act of State doctrine unless the President stated that such adjudication would embarrass the conduct of foreign relations. However, courts have interpreted the statute narrowly to apply only to disputes over property present in the United States. A number of U.S. courts have concluded that the Act of State doctrine does not apply to commercial acts (although others have held to the contrary). The U.S. Supreme Court held that the doctrine does not apply to ordinary business decisions of people running a state-owned enterprise, where the decisions did not appear to represent public policy of the government itself. *Alfred Dunhill of London, Inc. v. Republic of Cuba*, 425 U.S. 682 (1976). Finally, the Court in *Sabbatino* suggested that the doctrine would not preclude adjudication under a treaty or other clear mutually agreed rule. In a subsequent case, a U.S. court allowed adjudication of an expropriation claim against a foreign government under a bilateral treaty. *Kalamazoo Spice Extraction Co. v. The Provisional Military Government of Socialist Ethiopia*, 729 F.2d 422 (6th Cir. 1984).

Enforcement of Judgments and Arbitral Awards. Even if an investor receives a court judgment or an arbitral award against a foreign government, the government may refuse to satisfy it. Recovery will then depend on whether the judgment or award can be enforced.

With regard to judgments, the FSIA makes enforcement in the United States difficult because it provides immunity from execution for foreign sovereign property, subject to exceptions for certain property used for commercial purposes. Enforcement of arbitral awards is somewhat easier because the FSIA has a specific exception for enforcement of arbitral awards, but it is also limited to commercial property. In general, enforcement against an agency or instrumentality of a foreign sovereign that engages in commercial activity in the United States is allowed under the FSIA's exceptions.

INSURING AGAINST THE RISKS OF FOREIGN INVESTMENT LOSSES

Investments abroad often are subject to risks that are not significant concerns to a domestic investment. An investment in the United States is not at risk from military conflict, uncompensated expropriation, or losses from a currency that becomes inconvertible. Because these risks are not present in most developed, democratic nations, and because they present extremely complex risk measurement problems for investors in developing nations, ordinary insurance carriers may not offer adequate coverage for investments in high risk nations. Foreign investors thus often turn to government and multinational investment insurance programs.

INSURANCE FOR FOREIGN
INVESTORS—OPIC

National insurance programs, such as the U.S. Overseas Private Investment Corporation (OPIC), encourage domestic industries to engage in investment abroad. OPIC was established to "mobilize and facilitate the participation of U.S. private capital and skills in the economic and social development of less developed countries and areas, and countries in transition from nonmarket to market economies."

OPIC insurance covers three principal risks: (1) inconvertibility, (2) expropriation or confiscation, and (3) war, revolution, insurrection or civil strife, now called political violence. Expropriation "includes, but is not limited to, any abrogation, repudiation, or impairment by a foreign government of its own contract with an investor with respect to a project, where such abrogation, repudiation, or impairment is not caused by the investor's own fault or misconduct, and materially adversely affects the continued operation of the project." Political violence coverage includes loss of assets or income due to war, revolution, insurrection or politically motivated civil strife, terrorism or sabotage. The usual OPIC contract provides protection against injury to the "physical condition, destruction, disappearance or seizure and retention of covered property directly caused by war or by revolution or insurrection and includes injury to the physical condition, destruction, disappearance or seizure and retention of covered property as a direct result of actions taken in hindering, combating or defending against a pending or expected hostile act whether in war, revolution, or insurrection." With terrorism becoming a major focus in many parts of the world, this class of OPIC insurance may become the most important.

As with traditional insurance, the investor must pay OPIC a substantial premium, based on the amount insured and the riskiness of the investment. In the event of a loss, the investor must exhaust remedies before OPIC becomes obligated to pay any claim. All reasonable action must be taken by the investor, including initiating administrative and judicial claims, to prevent or contest the challenged action by the host government. Prior to the receipt of payment of a claim, the investor usually will be required to transfer to OPIC all rights, title and interest in the insured investment. The investor has an ongoing obligation to cooperate with the U.S. government in pressing claims against the host government.

OPIC insurance is only available for investments in host countries that have agreements with OPIC, currently about 150 countries. Not all countries are willing to enter into such agreements, sometimes regarding them as infringements of their sovereignty. In addition, the United States may deny OPIC insurance to countries that do not extend internationally recognized workers' rights to domestic workers or do not respect human rights, but the President has discretion to waive this prohibition.

Critics of government-backed insurance of U.S. investment abroad argue that the program encourages and subsidizes the transfer of productive facilities abroad, at the cost of jobs in the United States. Some members of Congress believe that OPIC's role should be assumed by the private sector. They reject the concept that the government should engage in private sector support activities and worry about the potential burden on U.S. taxpayers. While OPIC is supposed to write insurance adhering to private insurance industry principles of risk management on a self-sustaining basis, it does not always or even regularly do so, perhaps because OPIC insurance is backed by the full faith and credit of the United States. Because of the absence of significant expropriations over the past few decades, OPIC has been a financial success that has allowed it to build reserves in excess of $4 billion, while claims have been nearly non-existent. As long as insurance claims remain dormant, OPIC is likely to avoid serious criticism from Congress and others about the risk to the general public.

INSURANCE FOR FOREIGN
INVESTORS—MIGA

OPIC insurance is limited to U.S. investors. To encourage increased investment in developing nations, similar insurance is provided by the World Bank's Multilateral Investment Guarantee Agency (MIGA), which was formed pursuant to an international convention in 1985. MIGA now has over 180 member nations, including the principal destinations for foreign investment. It insures cross-border investments made by investors from any

MIGA member country into a developing member country.

MIGA coverage is generally similar to OPIC, although potentially somewhat broader. Risks covered by MIGA include inconvertibility, deprivation of ownership or control by governmental actions, breach of contract by the government where there is no recourse to a judicial or arbitral forum, and loss from military action or civil disturbance. The insurance may cover equity investments or loans made or guaranteed by holders of equity (probably including service and management contracts), and also licensing, franchising and production sharing agreements.

At MIGA's formation, many people urged that it offer insurance only in developing nations that adopted standards for protecting foreign investment, but the final Convention did not expressly include this provision. Such standards may nevertheless be a factor in writing insurance, if reasonable risk management principles are followed. In addition, MIGA states that "projects supported must be financially and economically viable, environmentally sound, and consistent with the labor standards and development objectives of the country."

The viability of MIGA depends on its care in selecting risks to insure and its ability to negotiate settlements after paying claims. Unlike national programs such as OPIC, MIGA has the backing of a large group of nations when it presses a claim. Creating MIGA within the World Bank structure offers benefits that a separate international organization would lack. MIGA has access to World Bank data on nations' economic and social status, thus helping assess risks. The World Bank has considerable credibility that favors MIGA, and encourages broad participation. For U.S. investors, MIGA acts to some degree as a gap filler when OPIC insurance is not available or inadequate for the project.

CHAPTER 8

EXTRATERRITORIAL REGULATION OF INTERNATIONAL BUSINESS

International business activities are generally subject to the laws of the country where the activities take place. They may also be regulated by the country where the business enterprise is based or by other countries in which the activities have effects.

To mitigate conflict among nations, international law limits nations' ability to regulate beyond their borders (called extraterritorial regulation). But it also recognizes broad authority of nations to regulate the activities of their own citizens abroad and at least some ability by nations to regulate extraterritorial activities of non-citizens that have effects within the nation's borders, although the scope of the latter is subject to some dispute. As a result, international business must contend with the laws of multiple jurisdictions.

Business operations that transcend national borders have focused concern about the extent to which a nation's laws should be confined to its territory. Absent a controlling and enforceable international law governing multinational business activities, it is at least a fair question to ask whether national laws are needed to regulate extraterritorial business activities. Reasons advanced to support extraterritorial application of U.S. laws (particularly antitrust laws) are founded on the idea that some extraterritorial extension is necessary to prevent circumvention of national laws by multinational corporations with the business sagacity to ensure that transactions having harmful effects in the United States are consummated outside U.S. territory. For example, extraterritorial extension of antitrust laws can help protect the export opportunities of domestic firms and ensure that U.S. consumers receive the benefit of competing imports, which in turn may spur complacent domestic industries. The effect of automobile imports on U.S. car manufacturers is an example. In an increasingly internationalized world, extraterritorial antitrust and other business regulation may merely reflect economic reality.

On the other hand, non-U.S. commentators and policymakers (especially in Britain) argue that extraterritorial regulation permits the United States to unjustifiably "mold the international economic and trading world to its own image." In particular, the U.S. "effects" doctrine creates legal uncertainty for international traders, and U.S. courts may pay little attention to the competing policies and interests of other concerned governments. As the British House of Lords stated: "It is axiomatic that in anti-trust matters the policy of one state may be to defend what it is the policy of another state to attack."

Extraterritorial regulation is thus a matter of balance. The executive, legislative, and judicial branches of the U.S. government have reached out extraterritorially in, for example, the law of admiralty, antitrust, crime, labor, securities regulation, taxation, torts, trademarks and wildlife

management. A balance drawn wrongly by one
nation invites retaliatory action by others. For
example, in the case of U.S. antitrust judgments,
such as the "Uranium Cartel" treble damages
litigation of the late 1970s, many nations considered
that the balance had been wrongly drawn and took
retaliatory action by enacting "blocking statutes"
(many of which remain in force) that attempted to
frustrate the progress and enforcement of U.S.
litigation. In more recent times, cooperation
agreements and judicial limits on extraterritoriality
have attempted to mitigate conflicts, but not always
with success.

THE PRESUMPTION AGAINST
EXTRATERRITORIALITY

For U.S. federal law, U.S. courts apply a
presumption against extraterritoriality. As stated in
Morrison v. National Australia Bank Ltd., 561 U.S.
247 (2010):

It is a longstanding principle of American law
that legislation of Congress, unless a contrary
intent appears, is meant to apply only within the
territorial jurisdiction of the United States. This
principle . . . rests on the perception that
Congress ordinarily legislates with respect to
domestic, not foreign matters. . . . When a
statute gives no clear indication of an
extraterritorial application, it has none.

In *Morrison*, the Supreme Court refused to apply
a provision of the U.S. securities laws to an allegedly
fraudulent sale on a stock exchange in Australia.

Similarly, in *EEOC v. Arabian American Oil Co. (Aramco)*, 499 U.S. 244 (1991), the Court refused to apply U.S. employment discrimination law to the actions of a U.S. company in Saudi Arabia. In these cases, although the laws were written in general terms, they did not (the Court said) contain sufficiently clear indications of Congress' intent to apply them outside the United States. Notably, the U.S. presumption against extraterritoriality, although similarly based on the international law concept of territorial sovereignty, applies even where international law would allow extraterritorial regulation. For example, international law generally allows U.S. regulation of U.S. corporations abroad, as in *Aramco*.

One difficulty may be determining what constitutes an extraterritorial regulation. In *Morrison*, for example, the alleged fraud involved the Australian bank's U.S. operations. A direct U.S. regulation of fraudulent conduct by a foreign bank in the United States would not be extraterritorial. The Court nonetheless held that the "focus" of the U.S. regulation in *Morrison* was the sale of the bank's stock, which occurred in Australia, and thus that the regulation as applied in *Morrison* was extraterritorial.

U.S. STATUTES APPLIED ABROAD

The U.S. Congress may regulate extraterritorially if it does so clearly (thus overcoming the *Morrison* presumption). For example, both the *Morrison* and *Aramco* outcomes were later partially overturned by amendments to the relevant statutes making clear their (partial) extraterritorial effect. As a result, a number of major U.S. statutes relating to international business apply extraterritorially despite the presumption. The Supreme Court has not always been clear or consistent on what showing is sufficient to overcome the presumption.

Antitrust. Perhaps the most important example of U.S. law applying abroad is antitrust (principally the Sherman Act). Although the Supreme Court initially held that the Sherman Act operated only within the United States, *see American Banana Company v. United Fruit Company*, 213 U.S. 347 (1909) (involving monopolization of banana production in Costa Rica), it quickly retreated from that proposition. U.S. courts have long asserted the right to apply U.S. antitrust laws to foreign activities intended to affect or actually affecting the U.S. market. *E.g., Hartford Fire Insurance Co. v. California*, 509 U.S. 764 (1993) (applying Sherman Act to activities in Britain that restricted competition in the U.S. insurance market). The U.S. Congress attempted to clarify aspects of the antitrust laws' extraterritorial effect in the Foreign Trade Antitrust Improvements Acts (FTAIA) of 1982, stressing "direct, substantial and reasonably foreseeable" effects on U.S. commerce as a prerequisite to antitrust jurisdiction. Applying the FTAIA, the Court declined to recognize U.S. antitrust liability for injuries to non-U.S. citizens in foreign markets. *F. Hoffmann-La Roche Ltd. v. Empagran S.A.*, 542 U.S. 155 (2004).

U.S. application of its antitrust law abroad has led to substantial tension with U.S. allies and trading partners. In some cases, the U.S. approach has been tempered to allow consideration of the interests of comity and foreign countries' economic policies in the outcome. But in the main, U.S. antitrust law has been applied to foreigners and overseas activities with a zeal sometimes approaching religious fervor. For example, in the *Hartford* case, the Court applied U.S. antitrust law to coordinating activities of U.K insurance companies in the United Kingdom, even though U.K. policy was to encourage coordination in the insurance market.

The potential for conflict in this field is enormous. As noted above, in response to extraterritorial application of U.S. antitrust law, a number of countries enacted blocking statutes to attempt to protect their companies from the extraterritorial reach of U.S. laws. For example, the U.K. blocking statute is the Protection of Trading Interests Act of 1980, enacted in the wake of the uranium cartel litigation. This Act (without specifying U.S. antitrust law) makes it difficult to depose witnesses, obtain documents or enforce multiple liability judgments in the United Kingdom. Violation of the Act may result in criminal penalties. Furthermore, under the Act's "clawback" provision, defendants with outstanding multiple liabilities in foreign jurisdictions (*e.g.*, U.S. treble damages) may recoup the punitive element of such awards in Britain against assets of the successful plaintiff. The Act invites other nations to adopt clawback provisions by offering clawback reciprocity. U.S. attorneys confronted with a blocking statute need to understand that multiple liability judgments combined with contingency fee arrangements are virtually unknown elsewhere.

As discussed further in Chapter 10, blocking statutes may put foreign defendants in U.S. courts in a difficult position, because the U.S. court may insist on discovery (in antitrust cases or in other areas) that the blocking statutes prohibit.

Foreign Corrupt Practices Act. A U.S. statute, the Foreign Corrupt Practices Act (FCPA), generally prohibits paying bribes to foreign government officials for favorable treatment in international business transactions. It expressly applies to subsidiaries and agents of U.S. businesses even where the regulated activity occurs outside the United States. The FCPA is discussed in detail in Chapter 9.

U.S. Export Regulations. U.S. export control regulations expressly apply to the international delivery of U.S. products and technology, even when shipped from one foreign country to another. *See generally* Ralph H. Folsom et al., *International Trade and Economic Regulations in a Nutshell* (6th ed. West 2016), Ch. 4. In addition, the United States has sometimes applied specific trade sanctions (such as the Reagan administration's restrictions of technology exports to the Soviet Union) to foreign subsidiaries of U.S. companies and/or U.S.-sourced components shipped from foreign countries. This extraterritorial application of U.S. law is strongly resisted by European countries, which may not recognize such prohibitions as excusing contractual obligations for delivery.

Alien Tort Statute. The U.S. Alien Tort Statute (ATS) provides that U.S. courts have jurisdiction over suits for torts that violate international law. In the modern era, this statute has been used to bring international human rights claims in U.S. courts against foreign government officials for conduct that occurred outside the United States. *E.g., Filártiga v. Peña-Irala*, 630 F.2d 876 (2d Cir. 1980) (suit by Paraguayan citizens against Paraguayan official for torture and murder that occurred in Paraguay). Prior to 2013, this statute was also widely used by foreign plaintiffs to sue multinational corporations in U.S. courts for complicity in human rights violations by the governments of developing nations in which they operated. For example, in *Kiobel v. Royal Dutch Petroleum Co.*, 133 S.Ct. 1659 (2013), Nigerian plaintiffs sued Royal Dutch, a British-Dutch company, for aiding and abetting violations of their international human rights by the Nigerian government in Nigeria. Similar suits against both U.S. and non-U.S. companies have been brought for alleged complicity in the abusive conduct of governments in, among others, Burma (Myanmar), Indonesia, South Africa, Sudan, Colombia and Argentina.

In 2013, the U.S. Supreme Court held in *Kiobel* that the presumption against extraterritoriality (discussed above) barred application of the ATS to claims that did not "touch and concern" the United States. It accordingly directed dismissal of the claim in *Kiobel*, and after *Kiobel* numerous ATS claims against multinational corporations have similarly been dismissed.

It is unclear which, if any, ATS claims remain viable after *Kiobel*. If the defendant is a U.S. corporation (instead of a non-U.S. corporation as in *Kiobel*), and especially if some of the corporation's decisionmaking regarding the alleged harmful acts took place in the United States, it is possible that the presumption against extraterritoriality would be overcome (or would not apply). However, post-*Kiobel* courts have generally not been hospitable to ATS claims.

Even if the ATS applies, there is a question what level of involvement in the government's harmful conduct is required for liability. As a threshold matter, there must be a violation of international law. Not all harms, even grievous ones, violate international law. *See Beanal v. Freeport-McMoran, Inc.*, 197 F.3d 161 (5th Cir. 1999) (claimed environmental harms were not violations of international law and so not cognizable under the ATS). In addition, in most ATS cases the primary wrongdoer is the foreign government and the allegation is that the multinational corporation assisted the violation. In *Presbyterian Church of Sudan v. Talisman Energy, Inc.*, 582 F.3d 244 (2d Cir. 2009), the court of appeals held that for ATS liability the defendant corporation must have intended that the government's wrongful conduct occur. However, other courts have allowed ATS claims if the corporation knew (or should have known) of the violations and acted in ways that facilitated them, even absent intent that they occur.

Although the threat of ATS litigation has diminished after *Kiobel*, U.S. companies need to carefully assess investments in countries with abusive governments. Some ATS litigation remains active even though the primary harms occurred outside the United States. In addition to the ATS, suits might be brought under other U.S. laws, or under foreign law. Various codes of conduct, developed by industry groups and international organizations, suggest ways that corporations can ethically conduct business in countries with such governments.

Other Extraterritorial Statutes. Each U.S. statute should be evaluated independently to determine its extraterritorial scope. It may not be easy to determine the scope simply by looking at the statute because the Supreme Court has applied different versions of the presumption against extraterritoriality over time. As discussed, U.S. courts allow extraterritorial application of U.S. antitrust law even though the antitrust laws themselves are not clear about their extraterritorial scope. Similarly, the Court held that U.S. trademark law applied to infringing activity of a U.S. citizen in Mexico, even though the relevant statute (the Lanham Act) did not specifically declare its extraterritorial application. As indicated by *Morrison*, more recently the Court has applied a stronger version of the presumption.

EXTRATERRITORIAL APPLICATION OF EU LAW

Although the United States may be the most aggressive nation in applying its laws extraterritorially, other nations do so as well. In particular, the European Union (EU), despite European objections to U.S. antitrust law, applies its equivalent (called competition law) to activities that affect the EU market. Thus, for example, the merger of two U.S. multinational corporations with sales or operations in Europe, even if approved by U.S. regulators, might be blocked by EU regulators because of the potential effect on the EU market.

The EU may also apply other laws to non-EU operations based on effects in the EU. For example, in *Google Spain SL and Google Inc. v. Agencia Española de Protección de Datos and Mario Costeja González*, the European Court of Justice (ECJ or CJEU) (the principal court of the EU) held in a controversial decision that EU privacy laws restricted the ability of Google (a U.S. company) to show internet search results regarding the embarrassing past activities of a Spanish citizen that no longer had public significance (the so-called right to be forgotten). Thus U.S. (and other non-EU) companies need to be aware that their operations may be subject to EU regulation if they have effects in the EU.

EU COMPETITION LAW

EU competition law is particularly significant for international business in this regard. It arises from Articles 101 and 102 of the Treaty on the Functioning of the European Union (TFEU). Articles 101 and 102 have a mandatory effect upon any international trade or investment touched by their reach. In general, Article 101(1) aims to prohibit arm's length competitors from agreeing between themselves to prevent, restrain or distort competition. Article 101(1) is roughly analogous to the prohibition against restraints of trade in Section 1 of the U.S. Sherman Antitrust Act. Broadly speaking, Article 102 prohibits dominant enterprises from abusing their position to the prejudice of competitors or consumers. This prohibition is more encompassing than monopolization as an offense under Section 2 of the Sherman Act. For detailed treatment, *see* Ralph H. Folsom, *European Union Law in a Nutshell* (8th ed., West, 2014).

Articles 101 and 102 are complicated and elastic. Although each article lists certain proscribed business practices, much of their specific substantive content has been generated by the European Commission (the EU's principal regulatory body) and the EU courts. Numerous treatises (including several multi–volume works) are devoted to European competition law. A notable feature is the law's applicability to publicly owned enterprises (of which there are many). For example, the European Court affirmed the applicability of Article 102 to RAI, the Italian state broadcasting monopoly, provided that such application would not obstruct its tasks.

The terms of Articles 101 and 102 are enforced, in the first instance, by the Commission, and by member state competition law authorities and national courts. The Commission has the power to investigate, *sua sponte* or upon complaint by interested persons or member states, possible violations. One notable decision upheld the authority of the Commission to conduct searches of corporate offices without notice or warrant when it has reason to believe that pertinent evidence may be lost. Another decision permitted a Swiss whistleblower who once worked for Hoffman–La Roche (a defendant in competition law proceedings) to sue in tort for disclosure of his identity as an informant.

The subject matter of Articles 101 and 102 is commerce, yet their impact is as political as commercial. Astute observers have noted that a significant number of the leading "test cases" have involved defendants from Japan, the United States, Switzerland and other non–members. It is, of course, politically much more acceptable when these Articles are applied to foreign firms. But they have also been applied extensively to European enterprises. The quantity and significance of competition law is sufficient to have generated a growing number of lawyers who specialize in giving advice about the effects of Articles 101 and 102 on transactions in the EU.

Businesses that ignore the reach of EU competition law may experience severe consequences, but nothing comparable to the felony criminal sanctions and private treble damages actions found in U.S. antitrust law. Article 101(2) renders offending business agreements null and void. Nullity is most often raised as a defense to enforcement of contracts, licenses and joint ventures in national legal proceedings. The Commission may levy fines for supplying false or misleading information or for holding back information in connection with inquiries about the applicability of the Articles, and may levy further fines if persons or activities are found to have contravened Article 101 or 102. Offending activity may be penalized per day until there is compliance with a Commission order. All Commission decisions imposing fines or penalties under competition law are subject to judicial review by the EU courts. In early years court decisions tended to reduce the amounts involved because of the developmental state of Article 101 and 102 law, but more recent decisions have upheld substantial fines and penalties imposed by the Commission in competition law proceedings.

Written communications with external EU-licensed lawyers undertaken for defense purposes are confidential and need not be disclosed. Written communications with in-house lawyers are not exempt from disclosure, nor are communications with external non-EU counsel. Thus communications with North American attorneys (who are not also EU-licensed attorneys) are generally discoverable. For example, the Commission obtained in-house counsel documents from John Deere, Inc., a Belgian subsidiary of the U.S. multinational. These documents were drafted as advice to management on how to avoid competition law liability for export prohibition restraints. They were used by the Commission to justify the finding of an intentional Article 101 violation and a fine of 2 million Euros. U.S. attorneys have followed these developments with amazement and trepidation. Disclaimers of possible nonconfidentiality are one option to consider in dealing with clients. At a minimum, U.S. attorneys ought to advise their clients that the usual rules on attorney–client privilege may not apply.

Article 101 and 102 fines are reducible to judgment in the courts of any member state. Article 101 or 102 sanctions may not preclude additional penalties for breach of a member state's business competition laws (e.g., laws which may authorize an aggrieved person to receive damages). Indeed it is possible, as several examples suggest, that multiple liability under British or German competition law (the most vigorous in the EU), EU law and U.S. antitrust law can simultaneously occur. With such a high level of risk, law in this area is ignored only at great peril to international business.

EXTRATERRITORIAL APPLICATION OF EU COMPETITION LAW

EU business competition rules have increasingly been applied with extraterritorial effect. For an agreement to be prohibited under Article 101(1) it must be "likely to affect trade between member states" and have "the object or effect" of impairing "competition within the Common Market." The EU court has repeatedly held that the fact that one of the parties to an agreement is domiciled in a non-member country does not preclude the applicability of Article 101(1) if the agreement is effective in the territory of the EU.

Swiss and British companies, for example, argued that the Commission was not competent to impose competition law fines for acts committed in Switzerland, and in Britain before it joined the EU, by enterprises domiciled outside the Union solely because the acts had effects within the Common Market. Nevertheless, those companies were held in violation of Article 101 because they owned subsidiary companies within the Union and controlled their behavior. The foreign parent and its subsidiaries were treated as a "single enterprise" for purposes of service of process, judgment and collection of fines and penalties. In doing so, the Court observed that the fact that a subsidiary company has its own legal personality does not rule out the possibility that its conduct is attributable to the parent company.

The Court has extended its reasoning to the extraterritorial application of Article 102. A U.S. parent company, for example, was held potentially liable for acquisitions by its Italian subsidiary which affected market conditions within Europe. In another case, the Court held that a Maryland company's refusal to sell its product to a competitor of its affiliate company within the EU was a result of united "single enterprise" action. It proceeded to state that extraterritorial conduct merely having "repercussions on competitive structures" in the Common Market fell within the parameters of Article 102. The Court ordered the U.S. company, through its Italian affiliate, to supply the competitor at reasonable prices.

In 1988, the Court widened the extraterritorial reach of Article 101 in *Ahlstrom and Others v. Commission* (the *Woodpulp Cartel* case), in which pulp producers from the United States, Canada, Sweden and Finland were fined for price fixing activities affecting Common Market trade and competition. These firms did not have substantial operations within the EU. They were primarily exporters to the Common Market. The decision's reliance upon a "place of implementation" effects test is similar to that used under the Sherman Act, although its full extent remains unclear.

More recently, the Commission has focused on restrictive practices of U.S.-based Microsoft Corp, relating to its Windows software. A U.S. settlement with Microsoft reached in 2001 was less demanding than the Commission's ruling of 2004, which required unbundling of media playback capabilities and imposed almost 500 million Euros in fines. In 2007, the Court broadly confirmed the Commission's 2004 decision. Legal battles continued through 2008, when the Commission fined Microsoft an additional 899 million Euros for non-compliance (reduced to 860 million by the EU court). Shortly thereafter, Microsoft settled the prosecution by altering its operating systems' licensing arrangements to favor "open source" software developers (e.g., Linux). In 2009, the Commission's investigation of Microsoft's bundling of its web browser produced a settlement that "unbundled" web browsers on Windows.

Other U.S. technology firms have also been under the EU competition law microscope, including Qualcomm, Intel, Google, IBM and Apple. In 2009, the Commission fined Intel 1.06 billion Euros for abusing its dominant position in microprocessors; the court upheld the fine in 2014 (although further appeals are pending).

EXTRATERRITORIAL REGULATION OF MERGERS

EU laws and regulations also give the Commission the power to oppose large-scale mergers and acquisitions that have competitive consequences in the EU. The process commences when a concentration must be notified to the Commission. The duty to notify is triggered only when the concentration involves enterprises with a combined worldwide turnover of at least 2.5 billion Euros and two of them have an aggregate region-wide turnover of 100 million Euros and at least two of the enterprises have a minimum of 25 million Euros turnover in the same three member states. As a general rule, concentrations meeting these criteria cannot be put into effect and fall exclusively within the Commission's domain. The effort here is to create a "one-stop" regulatory system.

Once a concentration is notified to the Commission, it has one month to decide to investigate the merger. If a formal investigation is commenced, the Commission ordinarily then has four months to challenge or approve the merger. During these months, in most cases, the concentration cannot be put into effect.

The Commission evaluates mergers in terms of their "compatibility" with the Common Market. This includes a prohibition against mergers that "significantly impede effective competition" by creating or strengthening dominant positions.

In 1997, the Commission dramatically demonstrated its extraterritorial jurisdiction over the merger of two U.S. companies, Boeing and McDonnell Douglas. This merger had already been cleared by the U.S. Federal Trade Commission. The European Commission, however, demanded and got (at the risk of a trade war) important concessions from Boeing. These included abandonment of exclusive supply contracts with three U.S. airlines and licensing of technology derived from McDonnell Douglas' military programs at reasonable royalty rates. The Commission's success in this case was widely perceived in the United States as favoring Boeing's European competitor, Airbus.

The Commission blocked the MC Worldcom/Sprint merger in 2001, as did the U.S. Department of Justice. Both authorities were worried about the merger's adverse effects on Internet access. For the Commission, this was the first block of a merger taking place outside the EU between two firms established outside the EU. More controversy arose when in 2001 the Commission blocked the General Electric/Honeywell merger after it had been approved by U.S. authorities. The Commission was particularly concerned about the potential for bundling engines with avionics and non-avionics to the disadvantage of rivals. On appeal, the Court rejected the Commission's legal reasoning. Nevertheless, the merger never took place.

INTERNATIONAL ANTITRUST COOPERATION

Some attempts have been made to coordinate extraterritorial regulation, especially in antitrust. International antitrust cooperation began as early as a 1967 recommendation of the Organisation for Economic Cooperation and Development (OECD), which provides for notification of antitrust actions, exchanges of information to the extent that the disclosure is domestically permissible, and where practical, coordination of antitrust enforcement. The OECD resolution served as a model for the 1972 Antitrust Notification and Consultation Procedure between Canada and the United States. Following the uranium cartel litigation, Australia and the United States reached an Agreement on Cooperation in Antitrust Matters (1982) to minimize jurisdictional conflicts. Australia has taken the position that U.S. courts are not a proper institution to balance interests of concerned countries within the context of private antitrust litigation.

The Agreement on Cooperation provides that when the Government of Australia is concerned with private antitrust proceedings pending in a U.S. court, the Government of Australia may request the Government of the United States to participate in the litigation. The U.S. government must report to the court on the substance and outcome of consultations with Australia on the matter concerned. In this way, Australia's views and interests in the litigation and its potential outcome are made known to the court. The court is not required to defer to those views, or even to openly consider them. It merely receives the report. Australia, in turn, has indicated a willingness to be more receptive to discovery requests in U.S. antitrust litigation and to consult before invoking its blocking statute.

Similar arrangements have been made between the United States and Canada. No such agreement has been reached with the United Kingdom, with whom the extraterritoriality issue remains contentious.

In 1991 the United States and the EU reached an antitrust cooperation agreement that commits the parties to notify each other of imminent enforcement action, to share relevant information and consult on potential policy changes. An innovative feature was the inclusion of "positive comity" principles, by which each side promised to take the other's interests into account when considering antitrust prosecutions. The agreement has had a significant effect on mergers of firms doing business in North America and Europe. After the failed General Electric/Honeywell merger, the United States and the EU further agreed to follow a set of "Best Practices" on coordinated timing, evidence gathering, communication and consistency of remedies.

CHAPTER 9

THE FOREIGN CORRUPT PRACTICES ACT (FCPA) AND THE OECD ANTI-BRIBERY CONVENTION

In the 1970s a broad investigation by the United States government revealed that bribery by U.S. corporations of foreign public officials was a serious, even rampant, problem. Congress responded in 1977 with the enactment of the Foreign Corrupt Practices Act (FCPA). At the same time, the United States began efforts to secure an international treaty on the same subject under the auspices of the Organisation for Economic Cooperation and Development (OECD). The result in 1998 was the OECD Convention on Combating Bribery of Foreign Public Officials in International Business Transactions (see below).

THE FOREIGN CORRUPT PRACTICES ACT

The Foreign Corrupt Practices Act is not a free-standing statute in the U.S. Code. Rather, the Act amended the Securities Exchange Act of 1934 in two important respects: First, in three substantive sections the Act makes it unlawful for a broad range of entities with connections to the United States to make corrupt payments to foreign officials. *See* 15 U.S.C. §§ 78dd–1, 78dd–2, 78dd–3. Second, the FCPA requires issuers of securities in the United States to maintain accurate financial records that would tend to disclose the existence of such payments. *See* 15 U.S.C. § 78(m)(b)(2).

Both the U.S. Department of Justice (DOJ) and the Securities and Exchange Commission (SEC) have a role in enforcing the FCPA. The DOJ's principal role is the criminal enforcement of the Act. For its part, the SEC has civil enforcement authority against issuers of securities on U.S. exchanges and their agents. Through such actions, the SEC may obtain injunctive relief, civil fines, future bans, and disgorgements of ill-gotten proceeds. In addition, the DOJ has a review procedure that allows certain U.S. entities to request an advance determination on whether the Department would prosecute on a stipulated set of facts. *See* 15 U.S.C. §§ 78dd–1(e), 78dd–2(f).

In recent years compliance with the requirements and limitations of the FCPA—as well as with a whole variety of similar regulatory regimes—has become a major line of business for law firms. Most firms, large and small, now have a "compliance" department with a thriving business in advising internationally active enterprises on how to avoid FCPA and related problems, and how to respond if such problems arise. Law firms also may become involved in the indirect enforcement of the FCPA through the "Whistleblower Bounty" provisions of the Dodd-Frank Wall Street Reform and Consumer Protection Act of 2010. Under those provisions, a person who informs the SEC of FCPA violations by a covered company may recover between 10% and 30% of collected monetary sanctions. *See* 15 U.S.C.

§ 78u–6(b). FCPA violations also may trigger prosecution for a variety of related criminal offenses, such as conspiracy, aiding and abetting, violations of the Travel Act, Mail Fraud, Wire Fraud, and the criminal side of Racketeer Influenced and Corrupt Organizations (RICO) Act.

THE FCPA'S ANTI-BRIBERY PROVISIONS

The principal way in which the FCPA combats corruption in international business transactions is through a direct prohibition on bribing foreign public officials. The Act achieves this goal in three separate provisions covering different entities connected to the United States: 15 U.S.C. §§ 78dd–1, 78dd–2, and 78dd–3. These three parallel provisions define the following elements of the criminal offense of bribery of a foreign official (although some commentators cut the pie somewhat differently): (1) a covered entity; (2) nexus with interstate commerce (with important exceptions); (3) corruption and intent; (4) prohibited act; (5) prohibited recipient and purpose; and (6) goal to obtain or retain business.

1. Covered Entities. As noted, the FCPA's prohibitions cover three separate sets of "persons":

(a) Section § 78dd–1 covers any "issuers" of securities on a national exchange (*see* 15 U.S.C. § 78*l*) as well as any entity that—basically because of its large size—is required to file periodic reports with the SEC (*see* 15 U.S.C. § 78*o*(d)).

(b) Section 78dd–2 covers any "domestic concern." This very broad term includes (i) nationals of the United States, (ii) "any corporation, partnership, association, joint-stock company, business trust, unincorporated organization or sole proprietorship organized under the laws of the United States," (iii) any resident of the United States or any territory or possession; and (iv) any entity with a principal place of business in the United States or any territory or possession.

(c) Section 78dd–3 is even broader. It covers "any person" who does "any . . . act in furtherance of" a foreign bribery "while in the territory of the United States." Thus, the FCPA extends even to a foreign person engaged in a foreign bribery scheme for a foreign company on a foreign transaction if she commits a single relevant act while in the territory of the United States (such as sending an email while on vacation here).

Each of these provisions also extends to "any officer, director, employee, or agent" of a covered entity as well as "any stockholder . . . acting on behalf of" such an entity.

2. Nexus with Interstate Commerce. Prior to certain amendments in 1998, the FCPA required for all violations the "use of the mails or any means or instrumentality of interstate commerce" in furtherance of an act of bribery. As a result of those amendments, however, this nexus with interstate commerce now is not required for extraterritorial acts by the entities covered by § 78dd–1 (see above) as well as by any "United States person." This latter term includes U.S. nationals and any business entity organized under the laws of a state or of the United States. *See* § 78dd–1(g), § 78dd–2(i). Such persons are subject to criminal liability under the FCPA for an act committed anywhere in the world, even one that otherwise has no nexus to the United States.

3. "Corruptly" and Intent. A violation of the FCPA also requires that a prohibited act be done "corruptly." The Act does not define this term, but the legislative history indicates that it connotes an "evil motive or purpose" or a "wrongful" intent to influence a prohibited recipient. In broader terms, the government must prove that a criminal defendant—including any corporate entity acting through its authorized representatives—had knowledge of the prohibited acts as well as that such acts were unlawful. For the criminal liability of natural persons, including officers, directors, etc. of covered entities, the FCPA also requires that the prohibited acts be done "willfully." *See* §§ 78dd–2(g), 78dd–3(e), 78ff(2).

4. Prohibited Act. The FCPA prohibits any "offer, payment, promise to pay, or authorization of the payment of any money" as well as any offer, promise, gift, etc. of "anything of value" to the prohibited persons defined below. The DOJ and the SEC have defined the term "anything of value" very broadly.

5. Prohibited Recipient and Purpose. In broad terms, the FCPA prohibits corrupt payments to any foreign official. But this notion is much broader than might appear at first glance. First, the term "foreign official" includes not only "any officer or employee of a foreign government or any department, agency, or instrumentality thereof" but also "any person acting in an official capacity for or on behalf of any such government or department[.]"

Second, the courts have interpreted the term "foreign official" to include not only formal *government* officials, but also officials, agents, and employees of state-owned and state-controlled companies (even if only majority owned by the foreign state).

Third, the set of prohibited recipients includes "public international organizations" as designated by the President.

Finally, and perhaps most important, the FCPA prohibits corrupt payments to "any person . . . while knowing that" any portion of the payment will be offered or given to any foreign official as described above. Moreover, the definition of "knowing" includes an awareness that a prohibited use of a payment is "substantially certain to occur" or knowledge of a "high probability" of such a prohibited use. The courts in turn have interpreted this definition to embrace a "willful blindness" (or "conscious ignorance") test. Thus, a covered person may commit a criminal act under the FCPA if he is aware of a "high probability" that a consultant, broker, or "fixer" will direct any part of a payment to a foreign official if the covered person deliberately refrains from investigating further.

The prohibited payments also must be for a defined corrupt purpose. These include the *direct* purposes of (a) influencing any act or decision of such foreign official "in his official capacity," (b) inducing such foreign official to do or omit to do any act "in violation of the lawful duty of such official," and (c) the securing "any improper advantage." They also include the *indirect* purpose of inducing an official "to use his influence" with a foreign government or official to affect or influence any act or decision.

6. Business Goal. Finally, the focus of the FCPA is corrupt business activities. Thus, a violation of the Act requires a goal of assisting a covered entity "in obtaining or retaining business for or with, or directing business to, any person." Such a business goal may cover a broad range of advantages, including government contracts, concessions, tax reductions, customs clearance, or virtually any benefit to a business enterprise.

Exception and Defenses. The FCPA expressly recognizes an exception and two defenses. The exception is for so-called "grease payments." *See* §§ 78dd–1(b), dd–2(b), dd–3(b). This covers any "facilitating or expediting payment" made to a foreign official "to expedite or to secure the performance" of a "routine governmental action." The Act defines this last term as a nondiscretionary act that is "ordinarily and commonly" performed by a foreign official, such as "obtaining permits, licenses, or other official documents," "processing governmental papers," providing basic services (*e.g.*, police protection, power and water supply, etc.), and "actions of a similar nature."

The FCPA also recognizes two narrow "affirmative defenses." *See* §§ 78dd–1(c), dd–2(c), dd–3(c). The first is for payments that are lawful under the "written laws" of the foreign country (a quite rare circumstance for bribery). The second is for "reasonable and bona fide" expenditures directly related to promotion of a product or performance of a contract with a foreign government. The idea here is that payments to support customary marketing and promotions practices (such as for reasonable lodging or dinners) do not constitute a violation of the Act provided that they do not have a corrupt purpose.

Criminal Liability for Substantive Violations. Corporate entities that violate the FCPA's substantive prohibitions are subject to criminal fines of up to $2 million per violation and civil fines of $10,000. In addition, the DOJ may seek injunctions against violations and the SEC may pursue administrative sanctions (such as civil fines and injunctive relief). Individuals who "willfully" violate the FCPA's substantive prohibitions are subject to criminal fines of up to $100,000 and imprisonment of up to five years (or both) as well as civil fines of up to $10,000. Any criminal fine imposed on a person under the FCPA may not be paid or indemnified by her employer, whether directly or indirectly.

In practice, the DOJ and SEC resolve nearly all FCPA cases against corporations through "deferred prosecution agreements" (DPAs) or non-prosecution agreements (NPAs) founded on an agreed payment of fines (often very substantial ones). Corporations usually prefer to accept a negotiated fine rather than litigate and risk the potentially huge "collateral consequences" of a criminal conviction (loss of required business licenses, bans on government contracting, among others). The result has been a series of high profile, and high number, fines accepted by multi-national corporations, most often from "self-reporting" of potential violations to the DOJ and SEC.

THE FCPA'S ACCOUNTING PROVISIONS

The second pillar of the FCPA is directed to accounting practices. In general terms, the Act requires issuers of securities in the United States to maintain sufficiently detailed financial records and to put in place internal controls to ensure that those records remain accurate. *See* 15 U.S.C. § 78(m)(b)(2). The simple idea is that these separate requirements directed to a firm's accounting and compliance departments will serve as checks on the activities of the sales and marketing departments.

The accounting requirements apply both to formal "issuers" of securities under the Securities Exchange Act (*see* 15 U.S.C. § 78*l*) and to those other companies that are required to file periodic reports under that Act (*see* 15 U.S.C. § 78*o*(d)). In addition, such entities are required to ensure compliance with the accounting provisions by any majority owned (*i.e.*, more than 50%) foreign subsidiary.

The Record-Keeping Requirements. The basic accounting requirement is to "make and keep books, records, and accounts, which, in reasonable detail, accurately and fairly reflect the transactions and dispositions of the assets of the issuer." The FCPA defines "reasonable detail" to mean a "level of detail . . . that would satisfy prudent officials in the conduct of their own affairs." As noted above, the goal of such requirements is to facilitate detection— by other company officials as well as the SEC—of corrupt practices including, of course, bribery of foreign officials. And as noted below, these requirements have teeth, for violations may subject covered entities, as well as their officials and employees, to criminal liability.

The Internal Controls Requirements. As further support for the goal of combating corruption, the FCPA requires covered entities to "devise and maintain a system of internal accounting controls sufficient to provide reasonable assurances" of accurate books and records. In more specific terms, such internal controls must ensure that (i) transactions are executed in accordance with management's authorization; (ii) transactions are recorded sufficiently to prepare accurate financial and asset statements; (iii) access to assets is permitted only in accordance with management's authorization; and (iv) the records are compared with existing assets at reasonable intervals. The term "reasonable assurance" again means "such . . . degree of assurance as would satisfy prudent officials in the conduct of their own affairs."

Criminal Liability for Violations. Knowing violations of the accounting or record-keeping requirements may subject covered entities and their employees to criminal liability. In specific, the FCPA provides that it is a crime for any person "knowingly" (i) to "circumvent or . . . fail to implement a system of internal accounting controls" or (ii) to "falsify any book, record, or account." Corporate entities may be subject to fines of up to $25 million per violation and individuals to fines of up to $5 million and imprisonment of up to twenty years. In addition, the SEC has been particularly active in pursuing administrative actions— including civil penalties and injunctions—against covered entities for violations of the FCPA's accounting and internal controls provisions.

THE OECD ANTI-BRIBERY CONVENTION

Almost immediately upon the adoption of the FCPA in 1977, the United States began efforts to secure an international treaty to combat bribery of foreign public officials. It pursued this goal principally through the Organisation for Economic Cooperation and Development (OECD). The reason for this choice was that the OECD's thirty-four member states represent the most economically developed countries in the world and thus the most likely sources for "outbound" bribery of foreign public officials. These efforts bore fruit in 1998 in the form of the OECD Convention on Combating Bribery of Foreign Public Officials in International Business Transactions. The United States promptly ratified this Convention and then implemented it through amendments to the FCPA in 1998.

The OECD Anti-Bribery Convention is a formal international treaty, but in its substance it is very similar to the rules that already existed in the FCPA. In its most fundamental provision, the Convention creates an obligation for member states to criminalize under domestic law the offense of "bribery of a foreign public official." The elements of this offense, as stated in Article 1.1, are quite similar to those in the FCPA: (a) an act by "any person" (b) "intentionally" (c) "to offer, promise or give any undue pecuniary or other advantage," whether directly or indirectly, (d) to "a foreign public official" (e) in order that the official "act or refrain from acting in relation to the performance of official duties" (f) in order to "obtain or retain business or other improper advantage in the conduct of international business." A separate provision in Article 1 requires the criminalization of "complicity in, including incitement, aiding and abetting, or authorization of" an act of bribery of a foreign public official. Article 3 then requires that such offenses be "punishable by effective, proportionate and dissuasive criminal penalties."

Again similar to the FCPA, the OECD Convention also has accounting provisions. In specific, Article 8 mandates "effective, proportionate and dissuasive civil, administrative, or criminal penalties" for a failure to establish and maintain accurate "books and records, financial statement disclosures, and accounting and auditing standards." Other noteworthy provisions address consultation on issues of parallel prosecution (Article 4.3), money laundering (Article 7), and required international cooperation through mutual legal assistance and extradition (Articles 9 and 10).

For purposes of U.S. law, the most significant provisions of the OECD Convention were on jurisdiction, for in two respects the Convention required an expansion of the scope of the FCPA. First, Article 4.1 requires member states to criminalize foreign bribery if an offense "is committed in whole or in part in its territory." It was this provision that led to the adoption of § 78dd–3 (see "covered entities" above), which criminalizes any act in furtherance of foreign bribery by "any person . . . while in the territory of the United States." Second, Article 4.2 requires that member states establish the legal grounds for prosecuting their own nationals "for offences committed abroad." This provision triggered the removal of the requirement of the use of interstate commerce for issuers and other "United States persons" (again, see "covered entities" above).

Implementation the OECD Convention. All thirty-four OECD member states have ratified the Convention (as have seven other nations), and it formally entered into force on February 15, 1999. Between 1999 and early 2004, these states also implemented the Convention by amending their domestic law to criminalize the "bribery of a foreign public official" as defined in its Article 1.

One important issue in the implementation of the OECD Anti-Bribery Convention is that it states a floor, not a ceiling. A prominent, and in part controversial, illustration of this point is the UK Bribery Act 2010. This Act differs from the FCPA in the following important respects: (a) It prohibits bribes even to *private* foreign entities; (b) it does not require a "corrupt" intent; (c) it makes it a crime to *receive* a bribe; and (4) it does not have an exception for payments that facilitate "routine governmental actions."

Other International Anti-Corruption Efforts. The OECD Anti-Bribery Convention is by no means the only international effort to combat corruption. In 1996, the Organization of American States concluded the Inter-American Convention Against Corruption, which effectively every nation in the Western Hemisphere has ratified. At roughly the same time, the United Nations began work on a comprehensive treaty on the same subject. The result was a 2003 treaty, the UN Convention Against Corruption, which is much broader in scope than the OECD Convention (in particular regarding purely domestic forms of corruption). Over 170 nations have ratified this treaty, including the United States in 2006 (although it took the position that ratification did not require amendment of the FCPA).

CHAPTER 10

RESOLUTION OF INTERNATIONAL BUSINESS DISPUTES: LITIGATION AND ARBITRATION

Parties to an international business transaction may not want to think about what will happen when disputes arise, preferring to focus on the success they hope their venture will enjoy. But despite thorough planning of the transaction, exhaustive assignment of risks, and careful drafting of documents, disputes can and will arise that cannot be resolved by the parties themselves. The time to think about how to resolve these disputes is *before* they arise. Important decisions about dispute resolution can be made in the contract documents. And even where the parties cannot agree on dispute resolution procedures (or where there is no contractual relationship between them, as in many international tort disputes), understanding the likely course of dispute resolution and the challenges to successfully bringing claims will influence the parties' assessment of their risks and may shape their business strategy.

In selecting a method of dispute resolution, the most basic choice is between litigation in national courts and international arbitration. (There are few if any international courts suited to hear business disputes involving private parties). If choosing arbitration, the parties need to think about how and where the arbitration will be conducted and how the outcome of the arbitration (the arbitral award) will be enforced.

If the parties prefer litigation in national courts, they will want to consider specifying *which* nation's courts. They also may wish to specify the governing rules for their relationship. They may agree that a particular nation's law applies, or they may stipulate that a contract for the sale of goods is governed by the International Chamber of Commerce (ICC) INCOTERMS (see Chapter 3) or other sets of privately developed rules. The parties may choose to opt out of the otherwise applicable Convention on International Sale of Goods (CISG) (see Chapter 2), instead preferring the UNIDROIT Principles of International Commercial Contracts or a particular nation's sales law.

If no method of dispute resolution can be agreed in advance, the parties still need to understand how dispute resolution will unfold. For example, a U.S. business contemplating a transaction with a foreign company should consider: What if the foreign company does not fulfill its obligations—can it be sued in U.S. courts? Would the U.S. company actually be better off in foreign court? What procedural defenses might the defendant raise? Are there things the U.S. company can do in advance to make those defenses less likely? What law will govern the question whether the contract was breached? If the U.S. company obtains a judgment, will it be able to collect it, if the foreign company has no assets in the United States? Are there things that can be done to make a judgment more capable of enforcement? What if the foreign company wants to sue the U.S. company—will it be able to sue in foreign court? Would the U.S. company be better off in U.S. court? Will the law be different in foreign court? Will a judgment against the U.S. company in a foreign court be enforceable in the United States?

As we will see, many of these questions have no easy answers, but thinking about them in advance, before the deal is concluded, is crucial to understanding what risks are being undertaken.

Each form of dispute resolution has advantages and disadvantages to the parties from their perspectives at the time of drafting the contract and from their perspectives when a dispute has arisen. Clients will expect to be advised as to the most favorable form of dispute resolution for their own individual interests, not some philosophical value judgment of the "fairest" method of dispute resolution or the "best" legal system.

This chapter begins by discussing international business litigation before turning to its principal alternative, international commercial arbitration.

THE PROCESS OF INTERNATIONAL BUSINESS LITIGATION

The next nine sections describe the basic procedural challenges of litigating international business disputes in national courts. Many of them may be familiar from the introductory civil procedure course. For international disputes, however, they are often especially complex and daunting.

(1) *Choice of Forum*. In what country's courts will the dispute be litigated? Often parties attempt to resolve this question through a forum selection clause in their contract; absent a contractual selection, the plaintiff will make the initial choice by choosing the court in which to file suit, subject to the defense's attempts to defeat it.

(2) *Jurisdiction*. In international litigation, personal jurisdiction can be a particular challenge. It may be the case that a non-U.S. party cannot be sued in U.S. court, or can be sued for only a limited number of claims.

(3) *Service of Process*. After filing their claims, plaintiffs must assure that adequate notice is "served" on defendants. This may seem like a technical step, and it is, but if not done properly it may be grounds for dismissal—and serving process on defendants located abroad can be challenging.

(4) *Forum Non Conveniens*. Even if a U.S. court has jurisdiction, a defendant may argue that the courts of some other nation are more convenient for resolving the

dispute (often as a strategic matter to achieve a forum less favorable to the plaintiff).

(5) *Parallel Proceedings.* A defendant in litigation in one country's courts may file as plaintiff in another country's courts. The original defendant will then try to dismiss or stay the original proceeding, while the original plaintiff may seek to enjoin the second proceeding.

(6) *Discovery.* U.S. rules of discovery differ dramatically from the rules in many other countries. How can U.S. plaintiffs obtain U.S. style-discovery of witnesses and documents located abroad?

(7) *Choice of Law.* What substantive law will govern if the dispute touches multiple jurisdictions? A court will always apply its own procedural law, but it might apply foreign law to the merits of the claim. As with forum selection, parties may seek to resolve this uncertainty in advance by contract through choice of law clauses.

(8) *Enforcement of Judgments.* Even if the plaintiff obtains a judgment, it may be of little value unless it can be enforced in a jurisdiction in which the defendant has

assets. But foreign judgments are not automatically enforced in most jurisdictions (in some, they are not enforced at all, requiring re-litigation).

(9) *Special Issues Involving Litigation Against Foreign Sovereigns.* Where a foreign sovereign (or an agency or subsidiary of a foreign sovereign) is a defendant, there may be additional complications. As discussed in Chapter 7 regarding takings, foreign sovereign immunity, the act of state doctrine and difficulties in enforcing a judgment may preclude a successful claim.

One matter needs to be stressed repeatedly. Each of these areas should be evaluated separately before making decisions regarding any one of them. For example, bringing suit in a nation favorable to the plaintiff with regard to ease of proof and the availability of substantial damages may prove futile if a favorable verdict is gained but the defendant's assets are located in another nation that does not enforce any foreign judgments or does not enforce judgments of the chosen forum. Choosing the best forum for a plaintiff means working through each stage for obstacles and solutions.

After you review all these challenges and uncertainties with your clients, they may be ready to consider an alternative to the vagaries of national courts: arbitration. Arbitration is discussed in the second part of this chapter.

THE CHOICE OF FORUM

Forum selection clauses. International business contracts (like many domestic contracts) often include a forum selection clause. A typical one might read:

All suits arising out of or relating to the subject matter of this contract shall be decided solely and exclusively by the state or federal courts located in New York City, New York.

In drafting the clause, it is important to distinguish between mandatory and permissive selections. The clause quoted above is mandatory (it requires New York courts). A permissive clause would allow, but not require, litigation in New York courts. In addition, parties should draft the clause broadly to include disputes "relating to" their contractual relationship, to include not just breach of contract claims but also for example related tort claims.

In negotiating a contract, the parties should always at least consider the appropriateness of stipulating a chosen forum. If a choice is not made, there may be substantial uncertainty and costly disputes over the location of the litigation. The parties may not be able to agree and so do nothing, but at least they will have considered the issue.

A forum selection clause does not assure that other courts will not hear the case. Indeed, until the modern era few courts were willing to enforce forum selection clauses because they were perceived as attempts to interfere with judicial administration by depriving a competent court of jurisdiction. But the attitudes of modern courts changed beginning with the U.S. Supreme Court's decision in *M/S Bremen v. Zapata Off-Shore Co.*, 407 U.S. 1 (1972). In that case, the Court upheld a clause in which the parties had chosen, not the courts of one of their own countries (the United States and Germany), but the courts of London—a neutral forum that had no other relationship to the transaction. "[I]n the light of present day commercial realities and expanding international trade," the Court held, "we conclude that the forum clause should control absent a strong showing that it should be set aside."

The *Bremen* decision left open the question what showing would be sufficient to set aside a forum selection clause, although it indicated that where sophisticated parties had bargained over the clause, it would almost always be enforced. In *Carnival Cruise Lines, Inc. v. Shute,* 499 U.S. 585 (1991), the Court went much further and upheld a forum selection clause that was not bargained for and was contained in the middle of 25 paragraphs of boilerplate on the back of a cruise ship passenger's ticket, issued after the passenger had paid in advance for the trip. The Court found the clause "reasonable" because it saved "judicial resources" and might lead to lower ticket prices.

Carnival Cruise, however, involved the choice of a U.S. forum (Florida) with connections to the defendant (which was based in Florida). A U.S. court might still refuse to enforce the choice of a foreign forum that was manifestly inadequate or unfair (so that the plaintiff could not get a reasonable hearing) or that was so inconvenient it appeared to have been selected to discourage litigation. In *Petersen v. Boeing Co.*, 715 F.3d 276 (9th Cir. 2013), the court of appeals reversed a district court's enforcement of a forum selection clause choosing Saudi Arabian courts where it appeared that the U.S. plaintiff could not get a fair hearing in Saudi courts and had agreed to the selection as a result of fraud and overreaching.

Bremen and *Carnival Cruise* both involved U.S. federal maritime law. It is not clear whether enforcement of forum selection clauses in federal diversity cases is governed by state law or federal common law, and in U.S. state court enforceability is governed by state law. But state courts have been influenced by the Supreme Court's conclusions and in general appear similarly willing to enforce forum selection clauses absent unusual circumstances.

European Union (EU) law also generally recognizes forum selection clauses under its applicable regulations. However, courts of other non-U.S. jurisdictions may not be as hospitable to them, perhaps retaining the historical hostility to the idea of limiting a court's power by contract. Careful inquiry regarding the law of the relevant jurisdiction is essential.

Choice by a U.S. Plaintiff. Where no forum has been selected in the contract, the party filing the suit will initially choose the forum (although the defendant may try to move the dispute to a different forum using various doctrines described later in this chapter). A U.S. plaintiff will usually assume that a

U.S. forum is the best choice. That may not be true. A foreign forum may be the only place where the defendant is subject to jurisdiction, or where the law is favorable to the plaintiff, or where the defendant has its assets.

It is important to note that suing in the United States does not assure that U.S. law will apply to the merits of the dispute. As discussed below, U.S. courts routinely apply foreign law to disputes that arise in other countries, including ones that involve only U.S. parties. Although the choice of forum may influence which substantive law is used, choosing the forum is distinct from choosing the applicable law. Suit in the United States does assure that U.S. procedures (such as U.S. discovery rules and, if applicable, jury trials) are used—unless and until, of course, the defendant can successfully claim that the case does not belong in U.S. court.

Choice by a Foreign Plaintiff. Foreign plaintiffs increasingly seek a U.S. forum, even to decide matters that have far more links to their own nation. The reason for such forum shopping, especially where the claim is a tort, is usually the prospect of damages not available in the foreign plaintiff's nation, such as pain and suffering and punitive damages. But even for commercial litigation the U.S. system may appear the better choice to foreign plaintiffs, with its more extensive discovery, jury system and possible contingent fee arrangements. In addition, choosing a U.S. forum may increase the chances (though not assure) that U.S. law will be used in place of unfavorable foreign law. In these circumstances, it may be the U.S. defendant who tries to move the case to a non-U.S. forum.

JURISDICTION

Personal Jurisdiction in U.S. Courts. As a constitutional requirement of due process, courts in the United States must have personal jurisdiction over the defendant. This requirement is generally described as a two-part test: first whether the defendant has *minimum contacts* with the jurisdiction and second whether the exercise of personal jurisdiction over the defendant is reasonable according to notions of *fair play and substantial justice. World-Wide Volkswagen Corp. v. Woodson*, 444 U.S. 286 (1980). Personal jurisdiction is often an issue in domestic cases in the U.S. system as well, but it can be more significant in international cases, where dismissal for lack of personal jurisdiction may require litigation not in a different U.S. state but in a foreign nation with an entirely different legal system.

Plaintiffs may seek to establish either *specific* or *general* personal jurisdiction over the defendant. General jurisdiction exists where the defendant has such extensive contacts with or operations in a jurisdiction that the defendant is said to be "at home" there. For an individual this is typically the place of residence; for a corporation it may include the place of incorporation, the place of principal operations, and other jurisdictions where extensive business activities are conducted. If a plaintiff establishes general jurisdiction over a defendant, the defendant may be sued in that jurisdiction for any alleged injury, even one with no connection to that jurisdiction. Recent Supreme Court cases have limited the availability of general jurisdiction based on business operations. *See Goodyear Dunlop Tires Operations, S.A. v. Brown*, 131 S.Ct. 2846 (2011); *Daimler AG v. Bauman*, 134 S.Ct. 746 (2014). In the latter case, the Court held that Argentinian plaintiffs could not obtain general jurisdiction over Daimler (a German company) in California for injuries suffered in Argentina, even though Daimler (through a subsidiary) sold significant numbers of cars in California.

For specific jurisdiction, in contrast, the plaintiff need only show that the defendant's alleged harmful conduct had some direct connection to the jurisdiction. However, unlike general jurisdiction, specific jurisdiction only allows suits arising from the acts connected to the jurisdiction. For example, in the *Daimler* case mentioned above, plaintiffs had to rely on general jurisdiction because the alleged wrongful acts occurred in Argentina. If the alleged wrongful acts had occurred in California, the plaintiffs could have established specific jurisdiction (but only for suits arising from those acts).

Sometimes it is clear when a wrongful act has enough connection to a place to establish specific jurisdiction, but often it is not. For example, in *Asahi Metal Industry Co., Ltd. v. Superior Court*, 480 U.S. 102 (1987), plaintiff was injured in a motorcycle accident in California, allegedly due to a defective part manufactured in Japan by a Japanese company (Asahi). Asahi had not sold the part in the United States nor taken action to cause it to be sold or used in the United States. The question was whether there was specific personal jurisdiction in California over Asahi. The Court held there was not, but the multiple opinions made it difficult to identify the exact rationale. A more recent case on similar facts, *J. McIntyre Machinery, Ltd. v. Nicastro*, 131 S.Ct. 2780 (2011), involved a machine manufactured in Britain that caused injury in New Jersey. The Court found no specific jurisdiction in New Jersey, apparently because the British company had not deliberately caused the machine to be sold there, again without a unified majority opinion.

In contract cases, it may be simpler to establish specific jurisdiction based on where the contract was negotiated and performed. However, even these cases are not always clear. A divided court of appeals in *Benton v. Cameco Corp.*, 375 F.3d 1070 (10th Cir. 2004), for example, found no specific jurisdiction over a Canadian company in Colorado court, in a breach of contract case between a Colorado company and the Canadian company, even though the contract was negotiated in part in Colorado and involved activities in Colorado.

Of particular interest to international business, another possible way to establish personal jurisdiction is through the contacts of a subsidiary, affiliate or agent. It remains unclear to what extent the contacts of a related party may be attributed to a defendant for purposes of showing minimum jurisdictional contacts. If a parent is the alter ego of its subsidiary, it seems clear that the subsidiary's contacts may be attributed to the parent. Some courts have gone further and allowed attribution for the acts of agents or formally separate subsidiaries, but others have not.

Note that in most U.S. cases, the question is whether the defendant had sufficient contacts with the *state* in which the litigation is brought (even if the litigation is in federal court). Some states have statutory or common law limits on personal jurisdiction beyond what is required by the U.S. Constitution, so these also must be considered. For claims under U.S. federal law, there are special rules that may allow jurisdiction based on the defendant's contacts with the United States as a whole.

Lack of personal jurisdiction can be waived, either expressly or by failing to object at the appropriate time. A forum selection clause is generally treated as an implicit consent to personal jurisdiction in the chosen forum, but parties often include an express consent to jurisdiction as part of the forum selection clause.

Subject Matter Jurisdiction in U.S. Courts. In the United States, the term subject matter jurisdiction typically refers to whether the dispute should be brought in state or federal court. Federal courts have limited subject matter jurisdiction while state courts have general subject matter jurisdiction. For international disputes, federal subject matter jurisdiction is most often established by "diversity," meaning that the dispute is between a U.S. party and a party from a foreign country, or between parties from different U.S. states. There is no diversity jurisdiction where all parties are non-U.S. citizens, or where the plaintiff is from the same state as at least one of the defendants. Diversity jurisdiction also requires that at least a certain amount (currently $75,000) be at stake in the case. The other principal way to establish federal jurisdiction is if the claim arises under a federal statute, treaty, or the Constitution (called "arising under" jurisdiction).

If there is federal subject matter jurisdiction, typically a defendant may "remove" a case filed in state court to federal court. If there is no federal subject matter jurisdiction, usually the case can be brought in state court instead (unless it is a matter over which no U.S. courts have jurisdiction, such as some claims against foreign sovereigns). Unlike personal jurisdiction, lack of subject matter jurisdiction cannot be waived, either by contract or by failure to object at the outset of the case.

Jurisdiction in Foreign Courts. While U.S. law distinguishes between subject matter jurisdiction and personal jurisdiction, that is not a characteristic of the civil law tradition, where the two concepts tend to be fused under the doctrine of judicial competency. Rules regarding competency are usually contained in codes of procedure or private international law. The rules usually seek to achieve much the same result as in the United States:

proper links to the court (subject matter) and fairness in bringing the defendant before the court (personal). In civil law nations there is often a rule that a matter may be decided at the location of the defendant's domicile (general jurisdiction) but may also be decided under an often complex framework addressing the location of the performance of a contract or the place of the commission of a tort (special jurisdiction). These rules place an emphasis on the relationship between the court and the claim, as opposed to the U.S. emphasis on the relationship between the court and the defendant. Unlike the U.S. rules, issues of contract and issues of tort occurring in the same case may have to meet separate special jurisdiction tests.

A principal practical difference between U.S. courts and other courts has been that U.S. courts are more willing to find general jurisdiction over companies based not just on domicile but also on the basis of business operations (thus potentially allowing general jurisdiction in multiple places). However, the Supreme Court's recent decisions limiting this practice, discussed above, may be narrowing these differences.

As discussed below, foreign countries may be reluctant to enforce judgments obtained under U.S. theories of personal jurisdiction that the foreign legal system does not recognize.

SERVICE OF PROCESS

Service of process refers to delivery to the defendant of notice of the claim against it. In the

United States, adequate notice is required by the Constitution's due process clauses and is done by the plaintiff pursuant to the rules of the court in which the claim is filed. For example, in federal court, service of process is governed by Rule 4 of the Federal Rules of Civil Procedure, although the Federal Rules partly incorporate state law procedures. Plaintiffs must select a method of service of process on defendants that meets the requirements of the law of the forum. Failure to make adequate service may cause the complaint to be dismissed. This may occur even on appeal after the plaintiff has won a judgment in the lower court.

Service in U.S. domestic cases is usually straightforward. For non-U.S. defendants, service is more complicated. First, there is an international treaty, the Hague Convention on the Service Abroad of Judicial and Extrajudicial Documents in Civil or Commercial Matters (called the Hague Service Convention) that addresses service of process. Over 65 nations including the United States are parties to the Convention. According to the U.S. Supreme Court, the Convention is the exclusive means of serving process outside the United States in countries that are parties.

The Hague Service Convention requires each party to establish a Central Authority to receive requests to carry out service in their territory. The Convention provides procedural steps that reasonably assure the plaintiff that compliance with the Convention will greatly reduce if not eliminate the possibility of a successful challenge to the service of process or other documents. The Convention allows nations to take reservations and make declarations to modify or limit obligations under certain provisions of the Convention. For example, the United States has made a declaration under Article 16 that an application for service will not be entertained under certain time-of-filing limitations. A number of foreign nations have made declarations or reservations under Article 10 prohibiting service by mail directly on defendants in their jurisdictions.

Where service on a non-U.S. defendant can be done in the United States, service may be made under U.S. domestic law and the Hague Service Convention does not apply. For example, the Supreme Court allowed a plaintiff to serve the German company Volkswagen by serving its U.S. subsidiary in Illinois, without regard to the Hague Service Convention. *Volkswagenwerk Aktiengessellschaft v. Schlunk*, 486 U.S. 694 (1988).

Finally, where service must be made in a country that is not party to the Hague Service Convention, plaintiffs may have to proceed through a process called a letter rogatory. This is a formal diplomatic request from the U.S. State Department to the foreign country to serve process on the defendant. In some cases, where the letter rogatory process appears futile, courts may allow plaintiffs to serve defendants abroad through other means, including mail or even email or social media.

If the defendants are in a foreign country, service in accordance with U.S. law may offend the nation in which the foreign defendant is located. Service by mail, for example, is not recognized in many nations. It may constitute sufficient notice in the U.S. forum, but any decision in plaintiff's favor might not be recognized and enforced in the nation of a defendant who was served by mail. Thus, plaintiffs in international litigation must consider complying with the service of process laws of multiple nations—where the plaintiff has filed suit and where each defendant has assets.

FORUM NON CONVENIENS

The common law doctrine *forum non conveniens* ("inconvenient forum") allows courts, even when they have jurisdiction, to decline to decide cases that seem more appropriate for resolution elsewhere. *See Piper Aircraft Co. v. Reyno*, 454 U.S. 235 (1981). *Forum non conveniens* motions are particularly common in international tort cases (though they may be made in contract disputes as well). That is because of characteristics of U.S. law that encourage plaintiffs to file in the United States, including contingent fee arrangements, civil juries, extensive discovery and, most importantly, pain and suffering damages and even the pot of gold at the end of the international rainbow, punitive damages.

The source of *forum non conveniens* doctrine is almost exclusively case law, except in a few states that have enacted statutes modifying or eliminating its use. U.S. federal courts apply a federal law of *forum non conveniens* that does not depend on the law of the state in which they sit, although the approaches are usually similar.

In considering a motion to dismiss based on *forum non conveniens,* a court may be influenced by whether the plaintiff is a U.S. resident or a foreign resident. A foreign resident's choice to sue in U.S. court may be less respected, because it may appear that the foreign plaintiff forum shopped for the reasons expressed above, such as high damages. For example, in the *Reyno* case mentioned above, the real parties in interest were Scottish, which the Court found significant in deciding to dismiss the claim. In contrast, it is often said that a U.S. plaintiff's selection of a U.S. court is generally respected. However, *forum non conveniens* dismissals have been upheld even against U.S. plaintiffs. In *Loya v. Starwood Hotels & Resorts Worldwide, Inc.*, 583 F.3d 656 (9th Cir. 2009), for example, the court of appeals affirmed a *forum non conveniens* dismissal of a claim brought by a U.S. plaintiff against a U.S. company for wrongful death at the defendant's hotel in Mexico.

A second key consideration is whether there is an available and adequate foreign forum. In the *Reyno* and *Loya* cases, the U.S. courts found that the courts of Scotland and Mexico, respectively, were available to hear the plaintiffs' claims and would provide plaintiffs with adequate remedies. Adequacy usually considers whether the foreign forum recognizes theories of action that the U.S. recognizes, such as strict liability, antitrust, class actions or consumer protection. But adequacy also has become enmeshed with considering whether the foreign forum is so corrupt, inefficient, inadequate and/or intimidating that it would be unjust to transfer the matter abroad only to meet a certain doom. Courts do not like to classify other nation's courts as incapable of providing justice, but the reality is that there are many nations that are so incapable, and in some cases *forum non conveniens* motions have been denied on these grounds. *E.g.*, *DiFederico v. Marriott Int'l, Inc.*, 714 F.3d 796 (4th Cir. 2013) (finding courts in Pakistan inadequate to resolve U.S. plaintiffs' claim for injuries in a hotel bombing in Pakistan). A defendant must show an adequate alternative forum as a prerequisite to *forum non conveniens* dismissal.

The third consideration by the court involves balancing various private and public factors set forth by the Supreme Court in *Reyno*. Private factors include where evidence is located and difficulties in getting it to the forum; the inconvenience of bringing parties, witnesses and experts to the forum; the need to translate documents and testimony; the ability to implead third-party defendants; the necessity of applying foreign law; and implications from fragmenting the suit if it were dismissed in favor of courts of different nations. Public factors include each nation's interest in being the location of the litigation, the burden on the court system and interest of jurors in serving, and sometimes deterring U.S. companies from producing defective products for export.

Courts often condition *forum non conveniens* dismissal on promises by the defendant. The most prevalent condition is that the defendant submit to the jurisdiction of the foreign court. Others may include waiver of foreign statutes of limitations and agreement to pay any judgment rendered in the foreign court—a promise that may be regretted if the foreign court renders a very large judgment. Defendants should recognize that *forum non conveniens* only removes the case from U.S. court; it may be refiled in the alternative forum, which might be less advantageous.

Internationally, *forum non conveniens* is essentially unknown outside some common law tradition nations. The EU's regulations on jurisdiction do not recognize it, a point confirmed by the European Court of Justice in 2005, when it ruled that Britain's use of *forum non conveniens,* even with non-EU defendants, was inconsistent with Britain's obligations under the EU jurisdiction regulation. The court believed that *forum non conveniens* led to needless unpredictability and that courts vested with jurisdiction under EU rules were obligated to hear the matter if a case was filed. *Owusu v. Jackson*, Case C–281/02 (ECJ 2005) (finding that British courts were obligated to hear case involving injuries at a resort in Jamaica).

PARALLEL PROCEEDINGS

Sometimes international claims are filed in more than one nation. For example, one party might file for damages for breach of contract in U.S. court while the other party seeks rescission, or a declaration that no breach has occurred, in a foreign court. Thus the plaintiff and defendant in the U.S. court may be, respectively, the defendant and plaintiff in the foreign nation. This is called parallel litigation.

The U.S. defendant's response to parallel litigation may be to ask the U.S. court to dismiss the proceedings or stay them until the foreign litigation is resolved. This is called *lis alibi pendens* (proceedings pending elsewhere) or abstention. The U.S. plaintiff's response to parallel proceedings may be to ask the U.S. court to enjoin the defendant from pursuing the suit in the foreign court. This is called an anti-suit injunction. In either situation there must be substantial identity between the parties and issues in the two proceedings.

Generally there is no presumption against parallel litigation in U.S. courts, and both *lis alibi pendens* and anti-suit injunction motions will (it is said) be granted only in unusual circumstances. Nonetheless, some courts appear more willing to find unusual circumstances than others, and the Supreme Court has not provided guidance on either doctrine.

EU law, in contrast, has a strong rule against parallel litigation and a strong preference for the location in which suit is first filed.

DISCOVERY

In a domestic U.S. case, discovery in another state is not significantly different than in the forum state. But when the dispute involves two different nations, access to witnesses and evidence in the foreign nation may be very difficult. In particular, foreign nations may be unwilling to accommodate U.S.-style discovery, which typically involves much more extensive and intrusive requests than other legal systems permit.

In U.S. federal court, discovery is governed by Rule 5 of the Federal Rules of Civil Procedure; state courts generally have similar sets of rules. Because the federal rules allow extensive discovery from parties and grant courts broad powers to enforce discovery orders against parties, international discovery of evidence in parties' possession may generally be obtained. Refusal of non-U.S. parties to comply with U.S. discovery orders, even where refusal is required by foreign law, may result in monetary penalties and unfavorable rulings on the merits.

Obtaining discovery from non-party witnesses who are not in the United States poses a greater problem. Typically a U.S. court will not have jurisdiction over these witnesses and so cannot order discovery nor impose sanctions. Instead, the requesting party must attempt to obtain the cooperation either of the witness or (if the witness is unwilling) of the foreign nation to compel discovery. Prior to the Hague Evidence Convention (discussed below), requests to the foreign nation were generally made through letters rogatory (diplomatic instruments issued by the U.S. State Department requesting assistance) and were often unsuccessful due to differing foreign attitudes toward discovery.

The Hague Convention on the Taking of Evidence Abroad in Civil or Commercial Matters (called the Hague Evidence Convention, and not to be confused with the Hague Service Convention discussed above) is an attempt to manage international discovery. It has been adopted by some 58 nations including the United States. The Convention tries to meet the needs of the forum court to obtain evidence while not imposing upon foreign entities demands that are excessive under the rules of their nation. For EU members, Council Regulation No. 1206/2001 has essentially replaced much of the Hague Convention.

An important early question for U.S. courts was whether the Convention procedures were mandatory or an alternative to the rules of the forum. If optional, a second question asked whether the Convention procedures had to be tried first and only if they proved inadequate could the court use discovery rules of the forum. The U.S. Supreme Court ruled that use of the Convention was optional and there was no need to try the Convention first. *Société Nationale Industrielle Aérospatiale v. United States District Court*, 482 U.S. 522 (1987). As a result, U.S. parties may avoid using the Convention for discovery requests to opposing parties, since U.S. rules are often more effective.

Like the Hague Service Convention, the Hague Evidence Convention requires nations to establish a Central Authority to process requests. Countries may decline to honor discovery requests for various reasons. One problem for the United States is reflected in Article 23 of the Convention. It allows members to restrict pretrial production of documents, which many in the United States believe reflects a lack of understanding by civil law nations of common law trial procedure. Article 23 is often cited by foreign nations in rejecting U.S. requests for discovery.

A particularly contentious issue in U.S. discovery arises from requests for disclosures that would violate the law of a foreign nation. In that situation, U.S. courts balance the importance of the information and the hardship to the parties that would arise from disclosure or non-disclosure. Although there are a range of decisions, U.S. courts commonly order disclosure even in violation of foreign law. This is particularly true where the foreign law is a "blocking statute"—that is, a law seemingly enacted for the purpose of frustrating U.S. discovery.

CHOICE OF LAW

A court will always apply its own procedural law (that is, the law relating to how the case is conducted, including pleadings, motions, discovery and evidence, and whether the outcome is determined by a judge or jury). But it will not necessarily apply its own law to the merits of the dispute (that is, to substantive issues such as whether a contract was breached or whether a tort occurred). Instead, as discussed in Chapter 2 regarding international sales transactions, the court may apply the law of another jurisdiction (another nation or, within the United States, another state) with a closer connection to the dispute. This is called choice of law or, particularly where the different laws lead to inconsistent outcomes, conflicts of law.

Choosing the applicable law is an important decision for a court because the outcome may be very different depending on which substantive law applies. For example, a decision to apply a foreign law that offers nominal damages is tantamount to a victory for the defendant. While U.S. parties may assume that U.S. law is more favorable, that will not necessarily be true.

Choice of Law Clauses. Similar to forum selection clauses (discussed above), contractual parties may use choice of law clauses to agree in advance on the applicable law and thus avoid uncertainty and costly disputes later. Often the choice of law and forum are included in the same section of the contract. A typical choice of law clause might read:

> *The rights and duties of the parties arising from or relating to the subject matter of this contract shall be governed solely and exclusively by the laws of the state of New York without regard to its conflict of law rules.*

As with forum selection clauses, it is important to draft choice of law clauses in obligatory rather than permissive language (assuming that is what is intended) and to draft them broadly to include not just contract claims but also tort claims arising from the parties' contractual relationship.

Like forum selection clauses, choice of law clauses were once disfavored but are now generally enforced. Broadly put, in both common law and European civil law jurisdictions, parties may choose the law which they wish to govern their contract relationship, at least as long as the law chosen is that of a place which has a relationship to the parties and the transaction and is not contrary to a strong public policy of the place where suit is brought. The Uniform Commercial Code (UCC) § 1–301 (formerly § 1–105) permits parties to choose the law governing the contract as long as the transaction bears "a reasonable relation" to the jurisdiction providing the governing law. Thus, party choice is permissible, but only within "reasonable" limits. That is not helpful to the merchants in a U.S.–German transaction who wish to use the law of some "neutral" country, such as England. For contracts not governed by the UCC, U.S. courts may allow even greater party choice. In the EU, applicable regulations also allow broadly unlimited party autonomy. See Regulation (EC) No. 593/2008 of the European Parliament and of the Council (17 June 2008). Parties may also choose sets of rules developed by private organizations such as the ICC or international organizations such as the U.N. The trend may favor few limits on party autonomy to choose applicable law in international transactions.

Also like forum selection clauses, choice of law clauses may be resisted on grounds such as fraud, overreaching and duress. In addition, a court may conclude that some aspects of forum law—called mandatory law—are so essential to public policy that parties cannot avoid them by agreeing to be governed by another nation's law. For example, U.S. antitrust law likely cannot be avoided by contract. *See Mitsubishi Motors Corp. v. Soler Chrysler-Plymouth, Inc.*, 473 U.S. 614, 617 n.19 (1985). However, a divided U.S. court of appeals concluded that U.S. securities laws could be avoided where the parties chose British rather than U.S. law. *Richards v. Lloyd's of London*, 135 F.3d 1289 (9th Cir. 1998) (en banc). The EU Regulation also embraces the idea of mandatory law, which it defines as "provisions the respect for which is regarded as crucial by a country for safeguarding its public interests."

Choice of Law Without Contractual Choice. Where no choice is made by the contract parties, or where the parties to a dispute do not have a contractual relationship, choice of law rules tend to select the jurisdiction most closely connected to the transaction or at least having a significant relationship to the transaction. In the EU and in most civil law systems, a detailed set of rules spells out what law will apply to particular types of transactions. In the United States, choice of law is mostly governed by state common law; federal courts apply the choice of law rules of the state in which they are located. The common law rules are often complex and unclear, and vary considerably from state to state.

In general, states either adopt a fairly rule-bound approach (*e.g.*, torts are governed by the law of the place of injury; contracts are governed by the law of the place where they are signed or performed) or a balancing test that seeks to identify which jurisdiction has the greatest interests in the dispute. These are often called the First Restatement and Second Restatement approaches, respectively, after the approaches endorsed by the American Law Institute's Restatement of Conflicts of Law and Restatement (Second) of Conflicts of Law. Some states have unique approaches that do not follow either Restatement.

As discussed in Chapter 2, choice of law for international sales of goods transactions has been partly harmonized by the UN Convention on Contracts for the International Sale of Goods (CISG), which provides a single set of substantive rules for international sales transactions within its scope. Where the CISG does not apply (either by its terms, or because the transaction involves persons or entities from a country that is not a CISG party) the governing law for sales transactions in the United States is usually the UCC, as adopted in the relevant state. However, also as noted in Chapter 2 and above, parties may opt out of the CISG or the UCC by contract.

Proving Foreign Law. Part of the analysis of what law should apply may include problems associated with proving foreign law. While a U.S. court is deemed to know U.S. law, it is not deemed to know foreign law. Foreign law must be proved. In U.S.

federal court, this process is governed by Rule 44.1 of the Federal Rules of Civil Procedure, which requires a party who plans to request the application of foreign law to give reasonable notice. It also allows the court wide latitude in determining foreign law. That usually includes the parties using experts to explain both the nature of the foreign legal system, such as how case law fits into the hierarchy of law, and the substantive characteristics of the applicable law. Experts usually provide affidavits that include translations of the applicable legal provisions. The extent to which courts should look beyond experts to published materials analyzing foreign law is disputed, although Rule 44.1 allows it.

RECOGNITION AND ENFORCEMENT OF FOREIGN JUDGMENTS

Frequently in international disputes a plaintiff may win a judgment in one jurisdiction but find that the defendant's assets are located in other jurisdictions. If the defendant does not satisfy the judgment voluntarily, the plaintiff must find a way to enforce the judgment elsewhere. In the United States, recognition and enforcement of the judgments of one state in another U.S. state is routine due to the Constitution's full faith and credit clause. However, the courts of most legal systems do not automatically recognize judgments from other jurisdictions. For example, in nearly two thirds of the countries of the world, judgments of U.S. courts either are not enforceable at all or are enforceable only if certain conditions are met. For foreign judgments brought to the United States, the full faith and credit clause does not apply to make them automatically enforceable, although there is no general rule prohibiting enforcement.

Effect of Foreign Judgments in the United States. Technically, there are two distinct issues in determining the effect of foreign judgments. "Recognition" refers to the U.S. court's decision to treat the foreign judgment as conclusive (for *res judicata* purposes, for example). "Enforcement" refers to the U.S. court's decision to issue its own order authorizing measures to compel the defendant to comply with the foreign judgment. Typically, however, there is a single process: U.S. courts will enforce foreign judgments which they recognize. In common speech, the process as a whole is often called "enforcement."

Enforcement of foreign judgments in the United States is governed by state law (with federal courts applying the law of the state in which they sit). Prior to the modern era this was often a matter of common law, as in the early U.S. Supreme Court case *Hilton v. Guyot*, 159 U.S. 113 (1895). The Court denied enforcement of a French judgment, announcing that it followed a rule of "comity," which required the opportunity for a "fair trial abroad before a court of competent jurisdiction," "regular proceedings," citation or appearance of the defendant, "a system of . . . impartial administration of justice," and the absence of "prejudice" or fraud. The Court did not fault French justice on any of these grounds, but it found that French courts did not recognize U.S. court judgments. Thus, the French judgment was denied conclusive effect, not because "comity" was lacking, but because "mutuality and reciprocity" were lacking.

Hilton is rarely controlling, for most attempts to enforce foreign judgments will depend upon state law, not federal law, and state courts are free to pursue their own policies and doctrines. For example, the New York Court of Appeals, stating that it was not bound by *Hilton,* has given conclusive effect to French court judgments, despite the lack of reciprocity.

In an attempt to bring harmony to the states' approaches, the National Conference of Commissioners on Uniform State Laws (the organization that developed the UCC) drafted the 1962 Uniform Foreign Money–Judgments Recognition Act (UFMJRA), which was adopted by more than thirty states. More recently, the Commissioners drafted a successor, the 2005 Uniform Foreign–Country Money Judgments Recognition Act (UFCMJRA), which is gradually replacing the UFMJRA in the adopting states. Under these similar Acts, recognition may be given to foreign money judgments that are final and enforceable where rendered. Enforcement of judgments not involving sums of money, such as injunctions or specific performance decrees, are not covered by the Acts, and remain subject to common law.

The Uniform Acts generally provide for recognition and enforcement subject to listed exceptions (UFCMJRA Sec. 4). The principal exceptions include where the foreign judicial system "does not provide impartial tribunals or procedures compatible with the requirements of due process," where the foreign court lacked personal or subject matter jurisdiction, where adequate notice was not given to the defendant, where the judgment was obtained by fraud, or where the judgment is contrary to public policy. The Acts do not require reciprocity for recognition of foreign judgments but several states have added non–uniform amendments requiring either reciprocity or "negative reciprocity." The latter requires only that the foreign nation has not refused to enforce a state's judgment, not that it has in fact actually enforced such a judgment.

In the absence of state statutory law, recognition and enforcement continues to be governed by common law, which often follows the general outlines of *Hilton* and the Uniform Acts.

Effect of U.S. Judgments in Foreign Courts. Non-U.S. jurisdictions take a variety of approaches to recognition and enforcement of U.S. judgments. Some jurisdictions will not enforce foreign judgments at all, absent a treaty specifically agreeing to enforcement; because the United States is not party to any such treaties, U.S. judgments are not enforced in these countries and the matter would have to be relitigated. Other jurisdictions may treat the U.S. judgment as persuasive but not conclusive.

A number of non-U.S. jurisdictions have enforcement rules similar to U.S. rules—that is, they generally enforce foreign judgments subject to exceptions such as lack of jurisdiction, lack of notice, fraud, and violation of public policy. Because U.S. law diverges from laws in many other legal systems on matters such as jurisdiction and service of process, as well as on substantive matters such as punitive damages, some U.S. judgments may not be enforced even in legal systems that generally enforce foreign judgments.

Judgments Rendered in Foreign Currency. If a foreign judgment is given in a foreign currency, how should a U.S. court design its award? In many states, a court's judgment must be in U.S. dollars. Although this should not induce a court to refuse enforcement, it does raise issues of the proper time for computing currency conversion. The Uniform Foreign Money Claims Act (UFMCA), enacted in more than twenty states, allows the court to issue a judgment in a foreign currency, gives three criteria for doing so, and requires any conversion to be computed on the date of payment.

Efforts at International Harmonization. Countries have tried to facilitate the enforcement of foreign judgments by bilateral treaties. Such efforts have been also the subject of multilateral treaties, such as the 1968 [EC] Common Market Convention on Jurisdiction and the Enforcement of Judgments (replaced by the EU Regulation on Jurisdiction and the Recognition and Enforcement of Foreign Judgment in Civil and Commercial Matters) and the 1979 Inter-American [OAS] Convention on Extraterritorial Validity of Foreign Judgments and Arbitral Awards. A major effort was undertaken to conclude a broad international convention on jurisdiction and foreign judgments, but it largely failed, producing only the narrower Hague Convention on Choice of Court Agreements, which requires recognition and enforcement where the parties chose the foreign court by contract. To date this Convention has been accepted by only one nation (Mexico), though the United States and the EU are actively considering it.

SPECIAL ISSUES IN LITIGATION INVOLVING FOREIGN SOVEREIGNS

In addition to the foregoing difficulties, special problems may arise if the defendant is a foreign government or the agency or instrumentality of a foreign government. As discussed in Chapter 7, international law generally recognizes immunity from suit for foreign sovereigns, subject to some exceptions. This rule is implemented in the United States by the Foreign Sovereign Immunities Act (FSIA).

Apart from takings (discussed in Chapter 7), the most likely business-related claim against a foreign sovereign is breach of contract. The FSIA's waiver exception should defeat immunity, assuming the foreign government will agree to a waiver in the contract. U.S. courts generally enforce waivers of immunity under the FSIA. Immunity might also be defeated by the FSIA's commercial activity exception, which denies immunity for claims arising from commercial acts in the United States or having a direct effect in the United States. In *Republic of Argentina v. Weltover, Inc.*, 504 U.S. 607 (1992), the

Supreme Court held that a suit resulting from Argentina's failure to make payment on bonds that were payable in New York arose from a commercial activity having a direct effect in the United States. Tort suits are unlikely to succeed because the FSIA's exception for torts requires that the tort occur in the United States.

It is important to understand that "agenc[ies] or instrumentalit[ies] of a foreign state" (which also have sovereign immunity under the FSIA) include state-owned enterprises (although only ones with direct, rather than indirect, sovereign ownership).

The act of state doctrine (discussed in Chapter 7) may be a barrier to some international business litigation as well. The doctrine generally prohibits U.S. courts from challenging the validity of acts of foreign states done in their own territory. It is unclear whether there is a commercial activity or waiver exception to the act of state doctrine. Some ordinary business activity of state-owned enterprises may not rise to the level of acts of the sovereign for act of state purposes.

The act of state doctrine may have relevance to international business litigation even if there is no foreign sovereign defendant, if the litigation calls into question the legality of a sovereign act. However, mere embarrassment of the foreign sovereign is not enough to trigger the act of state doctrine.

As noted in Chapter 7, a judgment against a foreign nation may be of little use because the FSIA limits execution against foreign sovereign property. If

possible it is important to obtain a contractual waiver
of enforcement immunity as well as jurisdictional
immunity, but much of the enforcement immunity is
not waivable. Private litigants may have to resort to
creative methods to encourage foreign sovereigns to
satisfy judgments. *See NML Capital, Ltd. v. Republic
of Argentina*, 727 F.3d 230 (2d Cir. 2013) (involving
efforts to enforce judgment against Argentina).

ALTERNATIVES TO LITIGATION

Most legal systems allow parties to choose
alternative dispute resolution (ADR) prior to or
instead of litigation. Some alternatives are designed
to encourage voluntary solutions, such as
requirements that the parties engage in good faith
negotiation, conciliation or mediation prior to filing
suit. Mediation, a popular choice, involves a third
party (the mediator) who encourages the parties to
resolve their dispute but has little power to compel a
resolution. Where parties agree to such procedures
by contract, courts typically require them to be
undertaken before litigation can proceed.

Parties may want to remove their dispute from
courts altogether and substitute a different
decisionmaker. Usually, this involves selecting
arbitration, in which the parties arrange for a panel
of neutral persons to hear the dispute and issue a
binding decision.

Courts initially resisted enforcing arbitration
clauses, holding that they deprived the parties of due
process of law (a reaction one might expect toward a
competitor). However, legislatures were more

sympathetic to arbitration, and began to enact statutes validating arbitration clauses. In the United States, commercial arbitration is governed by the Federal Arbitration Act (FAA), which broadly promotes the use of arbitration. Applying the FAA, U.S. courts have become very supportive of arbitration, and arbitration clauses in international contracts will usually be enforced. The U.S. Supreme Court has strongly embraced arbitration, to the extent of becoming very hostile to state laws that appear to limit it.

In addition to arbitration, there are other even less formal alternative dispute resolution mechanisms in use, such as the "mini–trial." The mini–trial comes in a variety of packages, each with a different impact on resolution of the dispute. It can be nonbinding if used with a "neutral advisor"; it can be semi–binding if its results are admissible in later proceedings; or it can be binding before a court-appointed master.

Internationally, the Convention on the Recognition and Enforcement of Foreign Arbitral Awards (called the New York Convention) encourages enforcement of arbitration clauses and arbitration awards. Most major commercial nations are parties, including the United States. After U.S. adoption of the New York Convention, Congress amended the FAA to assure U.S. compliance.

As discussed in Chapter 7, arbitration provisions also appear in many Treaties of Friendship, Commerce and Navigation (FCN Treaties), Bilateral Investment Treaties (BITs) and free trade agreements (FTAs) such as the North American Free

Trade Agreement (NAFTA). These agreements provide for arbitration to resolve investment disputes between foreign private investors and the nation in which the investment is located (called investor-state arbitration) (see Chapter 7).

WHY ARBITRATE?

Uncertainty about where a dispute may be heard, about procedural and substantive rules to be applied, about the degree of publicity to be given the proceedings and the judgment, about the time needed to settle a dispute, and about the enforcement of a resulting court judgment all combine to make arbitration a preferred mechanism for solving international commercial disputes. Thus the growth of international commercial arbitration is in part a retreat from the vicissitudes and uncertainties of international business litigation. More positively, it offers predictability, neutrality and the potential for specialized expertise. Arbitration also allows the parties to select and shape the procedures and costs of dispute resolution.

One of the most attractive attributes of international commercial arbitration is the enforceability in national courts of arbitral awards under the New York Convention (and the Panama Convention in Latin America), and related statutory frameworks such as the FAA. As discussed, there is no comparable international support for the enforcement of court judgments, which are subject to greater uncertainty.

Arbitration has potential disadvantages. Its procedures are relatively informal and not laden with legal rights. To quote Judge Learned Hand:

> Arbitration may or may not be a desirable substitute for trials in courts; as to that the parties must decide in each instance. But when they have adopted it, they must be content with its informalities; they may not hedge it about with those procedural limitations which it is precisely its purpose to avoid. They must content themselves with looser approximations to the enforcement of their rights than those that the law accords them, when they resort to its machinery.

American Almond Products Co. v. Consolidated Pecan Sales Co., Inc., 144 F.2d 448 (2d Cir. 1944).

Although arbitration is sometimes assumed to be cheaper and faster than litigation, that is not necessarily true, and both costs and delays appear to be increasing. One of the least attractive attributes of international commercial arbitration is the general lack of pre–trial provisional remedies. In addition, arbitrators may focus on splitting the differences between the parties rather than fully vindicating legal rights which in court might result in "winner takes all." But one-sided results could permanently disrupt longstanding and mutually beneficial business relationships, so "splitting the baby" through arbitration may really be the optimal outcome.

TYPES OF INTERNATIONAL
COMMERCIAL ARBITRATION

There are two basic types of international commercial arbitration: ad hoc and institutional. Ad hoc arbitrations involve selection by the parties of the arbitrators and rules governing the arbitration. The classic formula involves each side choosing one arbitrator who in turn together choose a third arbitrator. Typically the parties provide by contract a set of procedural rules (such as the UNCITRAL Arbitration Rules), or the ad hoc arbitration panel may select its procedural rules. Ad hoc arbitration can be agreed in advance or, quite literally, selected ad hoc as disputes arise.

Institutional arbitration involves selection of a specific arbitration center (sometimes confusingly called a "court of arbitration"), typically accompanied by its own rules and personnel. Institutional arbitration is in a sense pre–packaged, and the parties need only "plug in" to the arbitration system of their choice. There are numerous competing centers of arbitration, each busy marketing its desirability to the world business community. Some centers are longstanding and busy, such as the International Chamber of Commerce Court of Arbitration in Paris. Other centers are more recent in time and still struggling for clientele, such as the Commercial Arbitration and Mediation Center for the Americas (CAMCA).

Ad hoc arbitration presupposes a certain amount of goodwill and flexibility between the parties. It can be speedy and less costly than institutional arbitration.

The latter, on the other hand, offers easy incorporation into an international business agreement, supervisory services, experienced arbitrators and a fixed fee schedule. The institutional environment is professional, a quality that sometimes can get lost in ad hoc arbitrations. Awards from well-established arbitration centers (including default awards) are more likely to be favorably recognized in court if enforcement is contested. Many institutional arbitration centers now also offer "fast track" or "mini" services.

INTERNATIONAL ARBITRAL RULES: UNCITRAL AND ICSID

Two commonly used sets of arbitration rules are the UNCITRAL Rules and the ICSID Rules. The UNCITRAL Rules refer to the Model International Commercial Arbitration Rules issued in 1976 by the U.N. Commission on International Trade Law (UNCITRAL). The Iran–U.S. Claims Tribunal, discussed in Chapter 7, has used the UNCITRAL Rules in dealing with claims arising out of the confrontation between the two countries in 1979–80. Trade agreements such as NAFTA allow for the use of UNCITRAL rules in investment disputes. The UNCITRAL Rules are not identified with any national or international arbitration organization, a factor supporting their use as "neutral" arbitration rules.

Among other things, UNCITRAL rules provide that an "appointing authority" shall be chosen by the parties or, if they fail to agree upon that point, shall be chosen by the Secretary–General of the Permanent Court of Arbitration at The Hague (comprised of a body of persons prepared to act as arbitrators if requested). The UNCITRAL rules also cover notice requirements, representation of the parties, challenges of arbitrators, evidence, hearings, the place of arbitration, language, statements of claims and defenses, pleas to the arbitrator's jurisdiction, provisional remedies, experts, default, rule waivers, the form and effect of the award, applicable law, settlement, interpretation of the award and costs.

In addition to its 1976 Model Arbitration Rules, UNCITRAL has promulgated the 1985 Model Law on International Commercial Arbitration (amended in 2006), the 1996 Notes on Organizing Arbitral Proceedings, and the 2002 Model Law on International Commercial Conciliation. The 1985 Model Law has been enacted in approximately fifty countries (and the 2006 amendment in a half–dozen), as well as in a number of U.S. states. In Model Law jurisdictions, an arbitral award may be set aside by local courts on grounds that virtually track those specified as permissible for denials of recognition and enforcement of awards under the New York Convention (discussed below). Under the UNCITRAL Model Law, submission to arbitration may be *ad hoc* for a particular dispute but is accomplished most often in advance of the dispute by a general submission clause within a contract. Under Article 8 of the Model Law, an agreement to arbitrate is specifically enforceable. Although no language will guarantee the success of an arbitral submission,

UNCITRAL recommends the following model submission clause:

Any dispute, controversy or claim arising out of or relating to this contract, or the breach, termination or invalidity thereof, shall be settled by arbitration in accordance with the UNCITRAL Arbitration Rules as at present in force.

The ICSID Rules arise from the 1966 Convention on the Settlement of Investment Disputes Between States and Nationals of Other States, to which over 100 countries including the United States are parties. The Convention provided for the establishment of an International Center for the Settlement of Investment Disputes (ICSID) as a non–financial organ of the World Bank. ICSID is designed to serve as a forum for conciliation and arbitration of disputes between private investors and host governments. It provides an institutional framework within which arbitrators, selected by the disputing parties from ICSID's Panel of Arbitrators or from elsewhere, conduct an arbitration in accordance with ICSID Rules of Procedure for Arbitration Proceedings. Arbitrations are held in Washington D.C. unless agreed otherwise. An arbitral money award, rendered pursuant to the Convention, is entitled to the same full faith and credit in the United States as a final judgment of a court of general jurisdiction in a U.S. state.

Under the Convention, ICSID's jurisdiction extends only to legal disputes arising directly out of an investment "between a Contracting State or . . .

any subdivision ... and a national of another Contracting State" which the parties to the dispute consent in writing to submit to the Center. No party may withdraw its consent unilaterally. Thus, ICSID is an attempt to institutionalize dispute resolution between States and non–State investors. It therefore always presents a "mixed" arbitration. If one party questions jurisdiction, the issue of "arbitrability" may be decided by the arbitration tribunal. A party may seek annulment of any arbitral award by an appeal to an ad hoc committee of persons drawn by the Administrative Council of ICSID from the Panel of Arbitrators under the Convention. Annulment is available only if the Tribunal was not properly constituted, exceeded its powers, seriously departed from a fundamental procedural rule, failed to state the reasons for its award, or included a member who practiced corruption. ICSID awards may not be reviewed in national courts.

The Convention's jurisdictional limitations prompted the ICSID Administrative Counsel to establish an Additional Facility to conduct conciliations and arbitrations for disputes that do not arise directly out of an investment or in which one party is not a Contracting State to the Convention or the national of a Contracting State. The Additional Facility is intended for use by parties having long–term relationships of special economic importance to the State party to the dispute and which involve the commitment of substantial resources on the part of either party. The Facility is not designed to service ordinary commercial transaction disputes. ICSID's Secretary General must give advance approval of an agreement contemplating use of the Additional Facility. Because the Additional Facility operates outside the scope of the Convention, the Facility has its own Arbitration Rules and its awards can be reviewed by national courts. Numerous NAFTA investor–state arbitrations have operated under the Additional Facility.

ENFORCEMENT OF ARBITRATION AGREEMENTS

Even if parties agree to arbitration in advance, once a dispute arises one party may decide it prefers litigation (or it may refuse to participate in any dispute resolution). As a result, the usefulness of arbitration clauses depends on courts' willingness to enforce them. Where one party resists arbitration and files suit instead, the other party will seek to stay or dismiss the litigation and compel arbitration. If no such motion is made and a court judgment is rendered, the right to arbitrate may be waived.

The New York Convention and the laws of most major legal systems (including the United States) commit the courts in each member nation to recognize and enforce arbitration clauses and separate arbitration agreements for the resolution of international commercial disputes. Under the Convention, where the court finds an arbitral clause or agreement, it "*shall* . . . refer the parties to arbitration, unless it finds that the said agreement is null and void, inoperative, or incapable of being performed" (emphasis added). Article II(2) of the New York Convention requires national courts to recognize written arbitration agreements signed by the parties "or contained in an exchange of letters or telegrams." In most jurisdictions exchanges of fax, e-mail and the like embracing arbitration will also be recognized. However, arbitration clauses in unsigned purchase orders do not amount to written agreements to arbitrate.

Whether a valid agreement to arbitrate exists depends on the specifics of the arbitration clause, not the entire business agreement. The arbitration clause is severable, and issues of validity (such as fraud in the inducement of the arbitration clause and unconscionability) are directed to it. Many courts will stretch the limits of the New York Convention to uphold an arbitration clause. When there is a battle of forms, the same judicial bias towards arbitration is often found. But, in most cases, the disputes must "arise under" the business transaction to be arbitrable and legal claims falling outside the transaction remain in court.

Questions of validity and other issues concerning the appropriateness of arbitration are often submitted to the arbitral panel. For example, the U.S. Supreme Court has held that a claim that a contract containing an arbitration provision is void for illegality should be decided by an arbitrator rather than a court. *Buckeye Check Cashing, Inc. v. Cardegna*, 546 U.S. 440 (2006). Similarly, the Court held (in the context of investor-state arbitration) that the question whether the investor was excused from a contractual requirement to exhaust local remedies before pursuing arbitration should be decided by the arbitral panel. *BG Group, PLC v. Republic of Argentina*, 134 S.Ct. 1198 (2014).

The Court indicated in *First Options of Chicago, Inc. v. Kaplan*, 514 U.S. 938 (1995), that the question whether the parties agreed to submit a dispute to arbitration may be decided by the arbitrators if the parties manifested a clear willingness to submit that question to arbitration. However, silence or ambiguity should favor judicial resolution of the issue. Arbitration clauses that adopt the UNCITRAL Rules meet this requirement because Article 21 conveys jurisdictional issues to the tribunal.

An important consideration for enforcement of arbitration agreements is the question of arbitrability. It may be argued that certain types of public laws, because of their importance to society as a whole, should not be subject to private arbitration. Many lower U.S. federal courts once held that mandatory laws such as antitrust could not be the subject of arbitration, because of the public interest indicated by the legislative intent underlying the enactment of mandatory law and the public policy favoring judicial enforcement of such law. However, the Supreme Court firmly rejected that doctrine in *Scherk v. Alberto–Culver Co.*, 417 U.S. 506 (1974), holding that securities law issues arising out of an international contract were subject to arbitration despite the public interest in protecting the U.S. investment climate. In *Mitsubishi Motors Corp. v. Soler Chrysler–Plymouth, Inc.*, 473 U.S. 614 (1985), the Court held that antitrust claims arising out of an international transaction were arbitrable, despite the public interest in a competitive national economy and the legislative pronouncements favoring enforcement by private parties. *Vimar Seguros y Reaseguros, S.A. v. M/V Sky Reefer*, 515 U.S. 528 (1995), similarly rejected claims that foreign arbitrators could not apply the U.S. mandatory Carriage of Goods by Sea Act (COGSA).

In *dictum* in the *Mitsubishi* opinion, the Court stated that U.S. courts would have a chance at the award enforcement stage to examine whether the arbitral tribunal "took cognizance of the antitrust claims and actually decided them." Similar language appears in *Sky Reefer* regarding COGSA claims. It is not clear whether *Mitsubishi* invites U.S. courts merely to examine whether the arbitrators considered the antitrust issues, or also invites them to examine whether the arbitrators considered these issues *correctly* (review on the merits). The former can be evaded by a mechanical phrase; the latter can harm the arbitral process by introducing uncertainty and judicial second-guessing.

ENFORCEMENT OF ARBITRAL AWARDS: THE NEW YORK CONVENTION

As discussed, a key feature of international arbitration is the ability to enforce arbitral awards. The New York Convention generally requires enforcement of foreign arbitral awards subject to very limited exceptions, as does the FAA. The Supreme Court observed in *Scherk*: "[T]he principal purpose underlying American . . . implementation [of the New

York Convention] ... was to encourage the recognition and enforcement of commercial arbitration agreements in international contracts and to unify the standards by which agreements to arbitrate are observed and arbitral awards are enforced in the signatory countries." In an abbreviated procedure, U.S. courts entertain motions to confirm or challenge foreign arbitral awards.

Whether the New York Convention applies turns upon where the award was or will be made (called the arbitration "seat"). Thus it is important for parties to specify arbitration in a country that is a party to the Convention. Important seats for international commercial arbitration include Geneva, Stockholm, New York, London, Paris, Hong Kong and Singapore.

Under the Convention, grounds for refusal to enforce a foreign arbitration award include: (1) incapacity or invalidity of the agreement containing the arbitration clause "under the law applicable to" a party to the agreement, (2) lack of proper notice of the arbitration proceedings or the appointment of the arbitrators, (3) failure of the arbitral award to restrict itself to the terms of the submission to arbitration, or decision of matters not within the scope of the submission, (4) composition of the arbitral tribunal not according to the arbitration agreement or applicable law, and (5) non-finality or invalidity of the arbitral award under applicable law.

Enforcement may also be refused if it would be contrary to the public policy of the country in which enforcement is sought, or if the subject matter of the dispute cannot be settled by arbitration under the law of that country. Courts in the United States have construed the public policy limitation narrowly and applied it only where enforcement would violate the forum state's most basic notions of morality and justice. The Convention's other limitations on enforcement have also been greeted with judicial caution. *See Parsons & Whittemore Overseas Co., Inc. v. Société Générale de L'industrie du Papier*, 508 F.2d 969 (2d Cir. 1974).

There is uncertainty whether the implied ground of "manifest disregard of the law" bars enforcement of an arbitral award in U.S. courts under the New York Convention. The Convention does not expressly recognize manifest disregard of the law as a basis for denial of enforcement. However, as discussed, the Supreme Court in cases such as *Mitsubishi* and *Sky Reefer* strongly implied that arbitration awards involving U.S. laws such as antitrust and COGSA would be reviewed to assure that the arbitral panel actually applied U.S. law.

In addition to challenging foreign enforcement of an arbitration award, a losing party may contest the award's validity in the courts of the arbitral seat. For example, an award by an arbitral panel located in New York could be contested in New York court under U.S. law. Depending on the local law, there may be more grounds for challenging the award at the seat than there are for challenging the enforcement of the award elsewhere. Under an implied provision of the FAA, for example, some U.S. courts may invalidate a U.S. award for manifest disregard of the law (which, as discussed, is arguably not allowed under the New York Convention).

In general, if an award is invalidated at the seat, courts elsewhere will not enforce it. One U.S. court enforced an award invalidated at the seat because the parties had agreed by contract not to challenge the award at the seat. In subsequent cases, however, U.S. courts have refused enforcement of invalidated awards when there was no such agreement. *See Spier v. Calzaturificio S.p.A.*, 71 F.Supp.2d 279 (S.D.N.Y. 1999).

Another strategy to avoid arbitration is to seek an injunction against arbitration. Absent unusual circumstances this is not likely to succeed in developed legal systems (especially where the New York Convention applies). Courts in developing nations have sometimes issued injunctions against arbitral proceedings before they commence (perhaps to protect local companies). A party who proceeds to arbitrate after an injunction has been issued will almost certainly be unable to enforce the award in the enjoining nation on grounds of public policy (though it might be enforced elsewhere under the New York Convention).

In sum, arbitration does not wholly remove parties from national courts, nor does it resolve all uncertainties of international dispute resolution. However, it does provide a somewhat more settled legal regime, especially in terms of enforcement.

INDEX

References are to Pages